LOOKING FOR TROUBLE

Adventures in a Broken World

Ralph Peters

STACKPOLE
BOOKS

First published in paperback in 2010 by
STACKPOLE BOOKS
5067 Ritter Road
Mechanicsburg, PA 17055
www.stackpolebooks.com

Printed in the United States

First paperback edition

10 9 8 7 6 5 4 3 2 1

Front cover photo: Bolivia, 1994
Back cover photo: Uzbekistan, 1990
Cover design by Caroline M. Stover

ISBN-13: 978-0-8117-0689-6 (paperback)
ISBN-10: 0-8117-0689-3 (paperback)

Library of Congress Cataloging-in-Publication Data

Peters, Ralph, 1952–
   Looking for trouble / Ralph Peters. — 1st ed.
      p. cm.
   ISBN-13: 978-0-8117-3410-3 (hardcover)
   ISBN-10: 0-8117-3410-2 (hardcover)
   1. Peters, Ralph, 1952——Travel. 2. Voyages and travels. I. Title.

G465.P4773 2007
910.4092—dc22

2007042578

*To the road dogs who ran
with me.*

Knowledge and improvements are to be got by sailing and posting for that purpose; but whether useful knowledge and real improvements, is all a lottery—and even where the adventurer is successful, the acquired stock must be used with caution and sobriety, to turn any profit . . .

—Lawrence Sterne, *A Sentimental Journey*

CONTENTS

INTRODUCTION

THE ROAD TO IRAQ, 2004

I FLEW TO DIYARBAKIR LATE IN THE AFTERNOON, DRINKING AN EFES beer and reading Xenophon. My point of departure was Istanbul, a city whose claim to a Western identity suggests a refugee waving a canceled passport. Istanbul may "look West," but it does so over one shoulder as its spirit staggers east. Having killed or driven out the Armenians, Greeks, and Jews who supplied it with genius, the city is less cosmopolitian now than it was a hundred years ago, less cultured than it was five hundred years ago, and less important than it has been for more than fifteen centuries. Contemporary Istanbul is grandeur on crutches, cranky, with senile delusions. But when you reach the airport at Diyarbakir, the pretensions stop. You are thrust into the stubborn East, a city as resiliently Kurdish as its ancient walls are strong.

Flights arrive to hubbub and disorder. In the exuberantly chaotic parking lot, old cars smoke and drivers punch their horns as if striking an enemy. My greeter, a Kurd working for a Turkish company doing a favor for a Kurdish political party in Iraq, led me to a battered Japanese car. I met my driver, Haji Mustapha. He regarded me with distaste and barely tried to conceal it. I was not only an infidel and clean shaven (in contrast to the haji's manly beard), but an American.

I was, however, a job. In a poor country.

The haji spoke no English. My Turkish is slight.

"Is he really a haji?" I asked the greeter, the inevitable middle-man of the East.

"Oh, yes. He has been to Mecca. Twice. Maybe three times."

The haji stroked his salt-and-pepper beard.

The heat eased, the light softened. We had a seven-hour drive ahead of us. I would stay overnight in Cizre—a city once great, now forlorn—then cross the Iraqi border on foot in the morning. A fixer would tell the Turkish border police that I was a hydrology engineer, a disguise I could not have sustained for fifteen seconds. But all that was still to come.

The airport greeter was eager to pack us off, but first I asked him to express my respect for the haji, his devotion, and his faith. The greeter told him something, God knows what. Haji Mustafa glowered, smiled, then gave me a murderous look. I climbed into the front seat of his wounded car.

And we were off. Really off. The haji hit the gas pedal the instant we cleared the lot. He didn't trifle with the horn: children, dogs, goats, and other drivers would avoid us, if Allah willed it. I had never seen a man look so intense behind a steering wheel. Even in the suburbs, he drove as if chased by Satan—*Shaitan* in his cosmology—taking the turns with the abandon of a cartoon character. A charm against the evil eye dangled from the rear-view mirror and swayed.

In less than five minutes, we stopped.

The haji pulled into a dirt lot by a service station, throwing a veil of dust over a confusion of long-haul trucks and crowded sedans. We didn't need gas. It was time for the haji to say his evening prayer. Excusing himself, he ducked into the lavatory to wash, dropped his slippers under a bench, and disappeared into a shabby prayer room.

I stood in the April evening and stretched out the airplane stiffness, unreasonably pleased to be back in Turkey, a country at once seductive and exasperating. I first succumbed as a backpacking sergeant in 1979, arriving at the Kusadasi wharf in a fishing boat after a short voyage from Samos—a journey deemed impossible, given the political situation.

But few things are impossible. A buddy and I were greeted dockside by an uncertain Turkish official who had difficulty finding his passport stamp. I traded a pair of blue jeans for an overnight bus ride for two to Istanbul and fell in love with a country so jostled by fate it could no longer pay for essential imports. Even with hard currency, you could not get a cup of Turkish coffee, and the old DeSoto and Chevy cabs drifted down the Sultanahmet streets with their engines shut off. But the people were proud and earnest.

I returned to Turkey whenever I could, seduced by the colors of a village wedding, by the regal hospitality of the poor and the gripping history of the land. My wife and I honeymooned there, reaching the shadows of Ararat on the border with Iran. Everywhere, the smiles had been shy and warm, the greed natural, the bargaining playful, the disappointments brief. Whenever I went to the Caucasus or Central Asia, I tried to fly through Istanbul, to steal a day or two to walk the city's hills in pursuit of secrets.

Now I had come back again.

In the spring, the light seeps away from the steppes, pulling shadows from the long mounds and low hills. The scent of wild herbs mingled with the diesel stench of the parking lot. The haji returned from his prayers, face more somber than ever. And he floored the gas pedal. We left the lot in a plume of dust, to the noise of cascading gravel.

Turks are fatalistic drivers, but they only occasionally seek death. Haji Mustapha drove as if tormented by a djinn, one of the fabled spirits that predate the Prophet Mohammed (peace be upon him). Diyarbakir's last drab buildings faded behind us. The broad road narrowed. Traffic thinned. The highway was a lifeline for northern Iraq, manipulated by the Ankara government to create just enough border-crossing delays and other mischief to wake Iraq's Kurds from their dreams of independence.

We passed trucks. Big trucks. The caravans of a new age, tracing an ancient route.

The haji's devotion didn't enhance his ability to calculate time and distance factors. Nor did his reverence extend to the use of brakes. I fastened my seatbelt—proof of a lack of virility anywhere east of Budapest. Had we struck one of those trucks, the seatbelt would have been irrelevant. But I hoped we might veer at the last instant and merely wind up flipped over in a ditch.

In dying light, we reached Mardin, another persistent city. A mountain rises from the plain. Before ascending, the highway funnels between featureless concrete dormitories of the sort the last century's governments imposed upon the workers of the world. The city's soul emerges as the road climbs. Ancient houses pack the slopes. Mardin is a museum of annihilated empires and vanished minorities, of arches, doorways, and pediments distinctive to Armenians, Syriac Christians, Chaldeans, Greeks, Jews, Kurds, Ottomans . . . a city of steps, narrow passages, and shame, of weathered crosses carved into walls and broken arabesques, of knocked-down faiths. From the road, a traveler might overlook the rubble of the fortress—often besieged, rarely taken—glimpsing only a radio relay tower and squat barracks on the mountaintop. Forgotten by the world, Mardin was once a prize sought by Arabs, Crusaders, Armenians, Seljuks, Mongols, and Ottomans. Today, it's as lonesome as a Midwestern town bypassed by the interstate.

We stopped at a roadside garage, its bay torn into the belly of an old house. Half a dozen men idled while one worked. The haji needed to replace a fuse under the dash panel. And he needed to pray again.

It was not the appointed time for prayer. And five times a day seemed quite enough to me. But the haji's spirit wanted reinforcement.

As we descended the far side of the mountain, I found out why. The haji didn't turn on the headlights. In rose-gray haze, we careened between barren hills and mounds of garbage. Poisoned earth steamed. A dead zone—the uncanny sort of place that raises your hackles—it made me think of Gehenna, the foretaste of Hell below holy Jerusalem.

Night fell as we regained the flatland. The haji finally reached for the light switch. But only the parking lights came on. In the former Soviet empire, drivers spared their lights, convinced that their use drained a car's batteries, but I hadn't encountered that superstition in Turkey.

We were racing along in a car without working headlights.

The international truckers drove by night. On the long straight stretches, their headlamps appeared as diamonds, tiny spots a continent away. Suddenly, a blaze engulfed us. Then darkness returned as the truck roared past, rocking our tiny car. A string of yellow lights on the horizon marked the border with Syria, a realm of guard towers, barbed wire, and land mines. This was Kurdish country, occupied by the Turks, a land of military sweeps through villages and ambushes in barren valleys, of demolished homes, unmarked graves, guns, and fantastic lies. And kidnappings. I knew all that. But I hadn't considered the risk of hurtling through the dark in a car without headlights.

When experience warned him that a truck was on a deadly trajectory, the haji reached under the dashboard and jiggled the wires. Sometimes, our headlamps flashed. Which might have alarmed the truckers into over-steering.

I could have signaled the haji to slow down. But I didn't. The torpor of his world had already claimed me. I would cross into Iraq as the guest of Kurdish friends, with trust in lieu of body armor. With years of experience in troubled lands, my approach was to avoid any suggestion of prosperity, get a deep suntan, and travel in beat-up cars. I had been a successful judge of what could be done and what could not. But I never had contemplated a head-on collision on a Turkish highway.

The lights may not have worked, but we listened to good music, the ornate improvisations that defy the borders of the Middle East. The haji spared me his tapes of Friday sermons. I sat back and let Allah and my Christian God roll the dice.

We stopped for a late meal in a roadside restaurant run by Kurds. Fat kebabs browned in a flaming oven. To my chagrin, there was no sign of alcohol. The restaurant was run by stern Muslims, with a section for prayer along the southern wall.

The haji prayed again. It was almost a relief this time.

We screamed back into the night, passing trucks with such abandon that an American state trooper would have fainted.

Cresting a ridge, we saw the lamps of Cizre. Behind the rooflines, the Tigris turned down into Mesopotamia. Wrenchingly potholed and rutted, Cizre's main street might have been designed by a wheel-alignment shop hungry for work. Except for a roadside hotel, the city slept. Haji Mustapha dropped me off by the lighted entrance. In the morning, I would be in other hands. The haji dismissed my thanks and evaded my hand.

His job was done.

The hotel drew a smile of recognition. Although this was my first passage through Cizre, I had entered that lobby countless times. Thick smoke. A blaring television replaying a soccer match. Old men on a sofa, fingering worry beads. Petty gangsters in the bar. A desk clerk wearing a collar two sizes too large, crumpled in by a polyester tie. He fingers your passport with too much affection and holds the currency you hand him up to the light. The punch of disinfectant, an unvanquished reek of urine. No women.

My home away from home.

Wise enough to have brought my own bar of soap, I washed then ripped down the bedclothes to check for wildlife. It was headache late. In three hours, I would need to rise and hurry past the twenty-kilometer line of trucks awaiting customs clearance. I needed to get across the border into Iraq, link up with the Kurds, and reach Suleimaniye with daylight to spare.

But sleep only teased me. I lay awake in the dark, listening to the grumble of an occasional truck jouncing along below my window. I found myself smiling over the lunacy of the drive. Cruising with the haji. As crazy as the races of my teenage years in coaltown Pennsylvania.

It struck me that I *needed* to write down a few of my traveler's tales. I had written novels, essays, columns, reports . . . since retiring from the U.S. Army to write full-time, I had lived well enough by the pen. Descriptions of places I'd been appeared here and there as background to a plot or to add color to a column. But my you-won't-believe-this stories from the road had been reserved for after-dinner chats, as we drank wine by the fireplace. Friends suggested I should do a book of travel anecdotes, but I never took it seriously.

Such things need to ripen. Suddenly, in Cizre, I felt an almost-painful urge to capture the past on the page, to preserve a few of the journeys I had been privileged to make, alone or in splendid company. Lying there, I yearned to reclaim the satisfaction, the follies and the occasional thrill of fear, to reimagine the landscapes and relive the perfect hours.

Above all, the characters begged to live again, those quirky beings travel conjures, men and women too extraordinary for fiction: the gleefully corrupt Thai police general who loved to impersonate Elvis to a karaoke machine in an industrial-size brothel, or the Armenian agent tasked to watch me, who could think of nothing but the child he and his young wife had lost for lack of basic medicine. Burmese colonels disarmed by a Westerner's invocation of the Buddha. The pimply, foul-mouthed ballerinas backstage at the Bolshoi, waiting to turn into swans before the audience. A Pakistani lieutenant who wrote passionate love poems, sometimes to an ideal bride, elsewise to Allah. The aging Jewess in La Paz, contemptuous of those with Latin blood, who told me that "We Germans must *all* stand together against *them*." And my companions on so many roads, men of great character and courage, each of whom understood that life is, indeed, a journey.

A good traveler has one thing in common with a novelist: He need not love humanity, but he has to be fascinated by human beings.

That night in Cizre, a few weeks short of my fifty-second birthday, I recalled what a grand ride it had been. Not only with Haji Mustapha, but for decades, in the Army and out of it, from Moscow to Mandalay, from the Upper Amazon to the corpse-littered banks of the Ganges. It wasn't the brief passages of fear that mattered, but the moments of wonder. The world was an endless drama. And a comedy, too.

I also told myself that I was crazy. At some point, every man's luck runs out. And I had been luckier than most. I adored my wife. I had a good life, living better than I ever had anticipated. There was no sense in crossing that border into the tumult of Iraq in the morning.

There was no reason to go anywhere more perilous than California or Italy (my two favorite foreign countries). It was time to enjoy life, to content myself with writing novels and reading the countless books I yearned to read. I had reached a stage in life where a wise man would just go home and count his blessings.

But I knew I wouldn't.

THE CAUCASUS

A BROKEN ROAD STOPPED US SHORT OF THE BORDER. CRUMBLING macadam had been churned with a plow. The track looked barely passable, if we drove it at a crawl and risked the car.

There was no need to pull to the berm while we made a decision. Our squat Lada—a tractor masquerading as an automobile— was the only vehicle in sight. The car idled in a narrow valley of the sort that bygone warriors liked for an ambush. The roads we had traveled all that day had been desolate, but never as forlorn as this.

Capt. Peter Zwack and I were in Soviet Armenia illegally. Two U.S. Army officers. In civilian clothes. Only a few kilometers from the Georgian border and safety. A day of adventure begun in confident spirits threatened to end in secret-police cells and a diplomatic incident that would, at the very least, strike us off the promotion list to major and send us hunting for private-sector employment. Courts-martial loomed.

The blue afternoon waned. Slowly. June in the high country. Our car throbbed, throwing heat as we stared up the gutted road.

Black flies settled on the white hood. With the windows down, the pollen in the air fell thick as fabric. We studied our second-hand map, which stubbornly refused to present an alternative. The road before us seemed our only hope.

It was my fault. I had done the map reconnaissance and planned the route.

"Well?" I asked Peter. With Italian sunglasses, an aquiline pro-file, and blond hair combed back like a silent-film Lothario, Peter always looked as if he should be prowling a Mediterranean piazza. Instead, we were deep in Indian country. In the decomposing Soviet Union.

Peter shrugged. "We could go a little farther. See if it gets bet-ter." He had an appetite for risk that would have suited a cavalry officer in a more decorative age. The eldest son of an aristocratic Hungarian family transplanted to America, Zwackie was splen-didly brave and every bit as capable as I was of doing spectacularly stupid things.

A shepherd sat by his flock a short climb up a hillside. Elevat-ing his cape on his staff, he had made a one-man tent to shield his face and flesh from the sun. Even with his features hidden, he was unmistakably aged, a man who had survived beyond his own expectations. Watching us with patient curiosity.

"I'll ask him what's going on," I said. "*If* the bugger speaks Russian."

"Good luck." Peter was being gracious about the mess I had produced. A mistake of his own, made earlier that day, easily rivaled mine. We had been reduced to bribing and bullying our way out of the grip of Azeri border guards.

The instant I got out of the car, the sun pressed my shirt to my shoulders. I started up the embankment. A stream slapped along on the other side of the roadbed. The valley wore the austere beauty common to barren lands.

Peter remained behind the wheel in case we had to move fast. Although our options were limited.

The shepherd rose—I could almost hear him creak—and stepped down the slope toward me as I climbed. The courtesy of the badlands toward the stranger. His dog followed arthritically, old tongue flapping, quiet. The hillside was rocky, the grass sparse. Low shrubs hummed with insects.

I greeted the shepherd in my finest Russian. His first response was short and unintelligible. Decades of sun had scorched his skin to rind.

"Can we get back to Georgia on this road?" I repeated. "Is it blocked up ahead? Is the border open? We're trying to get back to Tbilisi."

If my Russian was imperfect, his was that of an amnesiac schoolboy. Amid the region's amber irises, he had a child's eyes of startling blue, a legacy of the innumerable invasions that left their seed in the Caucasus. His teeth were stumps.

I tried yet again. Slowly. "Can we get back to Tbilisi on this road?"

Leaning on his staff, he nodded. Grasping my question at last. His smile was small, but friendly, almost fatherly. "*Da, da. A ostorozhno, malchik. Mini yest. Tam.* "He pointed up our route. "*Mini. Tam. Ponimaitya?*"

Yes. You can get to Tbilisi on that road, my boy. Just be careful of the land mines.

Peter turned the car around and we began a worried drive back to the border post we had driven through hours before without stopping. The backwater guards had been inattentive during the long mountain lunch break. But it wasn't siesta time now. We would have to run the border again. Hoping they didn't have the barrier down.

We rode in silence as the light softened, recrossing the Alaverdi Valley—turned to a moonscape by Soviet pollution—to climb back to the sweeping grasslands above. As we hurried over lonely roads, shadows filled the ancient earthquake fissures, maws in the landscape.

"We," Peter said at last, "are truly fucked."

That's how we missed a terrible dinner and met David the Madman.

———————

The evening seemed as long as a bad date. After two and a half hours of reckless driving, with frequent and worried discussions about the gas gauge, we neared the border at dusk.

"Just blow through?" Peter asked.

"No choice."

Just don't let the barrier be down. In those days, even internal Soviet borders were guarded. You needed a separate visa for each "republic" you hoped to visit. Our permission slips had gotten us from Moscow as far south as Georgia on a road trip of more than

2,500 kilometers. But we hadn't bothered to apply for visas to Armenia. Given the recent political turbulence, the bureaucrats at the Russian embassy in Bonn not only would have denied us the pleasures of Yerevan but probably would have forbidden our entire trip.

Still, I had a romantic vision of Armenia, a remnant land I had longed to visit since my teenage years, when I first read its tales of fallen kings and genocide. But Armenia was off limits to me for decades, first because of the old Soviet system's paranoia, then because of the security clearances I held as an intelligence officer. Now the world was changing with marvelous speed and there was a stretch—too brief—when dreams became reality.

I wanted to stand with both feet on Armenia's soil. So nearing the end of our month-long trip, I plotted a route along back roads of the sort only locals used. Given the terminal lethargy that had gripped the Soviet system, the risk seemed moderate enough.

Peter was game. Peter was always game. Slick as a seal's pelt, his old-world manners hid a historian's mind, a romantic spirit and a daredevil curiosity. The word "dashing" is out of vogue, but it fit him like a hand-made suit—an Errol Flynn from Budapest, by way of Park Avenue apartments, cast as an Army intelligence officer.

Napoleon wanted lucky generals. For all of the other virtues we may or may not possess, Peter and I have both been blessed with an otherworldly run of good fortune, escaping muddles that would have devoured our betters.

That evening in Armenia, God smiled through the twilight.

A constant challenge on our journey from Moscow had been fuel. Those rare service stations built by the state for the workers and peasants rarely had gasoline (and never offered service of any kind). Built only to fulfill a norm, they sat unattended and rusted. You filled your tank by immediately joining the tail end of any line of cars you saw backed up on the roadside. The queue signaled that a driver was selling fuel from his tank truck, one more part of the Soviet Union's unofficial economy. The traffic police, the *militsia*, were more apt to demand a cut than they were to make an arrest.

With our spare gas can already drained, we weren't sure we could make it back to Tbilisi—even if we got past the border post. Our drive had been far longer than we expected.

And there in the twilight, in a green field in the middle of nowhere, a fuel truck sat nursing a line of battered cars. Males in their combative years loitered near the front of the pack of vehicles. They didn't look Armenian. Too swarthy. And their features lacked the touch of Europe you saw in Georgian faces. Dozens of minor tribes and peoples salt the high plains and mountain gorges of the Caucasus. When Stalin drew the USSR's internal boundaries, he purposefully separated brother from brother, while thrusting hostile populations together—leaving the balance of power in Moscow's claws. Odd lineages and languages pressed against administrative divisions. The old ways learned to mask themselves, but never disappeared. Outside of the cities, clans ruled whenever the commissars were absent.

We pulled up to the rump of the line and got out of the car to stretch. Weary. Not thinking.

In a matter of seconds, we found ourselves surrounded. The natives did not appear friendly.

"*Russki? Vi Russki?*" a round-faced thug demanded. As he spoke the unconjugated word for "Russian," he spit invisible flames.

With Peter's fair hair and our European complexions, the hillbillies by the fuel truck assumed we were Russians, the blood enemies of their kind. Who had just treated them to seventy years of Communism, secret police interrogations, concentration camps, executions, and poverty.

We hastened to set things straight.

"*Mi Amerikantsi. Amerikantsi, druzya. Iz Ameriki. Amerika, bratya . . .*"

Nope. Not Russians. Not us. No way. Wouldn't even consider it. Never touch the stuff.

As if we had practiced a precision drill, Peter and I simultaneously produced packs of Marlboros, the currency of the hour. Neither of us smoked, but you did not go into the crumbling USSR without the world's most recognizable cigarettes to ease your progress.

"*Amerika?*" Our inquisitor's mood changed in an instant. The knot around us tightened, but the menace had evaporated. The new looks on the faces ranged from delight to wonder. As if unicorns had pranced in among them.

They took the Marlboros and passed them around, lighting up by the fuel truck while the driver went on pumping the gas. Someone put a lit cigarette between his lips and he nodded his gratitude to us, splashing gasoline over the earth.

Peter and I stepped back.

The hospitality of the Caucasus took over. The local toughs and their proud elders insisted that we, their honored guests, move right to the head of the line. We stammered some Anglo nonsense about waiting our turn, but they weren't interested. Our presence was an event, a sign that the world had arrived at their village doors, that the old days truly were passing, that the changes in distant Moscow would not bring just another disappointment.

I don't recall exactly how we explained our situation to the circle of roughnecks, who savored their Marlboros as if each puff were a sip of the rarest wine. We must have lied about straying over the border inadvertently, although our concerns about recrossing the frontier were genuine.

After a few magnificently obscene remarks about border guards in general, the gentlest of which described sexual relations with a marmot, our new friends offered to lend a helping hand. It's a sound rule of thumb in underdeveloped countries that the closer you get to the border, the less affection the population has for the gendarmerie. On its frontiers, humanity is a brotherhood of smugglers.

"You wish to cross the border? Into Georgia? No problem. You are our American friends, our guests. Just follow us," the round-faced thug commanded.

And we did.

With one local vehicle in the lead—the border guards must have been accustomed to seeing it—our nondescript Lada following and a third car bringing up the rear, we sped past the checkpoint as blithely as a Mercedes sedan would blow past a hitchhiking Jesus.

A kilometer inside Georgia, just past a bend in the road, our new friends pulled over and waved us on our way.

Instead of land mines or KGB interrogations, the only penalty for our shenanigans was going to be a missed dinner. We still had miles to cover on dark back roads, and our grim *Inturist* hotel, where mice patrolled the wainscoting of the dining room, did a single thing promptly: close the kitchen.

It had been a high-adrenaline day, troubled even before we broke into Armenia. We both were relieved, sweated-through, cranky, weary, and savagely hungry. There were no roadside diners back in the USSR. All we'd had since a monk's breakfast of brown bread and bad cheese had been a packet of sawdust cookies glued together by some people's cooperative and washed down by chemical-colored bottles of pop discovered at a ramshackle shop on a remote hill where only socialist logic could have placed it.

Coming round the mountain, we reached Tbilisi at ten. The hotel hosted a bizarre party, either a wedding or a wake, we couldn't be sure. Rotgut brandy perfumed the lobby. Drunken men danced through archways. Uncharacteristically of Georgians—an aggressively hospitable people—they regarded us with suspicion and distaste. There was no food for outsiders.

Forget the parsimony advised by sanctimonious guidebooks. In poor and troubled countries, buy friends with cash. Peter and I had been tipping right and left—small amounts went far in those marvelous days—and a floor matron quietly suggested that we go around the corner and walk down toward the river gorge until we saw a doorway lit pink. It was a not-quite-legal nightclub. We could get a *shashlik*, if the staff were in the right mood. *If* they let us in. Our fairy godmother's tone suggested that we ought to pack some Marlboros.

After declining sidewalk offers of heroin and hashish, we found the nightclub down a steep side street—miffed that we'd missed it on earlier explorations. After all, we were intelligence officers, supposed to be alert to every detail. As the padded door opened, grim noise escaped, over-amplified music of the sort Soviet bureaucrats deemed an acceptable expression of the local character. As in every other club or restaurant in the USSR, the speaker system had been over-cranked and blown long before, but the volume nonetheless remained at the maximum level the electrical grid could support. Static, thumps, and feedback punched our ears.

We passed muster with the doorman, who mumbled and made way. At the bottom of stairs lit red, we entered a cavern. Dreaming of Las Vegas, a singer in a lurid satin costume barked away, polishing the microphone with his mustache. Apart from a pair of barnacled waitresses, the crowd was entirely male, muscular and menacing. Shocks of dark hair clustered over tables laden with bottles. The smoke was corrosive.

If ever I saw a mafiosi hang-out in the former Bolshevik empire, we were in one.

Too worn to cross the room to greet us, a waitress gestured toward the last empty table. The crowd was already far more interested in us than in the stage show: Russians were little better-loved in Tbilisi than in the hinterlands, although the Georgians played pretend by day.

This was an urban crowd, able to spot Westerners by their clothes. But Peter and I were doubtful cases, dressed for socialist realism, our shirts misshapen by sweat. Worst of all, they might have thought we were spies. Not American spies—who would have been perfectly welcome—but state-security agents poking into mafia business (or, to put it more accurately, interfering with the competition).

As soon as I could draw a waitress to our table, I told her we were from America and that tales of the club's delicious *shashlik* had crossed the Atlantic Ocean. Peter joined in, stressing our American-ness and our eternal affection for all things Georgian. Could we get some dinner, please?

The waitress proved to be a good soul: earnest, helpful and flustered by our presence. When we declared that we were Americans, her right hand instinctively rose to her hair, as if she had been surprised by Hollywood talent scouts. Even in the bad light, you could see she had been a looker, and not so long ago. Life had worn her down with unjust speed. As it did every woman in the Soviet Union.

Her demeanor careened from flirtatiousness to motherly concern and back again. She rapidly put it about that we were Americans, which turned the mood celebratory. Instead of murderous looks, we received gift bottles of Crimean "champagne" and Georgian wine that made retsina seem nuanced. Glasses rose at distant tables to cries of "America! Very good!" The interest grew so fervent that the waitress assumed the role of our protectress. After rounding up plates of *shashlik* and rice from a kitchen officially closed for the night, she warned our fellow guests to let us eat.

Kind though she was, she could not save us from David.

He watched us from a table not quite next to ours. With the build of a wrestler losing his discipline and a heavy fist that hid the glass he held, he caught my eye soon after we sat down. He might have been descended from a minotaur and looked as if he found violence a helpful solution to a wide range of problems. By local standards, he appeared fiercely antisocial, brooding as if recently deceived. In a room of crowded tables, he sat with a single companion, a slender man who had just finished being a boy. The two of them looked like a gangland Laurel and Hardy.

We had not quite finished eating when the wrestler made his move. Instead of having the waitress deliver another bottle of wine, he brought it himself, trailed by his sidekick. Unconcerned with formalities and clearly a bit drunk, he sat down and thumped the bottle on the tabletop.

His companion hesitated for a few seconds, looking us over before sitting down himself. The thin man said less than a dozen words that night.

The wrestler made up for it. Sudden as a gunshot, his scowl became a grin. Vast and yellow-toothed, that smile transformed the atmosphere.

Leaning in to be heard above the music, he said, "*Vi Amerikantsi? Eto tak? Nastoyashiye Amerikantsi?*"

Yes, we were Americans.

"I speak English," he declared. "Hello. Goodbye. I love you."

Thereafter, we spoke Russian. Except for one fateful word.

"I am David," he announced, thrusting out a paw that encompassed first Peter's hand, then mine. He pronounced his name Duh-VEED.

We introduced ourselves and only then, as an afterthought, David introduced his companion.

"This is Khosrou. He is my friend. He is a Kurd, I am Georgian. But we are friends. As close as this." He intertwined big fingers.

We shook hands with Khosrou.

"How do you like Tbilisi?"

Peter and I implied that we liked it nearly enough to buy retirement property on the spot. I began praising the unique architecture, the old churches, the tolerated mosque, and the remarkable survival of Georgian culture.

David brushed all that away. "But there are no girls. This is a problem. No girls to make a celebration." He bolted a glass of stinging wine, emptied the bottle around the table and barked for more. "I would like to go to New York City. There are wonderful girls in New York City. Teach me American slang. I must improve my English. What is the new slang?"

I drew an unaccustomed blank. As did Peter. If nothing else, we were usually resourceful—good "tap dancers" in military parlance. But our brains were running on fumes. We were tired, semidrunk and struggling to hear above the musical thunder. Heard live in my youth, The Who had been demure by comparison with the Georgian folk troupe on the stage. After devouring a meal we would have fled anywhere else, we had too much alcohol and too little water in our guts. And it was after midnight.

We just wanted to go to bed. The simplest scrap of slang was leagues beyond us.

A bottle of sweet champagne arrived. The waitress had done a powder-room makeover on her hair. It made her look sadder.

David watched us in expectation. The world wants American slang.

"Cowabunga," I blurted out. "That's the latest. Cowabunga."

"Say this again, please?"

"Cowabunga."

"Kahva-punka?"

"Yes. Cowabunga."

"Kowfa-bunka." He tasted the glamorous word.

"Perfect. You've got it."

"But what does this mean?"

"It's . . . an expression of pleasure. Of great happiness. Of joy and wonder. You say it when something glorious and amazing happens. Cowabunga." Thinking for a moment, I added, "It's like *mashallah*." The young Kurd glanced at me. "Only much stronger."

"Cowabonka?" He really did almost have it.

"Perfect."

He smiled with teeth varnished by a lifetime of cigarettes. "I will remember this." He raised a glass. "Cowabunga!"

Peter and I assumed that our work was done, that we could plod back uphill to our hotel. We had great plans for the morning.

David stood up. "Now we go. You must meet my mother. She will be angry, if I do not take you to her. It is hospitality, it is necessary, it is our honor."

Over his protestations, we managed to pay for our own dinner. But we could not escape the thrall of his excitement.

With a face marked by countless regrets, the waitress watched us leave. Her chance contact with America, with a land of dreams, was over.

David laid his heavy arms over our shoulders, guiding us toward the exit. Peter and I were wonderfully fit, but David could have snapped our limbs.

His Kurdish sidekick followed after, the eternal hanger-on.

David released us into the backseat of a big, black Volga sedan, the Kremlin's answer to a 1959 Caddy. The interior smelled of cigarettes, cheap cologne, and vodka. David was a fearless driver. But that first leg of our long day's journey into night only covered a few blocks. We scraped against a curb farther up the mountainside, at the entrance to an old block of apartments, solid construction from the days before the politburo had taught the proletariat that quality was the enemy of the people.

We trudged up several flights, in stairwell light the color of corn syrup. Smells evoked poor miners' homes from my childhood. David let us into an apartment adorned with heavy chairs from the Stalin years, their plush whitened with wear as if ghosts sat upon them. The walls were bare but for one framed, hand-tinted photograph. The heavy face looked unmistakably like David.

"Your father?" Peter asked.

David's chest expanded. In the unshielded light, I saw the outline of a revolver under his jacket. "My father," he said, still panting from our climb. "He is dead. At only the age of thirty-six, he has a heart attack. He was an athlete. Like me."

"And how old are you?" I asked.

"Thirty-five. But he did not take care of his health like I do."

A withered woman appeared beneath an arch: the long-suffering matriarch in a film set anywhere between Athens and Tehran. Her expression mixed pride at the sight of her son with befuddlement.

David spoke to her in Georgian, not Russian. We caught the repetition of "America" as the old woman nodded and bowed. We bowed back. She bowed again. Then David shooed her off.

"She is very honored by your visit. Now we will drink the specialty of my family. My mother makes it the right way. It isn't weak like the piss you buy outside."

With practiced speed, the old woman returned bearing a tray of antique glasses and a decanter. A plate of candied orange peels flanked the booze.

After she had served us brim-full glasses, David cried, "*Do kontsa!*" Bottoms up.

That was the point at which Peter and I diverged in our willingness to embrace life at its fullest. I soon would see him at his most heroic, drinking like a hussar.

I had already downed enough alcohol to make me faintly woozy on the steps. Custom of the country be damned, I only sipped the cherry *samogon*. It burned with a ferocity unmatched since "Uncle" Daney died. His ramshackle house hid up a mountain road and the white lightning he produced was for connoisseurs. Pennsylvania, too, is a land of traditions. Dating back to the Whisky Rebellion.

My family has always done its part to uphold the local bootlegging culture, as attested by the raw tattoo, *BCJ 21* for "Bradford County Jail, 1921," that had graced my father's meaty calf. (Crude hearts and women's names occupied his other expanses of flesh.) For the Peters clan, Prohibition had been less of an ordeal than an opportunity. My own first drunk, in eighth grade, had been on a bottle of 1899 Madeira lifted from a crate in our basement, where we stored odd gifts of liquor from my father's more interesting business acquaintances. The FBI had known our address well, and I remain the black sheep of my family, having spent a career in service to our country—a course akin to snitching to the revenuers. We had always gone to the wars when called but minded our own business in between.

Peter was fighting his own battle with our host, exchanging shot for shot. I noted that the Kurd drank as little as I did. We concentrated on the orange peels, which were delicious.

I cannot remember what triggered it, but we found ourselves in a push-up contest on the wooden floor. As he gasped and heaved his bulk, I worried that David would have a heart attack on the spot. But he only laughed, too heavy to do many push-ups, and suggested arm-wrestling instead. Interrupted by his mother with more snacks, he forgot about the trial of strength and went into the next room to make a telephone call.

The air reeked of male exertion.

The young Kurd spoke awkward Russian, but he smiled a great deal. Peter and I agreed that our duty as goodwill ambassadors was done and that, surely, we could now return to our hotel.

David swelled into the parlor again. "My wife wants to meet you!" he cried. "She is so excited! She invites you to dinner! My uncles are coming. Let's go!"

"That's very kind of you, really, but we just ate and it's—"

"But you must come!"

"—one o'clock in the morning. We have to—"

"My wife, she expects you now! You must eat real Georgian food, not those slops they give you. My wife begs me to bring you to meet her, she must meet my American friends." He smiled, undaunted by our protest. "You *must* come!"

After a farewell-to-mom's-place round of brandies and an exchange of smacking kisses between David and his mother, we stumbled back down the steps. I remember Peter saying, "This is nuts."

There wasn't very much traffic between one and two in the morning in Tbilisi back in 1991. Which was a very good thing. David drove back downhill with terrifying enthusiasm. Lanes were irrelevant, as were traffic signs of any sort. Intersections didn't slow us at all. Still, it took twenty minutes to cross the valley and penetrate a warren of dirt streets on the opposite mountainside. The big sedan bounced and scraped from one miniature canyon to another. Hopelessly shabby even in those unlit lanes, a plot of unfinished construction loomed before us.

"This is not where I truly live," David explained. "I build a new house, a big house. On the hill. This is for the moment. Only an apartment. But my family lives here." He lifted a hand from the wheel and swept a big dark arm across the neighborhood. "My uncles, they will come to us." He hooted abruptly, pleased as a child. "My wife is so excited! She is a good woman. A very good woman. A woman of virtue." His tone darkened. "I kill anyone who will say a bad thing about her. I kill the man who looks at her without respect. No other man will ever touch my wife! Never!"

That was fine with us. We were not, however, as certain as David that his wife had been thrilled to be rousted out of bed to lay out a no-notice feed for the boys. While my own admiration for American women is boundless and unreserved, I know not one who would respond pleasantly to such an eruption of social responsibilities.

We bounced and clunked to a stop. David led us across a jigsaw sidewalk of boards pressed into mud. His quarters were on the ground floor of a two-story home, the upper half of which remained unfinished. The lights were on.

The hospitality of the Caucasus is irrepressible, shaming, and a key reason why male life spans are so short. The kitchen table had been covered over with *zakuski*, an array of snacks and heavier dishes that looked as if it had been prepared by a team of chefs and caterers.

The food was ready. But David's wife was nowhere to be seen.

"*Lyuda!*" he shouted. Then he said to us. "She sleeps again. Women are lazy. She must get up and meet you. She is excited, I tell you."

We protested that we didn't wish to disturb her rest any further and paid tribute to her wizardry in laying out a feast in the middle of the night.

David was unpersuaded. He stalked into the darkness beyond a doorway. Meanwhile, a pair of uncles came in, mustachioed and—

a credit to their wisdom—more interested in the food than in David's American guests. Their greetings were perfunctory, their appetites immense.

We heard a brief argument, presumably from the bedroom. One voice was a woman's, weary and pleading. The squabble did not last long.

David reappeared, smiling hugely. "She is coming soon, my beautiful wife. She is so happy to meet you!"

We barely heard his words. Our shock—the horror—was too great. David stood clutching the largest bottle of liquor Peter or I had ever seen. Above a glass pot belly, a serpentine neck slowly narrowed as it rose a yard into the air. The contraption was filled to the top.

"I save this for a celebration! Now we will drink! Armenian brandy, the best in the world!"

"Do you think he means *all* of it?" Peter whispered, with terror in his eyes.

I took a seat at the table, near a window. Between my chair and the panes, a potted plant struggled for life. For the rest of the night, I faked drinking my shots, pouring most of them into the pot, in imitation of some old comedy serial. A jury of botanists would have tried me for murder.

Everyone drank a toast to the undying friendship and unbreakable bonds between Georgia and America just as a woman appeared in a tattered bathrobe. She wasn't Georgian, but an ethnic Russian or Ukrainian, with dyed-blond hair falling unkempt around cheeks that had sagged from charm to disappointment. Disheveled, groggy, and doubtless younger than she appeared, the woman might have offered a hard comeliness five years earlier. Now she looked like a slattern at the end of a brutal shift. Her expression said that she just wanted her torments to stop.

One of her eyes was bruised.

"My wife," David said proudly.

She nodded a greeting, clutching her robe to her thickening body. Briefly, she mustered that coy expression Russian girls learn, a Slavic version of the *faux* shyness of southern belles. I only hoped that Peter, an inveterate ladies' man, would not be too effusive in his compliments. The combination of enormous amounts of alcohol and the revolver under David's jacket was food for thought.

"Isn't she beautiful?" David said. He rose from his chair, as if he meant to hug her, but stopped in the middle of the room.

Unsteady on a stool, Peter offered a toast to David's good fortune in possessing such a wife. I agreed, generously, that David was a lucky man.

Forgetting her presence, he sat back down and began to cry. "If any man touches her," he said, with an unnecessary look in my direction, "I'll beat him until God won't recognize him. I'll kill him, I'll . . ."

One of the uncles poured another round as David sobbed.

I was eating and enjoying it. Cold chicken *tavuk*, ripe tomatoes, strips of bread torn off to dip in the sauces. Despite my attempts at restraint, I was drowning in alcohol. The food was a lifeline. And it let me avert my eyes from our weeping host.

"*Ochen vkusno*," I told David's wife, who yawned like a mangy lioness. "Wonderful. Thank you so much for your—"

David leapt to his feet again, enraged not by what I had said but by imaginary demons. The revolver appeared delicate compared to the fist that held it. "If *anyone* insults my wife, I'll kill him on the spot! I'll kill him, *I'll kill him . . .*"

Some background there, I thought.

Having produced his pistol, David now seemed uncertain what to do with it. An expression grew on his face that suggested he had dropped his drawers in public.

None of us had a clue how to respond. So we didn't. The Kurd and I ate. Gorged, the uncles drank. Peter nibbled. Valiantly keeping pace with the hard men of the Caucasus, he had begun to acquire a hint of green in his cheeks. Hypnotized by the mutant bottle of brandy, his gaze grew otherworldly.

His wife said something soothing to David. He put away the gun. Not under his jacket this time. In a drawer. She shuffled back into her bedroom and David sat down, drying his face with the back of his hand.

"Georgian men are emotional," he explained. "We must protect our wives. We must take care of them. Women are weak."

The hours blurred. Even as I murdered the houseplant, I couldn't avoid drinking entirely. Peter had developed the stare of a zombie, but still managed to lift glass after glass. I knew that the Zwack family had owned distilleries in Hungary and, later, in Italy—implying a familial tolerance for alcohol—but I had never seen him drink so unrestrainedly. In fact, I had never known him to get drunk. Not even as a lieutenant, when indiscretion is an implicit duty.

The table had become a wasteland, pillaged by the uncles, who sat in silence, awaiting their chance to leave. The Kurd remained awake, accustomed to the role of retainer, but David had drifted into a grunting reverie. Peter was on Planet X.

I looked at him. He returned to earth and nodded.

Rousing David, we persuaded him that we *had* to go. And we really meant it. The hour must have been four. Given how smacked everyone was, we were determined to walk back to our hotel, the distance be damned. We did not intend to get into any car with David behind the wheel.

That didn't wash for an instant. It wasn't acceptable to Georgian hospitality. David roared. He wouldn't dream of letting us walk. He'd deliver us to our hotel door, and no man would stand in his way.

His wife reappeared, more weary looking than ever. She must have been listening from the bedroom, unable to sleep for the racket. She knew her husband wasn't in any shape to drive. But her admonishments, in a weave of Russian and Georgian, had no effect. Nor did she raise her voice to insist. She was doing her duty. And no more. I figured they had reached a stretch in their marriage where the battles were over little things, while serious matters only called up sullenness.

"Really, David . . . we'd *like* to walk. For the fresh air. You've been a great host and we—"

David grunted and rose from his chair.

The uncles hurried off, chewing scraps. Our effort to finish the bottle of brandy had failed. But there were only a few inches of liquid left in the bottom.

We climbed into the back seat again. On the positive side, the sedan was built as solidly as those old Cadillacs with which it had once tried—and failed—to compete.

"If it looks like we're going to hit anything, just get down on the floor," I whispered to Peter. "This thing's a tank."

Peter nodded. But I wasn't sure he understood what I said.

David drove too fast from the start. The gullies in the dirt alleys were almost ravines. He ignored them. As soon as we gained a hard surface, he punched the gas, bullying the car the way a mad rider whips a horse. At each dip, the chassis lifted into the air and thumped back to earth, then shot along with a groan.

On the long boulevard that leads down toward the river, David spurred the engine for all it was worth.

I spotted the roadblock ahead.

"*Militsia!*" I shouted. Unsure if anyone else had seen the barrier across the road or the languid figures—who jerked to life as they registered our approach.

David hit the brakes and we fishtailed. The car shrieked. We stopped just before hitting the police set-up.

This is going to be interesting, I decided.

The cops stood back, shaken. Waiting for David to get out of the car. Before he did, he reached across and opened the glove box. Inside, I saw a semiautomatic pistol and a half-liter bottle of vodka.

David drew out the bottle, not the gun. Which was a relief, relatively speaking. I assumed he would use the vodka as a bribe.

I was wrong. Instead, he flashed some credentials at the cops. It didn't suggest that he was some sort of security agent luring us into a trap. Not in the least. Every male in Georgia had a relative in the government, or in a criminal gang, or in both, who provided him with official credentials of some sort. Anyway, the police seemed less interested in the contents of David's wallet than in the vodka.

It was one of those practical Soviet bottles with a tear-off top, designed for industrial workers in need of a morning top-up before they got down to the serious task of avoiding any hint of labor. Those little vodka bottles were the Soviet equivalent of a take-out coffee.

David opened the bottle, drank, and passed it to the nearest cop. Smiling, he turned to insist that we all get out and have a drink. To friendship.

"This is unreal," Peter said.

We all drank. The bottle didn't last three minutes.

One of the cops waved us on with his baton. David immediately stepped on the gas.

He drove straight down the middle of the boulevard. Going seventy miles per hour, that seemed the safest course in the dead of night. At least we wouldn't crash into any parked cars.

A different problem materialized. As we raced down the hill toward the bridge, the lanes parted around a decorative island. A curb rose from the center of the roadbed. At least ten inches high. With ornamental shrubbery behind it.

We were going to hit it head-on.

When you are in serious danger, biological magic takes over. Time really does slow down. As we roared toward the island, I saw everything clearly. Meanwhile, the Kurd had lolled into a doze. Behind the wheel, David drove in an open-eyed trance.

Alerting just in time, Peter looked ahead and stated, with great aplomb, "We're going to die."

He threw himself to the floor.

I called to David, to wake him, but before I could get a hand on his shoulder we struck the barrier.

Instead of stopping, we launched into the air, ripped through the bushes, and thumped down on the grass and flowers of the island. Still rolling at speed, but with the front wheels wobbling madly, the rest of the car complained like the patients in a Manhattan emergency room on a Saturday night.

As he steered the shivering car back onto the road—with another *thunk*—David turned his big face back toward us. With a madman's delighted grin, he cried:

"Cowabunga!"

———————————————

David's enthusiasm seeped away as we crossed the river into the old town. He tried to put a good face on things, but he knew he was in the shit. He had gone distant and I suspected him of formulating the explanations his wife soon would demand. She had him now. And nailing David to the household cross would probably seem worth another black eye.

We made it to the hotel, with the car threatening to expire as it clanked up the hill to Rustaveli Prospekt. Peter and I inventoried our bruises and found we didn't have so much as a bloody nose between us. It was as close to a miracle as traffic incidents come. But we were suitably chastened as the sedan moaned to a stop.

The Kurd snored through our farewells.

David didn't just drop us off. He got out to shake our hands. The sky was already the color of gray flannel, with true light threatening. Sobered by adrenalin, Peter's eyes were crazed with a combat stare. But his continental manners never deserted him.

In a hollow voice, David declared that he would pick us up at eight o'clock, to give us a tour of the city, to take us on a picnic in the country, to show us ancient churches that every visitor must see, to . . .

His words ran out. The street was empty and chill with the mountain air down from the Caucasus. We were all drop-dead weary.

We shook hands a second time. Then David hugged us both goodbye. With genuine emotion. His whiskers scraped my cheek and his flesh was moist.

We never saw him again.

THE GREEN GRAVE

WE HAD COME FROM MOSCOW, A CITY I LOVE BEYOND SENSE. Moscow survived centuries of misrule, invasion, and lethal philosophy by hunching its shoulders and plodding onward, never without a worried backward glance. It accumulated so many peculiar beauties that even Soviet might could not destroy them all. In the worst years of the workers' paradise, neglect and grime protected the best of Moscow. Even now, in this new czarist age of money without manners, urban renovation has proven incapable of destroying the Third Rome.

Moscow is an unexpected seductress, and some are immune to her charms. For them, Moscow is a tarted-up slut of a town, a tramp priced as a princess.

To each his own. I have walked across Moscow in winter and summer, through neighborhoods where nothing has changed but the advent of dented European automobiles, through derelict industrial zones—the truest Soviet monuments—and down streets that have regained the names recited by characters in the works of

Tolstoy, Chekhov, and Bulgakov. In late May and early June, when another winter has been washed away, each sprig of greenery seems finer than it could be anywhere else. The pollution recedes and the air grows exhilarating. Blue skies lift your heart above the gray buildings. For all its madcap traffic and bad planning, Moscow is a splendid walking city, a realm of hidden lanes where time stands still, of complex memories, of human resilience.

I admit that I liked it best in the Soviet twilight, but that is the cruel nostalgia of the visitor. I enjoyed the hockey-puck jars of caviar, fresh and addictive, supplied for ten bucks by an enterprising chambermaid. In restaurants and ateliers, I exploited the power of the dollars in my pocket. But more than anything else, I liked the dying breed of true believers.

Communism was bankrupt in every respect. The bosses in the Kremlin knew it and commenced grabbing. The workers in the resource-chomping factories saw it, as did the young and the non-Slavs, the quarter-billion subjects without a future. But a generation of proud Soviets remained—aging, poor, and mostly women—who still made the country function, to the extent that it worked at all.

Only its women allowed the Soviet Union to endure as long as it did. Not the Red Army, nor the industrial gigantism, nor the succession of goofy five-year plans. Sober and devout, women in their forties through mid-sixties swept the streets, cooked the food, petted the drunk, and excused every delay on the path to the Communist promised land. They were honest, those women. Painfully so. Had I been minded to found a joint-venture corporation amid the Soviet rubble, I would have hired only women.

Russian men are hopeless, Arab in their assumption of male privilege, medieval in their appetites, Celtic in their weakness for daydreams, and Persian in their disdain for honest work. The women rolled up their sleeves and did what was necessary.

From countless examples, a minor one stays with me. On my first visit to Moscow in 1989, one of my pilgrimage stations was Anton Chekhov's house. The city was grim with winter; the goods on offer were sparse and the people's means were slight. A dollar bill amounted to an enormous, longed-for tip and I had become accustomed to the deference of bribed waiters and the desperation of guides. But the aging women responsible for Chekhov's house were deeply in love. With a long-dead writer. The reverence they showed for every overheated room in which the playwright had taken a (short, tubercular) breath could only be the envy of scribblers everywhere. Their pride in his rooms and possessions was as bright as their clothing was drab. If any of the Russians with whom a visitor came into contact in those days could have used a small tip, it was those women, ill-fed and prematurely old, defending a legacy of written words.

As I gathered my coat from the check desk, I attempted to slip the attendant a few rubles.

She recoiled. "*Nye nado, nye nado.*" Not necessary. Her words were polite, but her determination was fierce. She had her meager wages from the state and would make do. She *believed*. Even then. She believed in a system that had betrayed her and her country. She believed in men who counted her life as nothing. She believed in a golden future, even if she would not live to see it. Perhaps, so late in a hard life, she had no choice.

When I think of Soviet brutality, I think, of course, of the GULag, the deportations, the bullet fired into the base of the skull. But I also think of that educated woman at the coat check, who had given her life to a pair of gods who could not help her, a dead writer and a stillborn dream of a better world.

The Soviet system was hardest on the scrupulous.

Even in 1989, Stalin's shadow remained more palpable than the gloom cast by the Gothic skyscrapers he erected to tyrannize Moscow's skyline. You met him at the dinner table, where none of the men had the slightest hint of manners. The women, on the other hand, were dainty. Ladylike to the point of exaggeration, they might have passed muster in the grandest restaurants of Paris or New York. That schizophrenia of knives and forks had cruel political roots. Just as the early Chekhists—the secret police unleashed by Lenin and whipped to madness by Stalin—were infamous for arresting men with eyeglasses as bourgeois intellectuals, they watched avidly for any sign that a male had not been spawned by the proletariat. Proper manners became as sure a sign of an enemy of the people as moles on the flesh were of witchcraft centuries earlier.

Yet, Stalin and many another murderer bred in the realm of the mother-cult proved squeamish about harming women. While millions of women suffered and perished during the Soviet experiment, less than a tenth of the GULag's inhabitants were females. Born for mourning, a Soviet woman might appear well-mannered and yet survive. The result was that Russian mothers taught their daughters table etiquette, but let their sons revert to barbarism.

Once, after passing another drunk collapsed at midday, I asked a sparkling Moscow girl a question as naïve as any could be:

"How can Russian women put up with Russian men?"

"What choice do we have?" she answered bitterly.

And yet, I came to wonder about that, too. At times, Russian women seemed as drawn to misery as their men were to the vodka bottle.

But nothing seemed miserable in Moscow in the late spring of 1991, as Peter and I prepared to begin our road trip. There were lilacs in the courtyards—*sireni*, a perfect name for that haunting flower. The girls attending the art school off the Arbat came out on their breaks to gossip or smoke a cigarette, and the grubby side street bloomed. As they strolled arm in arm, they were beautiful every one, no matter their marred features or poor teeth. June adorned them. Chattering, excited, unknowing despite the cynical smirks they summoned, they weren't only running out the clock on the school year, but celebrating a timeless rite of spring. And when you saw an authentic beauty, the drab buildings set her off like a gilded frame.

As I got to know Moscow through the years, I understood the longing of those three sisters Chekhov exiled to the provinces.

Peter and I were headed to those provinces. It was an unprecedented trip for two U.S. Army officers back then, an unsupervised journey across the Soviet heartland—soon to fracture into different countries. It's impossible now, after the passage of less than twenty years, to recapture the sense of adventure. The world has changed so mightily—at least in some respects—that the height of that iron curtain has been forgotten. Peter and I were convinced that we were a modern-day Burton and Speke (with a spunky car in lieu of native bearers).

We had to pay our own way, since Army budgets had not even begun to adjust to the sudden opportunities to inspect our old enemy's entrails. (For years thereafter, billions in intelligence funds would continue to go to useless satellite programs, while captains and majors dug into our own pockets to prowl the Soviet debris.) Our commander had done what he could, granting us a month of free "administrative" leave to make our drive and running interference with the bureaucracy. In every other respect, we were on our own.

I believe we were given permission to go only because our chain of command was convinced that the Soviets would deny us visas.

But those were the days of marvels, when the impossible could be done at every turn. As the Soviet Union succumbed to lazy distress, the rules collapsed. Even one year before, such a trip would have been forbidden, given Kremlin paranoia. In subsequent years, the route we took could not be retraced for other reasons: a half-dozen backwoods wars, terrorism, banditry, and the kidnapping that hallmarked the revived Great Game. We had the run of the house in a golden year.

Peter and I had just completed our training at the U.S. Army's Russian Institute in Garmisch, Germany, an alpine setting not conducive to study and a notorious generator of divorces. I had the better command of Russian grammar and vocabulary, but Peter was a grand master of social interaction, one of those charmed beings who not only can make themselves understood anywhere, but who leave devotees in every room they exit. He was the kind of man the waitress speaks to first.

We had made several visits to the Soviet Union before. But this was the big one.

Leaving Moscow's ring road to head south felt like plunging into an unexplored continent. We had grown up and served in the shadow of nuclear war and global rivalry. The Soviets—the Russians, to state it plainly—were the enemy. Yet, we both had been fascinated by Russia and its conquered neighbors since childhood. I grew up in the Pennsylvania anthracite fields, amid a Babel of Slavic tongues and accents. The foundation stones of the churches were inscribed in Cyrillic letters and gilded onion domes pointed to Heaven. We ate Ukrainian, Russian, Slovak, and Polish dishes— "hunky food"—and on the summer weekends there was always a festival in some park or at a hose company where polka bands embarrassed the adolescents and Lithuanian priests sold books about resistance heroes murdered by Communists. I got an illustrated history of the czars (wonderfully lurid) from a local discount mart and read it ragged. Thirty years later, at a folk-music concert in Odessa, I knew every melody.

Peter's connection was darker. Ennobled by the Habsburgs, his family had grown wealthy distilling Unicum, the unspeakably wretched national liquor of Hungary (as Peter would put it, "an acquired taste"). The ancestors of Peter Zwack von Wahl had lived splendidly in a mansion atop the fortress hill of Buda, looking east across the river to Pest. When the Second World War arrived, it brought the first wave of danger: Although long-converted, Peter's family had Jewish roots. His father and grandfather survived the Nazi interval and the Aerocross rampage during the siege of Budapest—only to face the proletarian "justice" of the commissars who arrived with the Red Army. As the Communists strangled Hungary in the aftermath of war, capitalist distillers had tempting necks. Peter's grandfather escaped from the Soviets by sitting under a barrel on a truck bed, with a walking stick in hand and the secret recipe for Unicum in his pocket. A fictionalized account of the Zwack family's history became a movie starring Ralph Fiennes, but the film captured neither the inspiring drama nor the formidable charm of the Zwack dynasty.

Our first stop on the road south came at my insistence. Tolstoy's country house, Yasnaya Polyana, lay a short detour away. We could not have had a finer day to walk from the dusty car park, past the ice-cream stand with no ice cream, to the white-swabbed house that might have done for a small Mississippi plantation. The yards were ill-tended, but lush with that desperate northern explosion of foliage that makes the most of brief summers. Down a path between the birches, we paused at Tolstoy's grave, an unmarked, grass-covered mound. Birds warbled and the air had just enough sting to pierce a denim jacket.

We were alone, except for Tolstoy's ghost. His was a suitable spirit to launch us on our journey through the Caucasus, where his own young curiosity had drawn him into primeval valleys with the czar's white-jacketed troops. His visit had come near the end of a military drama that consumed Russian generals by the dozen.

Armed with his unassailable faith in Islam and protected by his mountains, Shamil, the Daghestani mullah and warlord, had defied St. Petersburg for a generation and more. Gorges and crags devoured imperial armies. Forests consumed regiments. Squadrons of dragoons died to a man. The czar draped orders and military crosses around the necks of his generals, but they could not cast a noose around Shamil. It took decades of death to bring him to surrender. A religious war and a struggle against modernity, the conflict with Shamil was the sort of affair that Washington insisted was obsolete in 1991.

Peter and I did not share the certainty of our superiors.

Tolstoy's tales of the Caucasus were irresistibly alluring to any officer with spunk, but even we could not foretell how swiftly the Chechens would reignite the long war that Shamil had fought so bitterly.

For me, Tolstoy was as true and real as the gravel beneath our feet. I tried to read *War and Peace* in the fifth grade, only to be defeated as surely as Napoleon was on his retreat from Moscow. I managed the battle scenes and a ball or two, but the bond between Prince Andrei and Pierre eluded me. Yet, on a white night many years later, another remarkable friend, Henry Nowak, would walk beside me on the promenade along the Neva, discussing man and God with just enough vodka in us to loose our guarded thoughts.

Tolstoy changes as the reader does. At first, Anna and Vronsky seem romantic; later, they appear swinish and inane. The reader's sympathy shifts to Karenin—it takes a forty-year-old to admire a bureaucrat's self-discipline and fairness. Even *Resurrection*, the late novel all too readily dismissed, acquires a truth in fifty-year-old eyes that it cannot reveal to the bright young soul of twenty.

It was fitting that our adventures in Russia and all the czar's old domains were born in the books we'd read. Writers like to think of themselves as a universal conscience; in Russia, they were the *essence*. In the country's darkest years, literature played as consoling a role for Russians as the Koran does for Muslims. (Pushkin, at least, was memorized almost as frequently.)

We drank bottles of awful Soviet pop by the car park, then headed into the cauldron of the Great Patriotic War.

The highway resembled America's two-lane blacktops before the Interstate Highway System amputated history. Even the small cities—Tula, Orel—that broke the spell of the landscape reminded me of my 1950s childhood. (Although we had far more even then than the USSR ever offered its cheated people.) Wherever we stopped, we found ourselves tugged back toward a slower world, an elusive innocence. Dusty rays pierced the gloom of shops that smelled of sawdust heated by the sun. I might have been in Coaldale, Pennsylvania, in 1959. The conjured memories were so rich they were almost wounding.

It was Peter's turn to choose the detour and we turned off toward the town of Prokhorovka in search of a monument commemorating the Battle of Kursk, the greatest tank fight in history. In a colossal encounter fought over hundreds of square miles, the Red Army defeated the last great concentration of Nazi panzers. Stalingrad stopped the Germans; Kursk shoved them back.

The Great Patriotic War remained the most powerful source of the Soviet Union's pride, that atrocious state's single respectable triumph. Thirty million dead? There can be no accurate accounting. But Adolf Hitler drowned in Russian blood. The sacrifice made by—forced upon—the various nationalities of the Soviet Union was so stupendous that the mind can only operate at the reality's edges.

We found the monument. It stood beside a rural road, amid rolling green terrain more sharply incised than any tank commander would choose.

The site was squalid.

A T-34 tank—arguably the most-effective combat vehicle of the Second World War—sat high atop a plinth, angled upward as if about to launch a round at God. Garbage decorated the monument's foundations and the unkempt grasses nearby had been used as a public convenience. The stone of the base was chipped, the plaque honoring heroism broken. As with so much in the former Soviet Union, no one gave a damn what happened to things. Once the monument was erected, the apartment or factory built, the norm was fulfilled. Dictionaries insist otherwise, but I'm convinced there is no Russian word for maintenance.

With his detailed knowledge of the battle's tactics and commanders on both sides, Peter was disappointed. It was like arriving at Gettysburg only to find a single broken cannon.

We stayed in simple hotels with dirty restaurants. At breakfast, we ate all the sour brown bread—*chyorni xhleb*—we could, with margarine so wretched its formulation must have occupied a roster of evil geniuses. The only alternative was the ubiquitous pink jam that poisoned travelers everywhere in the creaking USSR. The best food could be found by the roadside, wherever an enterprising man of the road, a gypsy, or an entrepreneur down from the Caucasus squatted behind a tiny grill, cooking skewers of *shashlik*. Enthusiastically pessimistic and credulous, the Russians warned us not to eat the meat sold along our route because, "It's all from Chernobyl." It wasn't. But even if it had been, the other food available to us was so miserable that we would have devoured those succulent chunks of lamb even had they been aglow with isotopes.

I recall sitting on a green bank under shade trees by the roadside, using grass as a napkin to wipe our fingers as Peter and I chewed the meat away from the fat, longing for a cold beer. We settled for *kvass*, made of fermented bread and sold from a dubious tank-trailer in a desolate mining town. We had reached the Donbas in eastern Ukraine by then, reminiscent again of my childhood, this time because of the derelict pitheads and the slag heaps pimpling the steppes.

We smelled Novocherkassk, ancestral home of Cossack brotherhoods and now spawning fascist xenophobes. As we neared the Don, the fields went as flat as western Nebraska. The vastness created an illusion of freedom.

The only time we ever felt ourselves under surveillance came in Rostov, where the plump and handsome floor matron in our hotel responded to our query about her ethnic origins with a proud, "*Ya Kasatchka!*" ("I'm a Cossack!")

She was, indeed. I always liked the floor matrons in the old Soviet hotels. They kept order; most were honest—a bit of blackmarketing didn't count—and you could win them over to your side very quickly. Almost invariably, they would ask either Peter or me if our teeth were really our own. American dental care seemed magical in the realm that stretched from Minsk to Vladivostok.

I first came up with the key to winning their hearts by accident. So many of them had bad teeth or gold teeth that I felt guilty about my own—after all, what could be much more personal than the condition of a fellow human being's teeth? So one night, to ease her dejection, I had told a *dezhurnaya*, "Yes, they're my own teeth. But it's because my mother sacrificed everything for her children . . . she did all she could, gave everything to protect our health." I was betting on the Russian mother-cult, but had no idea what a jackpot I would hit.

A mother herself, the woman grew teary eyed. We agreed that mothers are responsible for all that is good in the world (a proposition I, for one, find dubious). From that early visit to the USSR forward, I always played up the "mom's sacrifice" angle and received a prince's treatment from the key-keepers in the Inturist hotels. Sometimes they brought me little home-cooked treats, and instead of the stiff disdain they reserved for late returnees breathing alcohol, their attitude toward me was all kindness.

It wasn't the floor matron who kept watch on us in Rostov, where we had been forced to reserve our hotel room in advance. Instead, it was the clumsiest Keystone Cop undercover agent who ever drew a salary from an intelligence agency. The KGB was already in disarray the year before when Henry Nowak and I, sitting in the cabin of an Aeroflot jet whose departure from Leningrad had been delayed for a VIP, found ourselves—two American Army officers—chatting with our seatmate, Boris Yeltsin. Even though Yeltsin was on the outs that year, it would have been unthinkable to plop him down by a pair of American captains from the "Garmisch spy school" had the KGB not lost its grip on events. But those were the years when the empire's problems kept the security services busy with the internal jockeying that one day would push Vladimir Putin across the political finish line.

After a punitive dinner shared with two stranded souls from our State Department, we walked the streets, soaking up as much of the city as we could. The relentless gray of Rostov's boulevards softened in the long dusk and the shadows of the reborn trees grew deep. We spotted our watcher almost immediately and treated him nastily, stopping and starting, abruptly reversing direction, pausing to inspect the cadaverous goods on display in a shop window then resuming our stroll straight toward our minder—always careful never to let him feel certain that we were on to him. It was ungracious behavior on our part. The poor fellow was only trying to do his job, stuck with the thankless evening shift and two *opasniye inostrantsi* wearing out his precious shoe leather.

In the morning we crossed the Don and drove into the Kuban, sensing the mountains long before we saw them. This was the old invasion route, from east to west, west to east, south to north, north to south, channeling hordes and armies through the Caucasian bottleneck or between the Ural Mountains to the north and the seas flanking the mountains to the south. We were headed for Pyatigorsk, a favorite spot of our hero, Fitzroy Maclean, the Scottish giant who managed to befriend the Soviets without compromising himself, thanks not least to his heroism in the Balkans during the Second World War. No other Westerner in our time possessed such a tactile sense of the Caucasus. An excellent writer and sharp observer, Maclean had also been a soldier's soldier. He was as fine a role model as the miserable twentieth century provided.

Excited about visiting regions long forbidden to Americans, we had no intention, whatsoever, of getting ourselves arrested by the Ministry of Internal Affairs.

———————

The Kuban is made for horsemen, either the individual rider with his herd or a swarm of invaders. The horizon dominates the landscape—neither the sky nor the land, but the vanishing point, beckoning and hypnotic. The southern sun narrowed my eyes and my denim jacket disappeared into my bag.

The lack of natural defenses slowed the development of cities in the Kuban. Military settlements came first. Thereafter, the ailments of nineteenth-century aristocrats and the bothered lungs of the rising bourgeoisie financed a cluster of spa towns to the south, where the advance guard of the mountains first shadowed the steppes. Before the revolution, Pyatigorsk had been a drowsy watering hole that drew characters out of Chekhov, men with a light cough and perfectly pressed but fraying cuffs, and women who had outlived their family's best days. Small mansions and sanitoria rose in the decades after the czar's generals finally subdued the tribes of the high mountains. There were gardens, walks and views, cafes, and a promenade. The city's charm was such that even Soviet construction could not shatter its appeal.

We were startled to find a clean, brand-new hotel that sought to meet an international standard. It failed, but we were glad to have hot showers. Of course, it made sense: the region was Mikhail Gorbachev's political base, and politicians are politicians, and pork is pork. "Gorbie's" patronage also accounted for Stavropol Krai's new roads and repainted facades. Yet, food, in the fertile Kuban, remained far from abundant. The two great continuities between the days of the czars and those of the Soviets were the Russian penchant for grandiosity and the attention to surface effects instead of substance.

By day, we drove south in splendid weather, past Nalchik (now the site of camps for refugees from Chechnya) and into the northern valleys of the spectacular, snow-crowned mountains. With his avid interest in World War II, Peter couldn't wait to visit Mount Elbrus, the highest peak in the range. During the war, German mountain troops from Garmisch-Partenkirchen (where we had studied Russian) had scaled the summit to plant the Nazi flag. Peter planned to stake America's claim.

The road wound past ragged gravel pits and industrial plants rusted to a stop. The potholes might have served as antitank ditches. A pair of chipped lions guarded the "Gate of the Caucasus" and the tipple of a derelict wolfram mine. The gorge narrowed, the road climbed. We parked beside an abandoned café at the foot of Elbrus and took the cable car up to the highest station, assured by an operator that the cable itself was of the finest quality, having been purchased used from Italy a few years before.

We didn't have mountaineering gear with us, but pawed our way up from the terminal, winning our first sunburn amid the snows. We didn't reach the summit, but once past all the evidence of preceding vandals, Peter drew out a small Star-Spangled Banner of the sort children wave at parades. He planted it proudly on the Soviet Union's highest mountain.

Things were going marvelously, with the surrounding peaks glistening white above gray rock and green gorges. The air was as sweet as an unexpected kiss. We returned to the cable car, sliding and laughing, ready to do more exploring down in the valley. And we got a bonus thrill.

Halfway down, the car screeched, lurched, swung, and stopped, dangling high above a ravine and the pine tops far below. In Switzerland or Germany, there would have been little cause for alarm, but the Soviets did repair work with sledgehammers. The cable car groaned, lurched—nearly toppling us over—and ran free for a stretch. It shrieked to a stop a second time, hurling us against one another.

We looked down again. The view was not encouraging.

We waited. The performance repeated itself. And we waited.

At last, with the afternoon stolen from us, we got down to the valley station by gliding slowly, stopping, and coasting again. Peter and I had been friends long enough to have no need to out-macho each other. The day had turned unexpectedly nerve-racking, we had a few hours' drive ahead of us, and neither of us could see beyond the first *pivo*—beer—awaiting our return to Pyatigorsk. I had grown to quite like the thin Russian beer and even acquired a taste for the salty mineral water that kept a traveler safe from dehydration. But, then, I'm fond of Calcutta.

God knows what we had for dinner, but we each scored a couple of beers and that was what mattered. Our nerves had loosened and we decided to stroll down from our hotel through the nineteenth-century quarter. It was Saturday evening, just shy of dusk, and the hour for the promenade, a Mediterranean habit that sailed up the Bosporus, crossed the Black Sea, and even reached Baku on the Caspian. Perhaps Jason and his Argonauts left the habit behind when they deserted Colchis with the Golden Fleece. It was always lovely to see the young girls gleaming with hope, the old men with their medals on their lapels or across their breasts, the husky matrons laughing as they danced in the park to a consumptive accordion, and, always, the children dressed as neatly as their adoring parents could manage, slopping *moroxhenoe*—ice cream—down the front of their prim shirts. Videos had not yet arrived—not in force. Apart from a few privileged bureaucrats, everyone was poor together. They made their own entertainment, talking, judging, flirting, and lifting gold-toothed smiles. At that soft hour, the men were not yet obnoxiously drunk and the young had not paired off beyond recall.

The dark crept in and the crowd thinned from the square. Peter humored me and we strolled the back streets in the gloaming. Residential architecture fascinates me. I find it endlessly evocative and a useful reflection of how a culture desires to see itself. Intelligence officers worry too much about dead facts and too little about their antagonist's delusions. What men believe about themselves is often more important than their reality—and certainly more useful, if you must fight them. Measure the difference between an enemy's mundane existence and his self-image, and you arrive at the shortest distance your bullet need travel. For me, at least, thinking past the facades raised up by successive generations was a good exercise.

Like a child, I imagined the lives once lived behind the decaying doors of minor mansions. In the fresh night, the gardens were so rich with scent you could almost touch the fragrances. Weak streetlamps lit history.

Of course, grown men have to prioritize. It was almost time for another beer in the plastic-and-plywood hotel bar. The fact that they had a good supply was a miracle in those days.

Then, on a block perfumed with flowers and earth, I noticed a particularly impressive house, its facade straight from the Silver Age of Russian literature. We crossed the street to have a closer look and I leaned over the fence, aching to see.

Spotlights flicked on, dazzling us. An amplified voice barked, "*Shtoy! Shtoy!*"

Stop. Halt.

We did.

An officer shot from the doorway, buckling on his duty belt. The mansion I had admired was the local headquarters of the MVD, the Ministry of the Interior, the domestic version of the KGB.

"Who are you? What are you doing?" His voice was as stern as lead.

It did not seem a time for creative storytelling.

"We're Americans," Peter told him.

"I was just admiring the architecture," I added. I was being utterly honest and it sounded like a lie.

I'm not certain the officer with the major's rank on his shoulderboards even heard me. Peter's declaration had been enough.

"Americans?" the major asked, bewildered.

"Americans," we both answered. I reached for the passport buttoned in my shirt pocket, then thought better of it. I didn't want to let it out of my hands. Until I had to.

"Americans . . ." the major repeated. Then he nodded and pointed to the gate. "Come with me."

Peter and I exchanged glances: We're in the shit now. And we didn't even *do* anything.

Another face had appeared in the doorway. An enlisted man, a junior sergeant. Leading us inside, the major gave an order so sharp and swift neither of us caught it. The sergeant fled into the darkened corridor.

The door slammed behind us.

"*Pozhalysta,*" the major said, pointing into a lighted room. "Please."

We went inside. It was the duty office, bright, cluttered, and reeking of cheap tobacco. A sleepy Saturday night in a southern town. Drunks and maybe a fender bender. A yawning routine. Then the officer on duty hauls in two American spies prowling around the MVD headquarters.

"Sit down."

The sergeant reappeared from a back room and hurriedly swept papers from the chairs. We sat. The major sat. The sergeant stood. The major leaned back, inspecting us. Does he call his superiors now? Will the MVD try to handle the case itself? Or will they call in the KGB?

"Can you tell me," the major began at last, "how to start a joint-venture corporation? I want to be a businessman."

He sent the sergeant off to make us tea.

Joint ventures were the order of the day in Moscow. And the lure of instant wealth had penetrated the hinterlands. The major, probably our age, looked a decade older. He complained about his pay and the lack of opportunity—another minor character from Chekhov, the officer stuck in a town beyond the railway lines, the bureaucrat suffocating in the provinces and dreaming.

I didn't want any more surprises, so I completed our story. "We're U.S. Army officers on vacation. Traveling from Moscow to Tbilisi. We're not businessmen, I'm afraid."

"Tbilisi? Across the mountains?" He spoke as if the thing could not be done.

"We're taking the Georgian Military Highway." Named for its original purpose, it was now a road for all.

He shook his head, concerned. "Go by daylight. Please. You must do as I say. You must get through the high passes before the evening. There are bandits. Yes, bandits. I tell you this honestly, between us. *Mezhdu nami.* But you must know *some*thing about joint ventures? Even if you are only military officers? I don't know where to start. I need a partner. Someone who will invest, who will help me . . ."

Peter's family had remained in the distillery business, transferring their firm to Italy after scooting from the Communists, so he possessed a business vocabulary, bolstered by innate salesmanship. He bantered, bluffed, and bullshitted—essential techniques for an intelligence officer. The major hung on every word, conjugated properly or not, that his shining guest had to offer. The major, who seemed a good-enough sort, had no idea what he wished to create, import, or trade. He just wanted his share of the "bizness" craze sweeping the Soviet ruins.

The sergeant returned with tea. I still did not quite trust the situation. After all, what could be more suspicious than two Russian-speaking American officers peering at the MVD head-quarters after dark?

While he and Peter discussed high finance and international marketing, the major sent the sergeant into a room just behind the duty desk. As the heavy door opened, I heard bells and the clatter of teletypes. It was the MVD's communications center.

The sergeant returned and offered me a clipboard thick with printouts.

"Maybe you are interested in this?" the major said to me. "This is how we get our reports. I know every major crime that has been committed today. Go ahead, read it." He smiled, confer-ring a privilege. Mr. Hospitality.

The reports were all marked "secret."

Now, I like to think that I make the most of my opportunities. And Russian secret documents were not available to us every day. But I couldn't help remembering that I was a Russian-speaking U.S. Army intelligence officer sitting in a regional MVD head-quarters with classified documents in my hands. Just bring on the cameras and the handcuffs, and save us the wait.

"Go ahead. Read," the major said. "It's all right."

As Peter and he bantered on, I read. With the sergeant standing over me, in case I needed help making something out. It was stan-dard national gendarmerie stuff: A woman's body found in the shallows of a Siberian lake, another murder in a village south of Grozniy (a foreboding of the Chechen violence the advancing decade would bring?). A deadly traffic accident on the highway to

Smolensk . . . the road that Isaac Babel described as built on human bones.

The MVD was a multi-purpose agency, responsible for everything from law-and-order to fielding combat regiments to deal with internal unrest. MVD units had a reputation for being third-raters, but the officers wielded power second only to that of the KGB. To the dissidents in the streets of Yerevan or Vilnius, they were the enemy.

The major drew a bottle of vodka from a drawer.

"I don't drink on duty," he said. "But this is a special occasion."

I handed the clipboard back to the sergeant, relieved at how little I'd learned from the stack of reports.

"Would you like to *see* our communications room?" the major asked.

"No, thanks. It's really none of our business."

"But you can look. It's no problem. It belongs to me."

The desk jockeys at NSA would have wet themselves over the prospect of getting into an MVD code room. But if things turned bad, we were already in deep enough. Anyway, I could see the racks of teletypes. They looked identical to those the U.S. Army had used when I had been an enlisted man fifteen years earlier. Our equipment was so awful that we used to joke that even the Soviets must have better gear. We were wrong.

God bless him, Peter had worked his charm on the major, who, having gained no information of any use about founding an international business for himself, clearly felt much the wiser—and blindly hopeful, as so many Soviet citizens seemed in those days. Most would meet with wretched disappointment. I suspect that major did, as well.

At any rate, he ended by handing Peter his loaded pistol, a 9mm Makarov, which Peter duly admired and gave back. It was evident that the major longed for the night to stretch on and on. But we had another long day ahead of us. Our manners were polite, but our thoughts were callous.

We made our excuses. Everyone shook hands. The major walked us out into the street.

"Who would have thought," he asked in a well-pleased voice, "that I would spend my evening with two American officers? I think this is a very good thing. There will be peace. Life will be better." Had he brought along the vodka bottle, a toast would have been inevitable.

"Perhaps we will see each other again? Someday?" he said, almost timid now. A girl afraid the date of her dreams won't call a second time.

"*Mozhet biet,*" I said. "*Seechas . . . vsyo vozhmozhno.*"

Maybe. These days, anything's possible.

"In Las Vegas," the major added hopefully. "In Hollywood."

Another Russian dreamer, he watched us go. Neither Peter nor I spoke until we had turned a corner and put a few blocks between us and our new friend.

"That," Peter said, beginning one of history's great understatements, "was a trip."

But the fun had only started.

LORD OF THE
MOUNTAINS

BEFORE WE LEFT PYATIGORSK, WE HAD ANOTHER PILGRIMAGE STOP TO make: Lermontov's cottage. The author of *A Hero of Our Time*, Russia's first great novel in prose (Pushkin's "novels" were in verse), Mikhail Lermontov had been every bit as self-dramatizing—and doomed—as his antihero, Pechorin. A cavalryman commissioned into the elite Guards and stationed near the imperial court, he was sent down to the Caucasus for insolent behavior. Returning briefly to St. Petersburg, Lieutenant Lermontov fought a duel with the French ambassador's son and found himself ordered back to the Caucasus, by then a mill of death for Russian officers. Stripped of his cavalryman's glamour and assigned to a plodding infantry regiment, he wrote beautifully, dueled carelessly, and died at twenty-seven, shot through the heart by a fellow officer on the "field of honor" near Pyatigorsk.

The Caucasus long has been a place where myths and history, legends and facts, intermarry. The fictional Pechorin, galloping through the mountains in a Byronic blaze, could seem more real than the parade of Russian generals who fought, failed, and finally triumphed in their long war against Islamist insurgents. Yermolov, Voronzov, Prince Bariatinsky, Yevdokimov . . . who in the West hears a resonance in their names? Haji Mourad, the historical tribal warrior, is forgotten except as Tolstoy's reinvention of him as Haji Murat. For me, our visit to Lermontov's cottage, not our ascent of Elbrus, marked the true beginning of our journey into the Caucasus.

The house was *na remont*. Closed for repairs. Under Soviet conditions, that could mean shut for eternity. Yet, Sunday though it was, a caretaker puttered about, bent over a crimson flower bed. Our unsettling American-ness—"Do Americans know of Lermontov?"—overcame his standard-issue gruffness. With a smile and a gesture asking conspiratorial silence, he opened a door of the gutted cottage wide enough for us to have a look. Torn walls and empty space. Of course, our visit wasn't so much about seeing anything as just about being there, at a symbolic point of departure, and my homage to the days when maverick officers lived with a sword in one hand and a skilled pen in the other.

We crossed the Terek at Mozdok and skirted Nazran, reaching Vladikavkaz by noon. The city's name means "Lord of the Caucasus." Its enduring importance was as a military outpost, manned first against the wild mountain tribes resisting the infidel czar and used today as an anchor for the appallingly clumsy Russian campaign in Chechnya—a fight as difficult for today's Russian generals as the Murid Wars were for their predecessors.

But the early summer of 1991 was an interval of peace, or something like it. The skirmishing across the mountains between the South Ossetian secessionists and the Georgians had reached a stalemate, Azerbaijan and Armenia rested between internal riots and their squabbling over Karabagh, and the lesser rebellions that would gnaw at Georgia had not yet begun to bite. The outward somnolence of Chechnya lulled Moscow—that tormented land soon would erupt with a fiery independence movement led by a former Soviet general and local boy, Dzhokar Dudayev, a mustachioed hustler who, until his violent death, would astonish the world with a selection of hats as various as the shoes of Imelda Marcos.

It was a summer of high hopes and petty thievery, of calculation and watching. The sunlight fell rich as honey.

I remember surprisingly little of Vladikavkaz: another poor hotel, a shabby amusement park across the river, the gray and ochre Soviet buildings on another Stalinist boulevard identical to so many others, the bleakness of the official city shading the faded colonial gems on the side streets. But Vladikavkaz was only a base for us. Our goal was to find the City of the Dead.

———————

We knew that a sprawling necropolis lay hidden in the northern folds of the Caucasus. Centuries of corpses lay exposed to the elements. Fitzroy Maclean had mentioned it in passing and we were determined to find it—despite warnings of the mountain clans' unpredictability.

Those foothills, meandering valleys, and high passes sheltered an explosive mix of peoples: Chechens, Ossetians, Tcherkess,

Balkars, Kabardines, Ingush, Daghestanis and dozens more. Virtually all had fought with everyone else. The intermittent peace of exhaustion allowed time for clan vendettas, which might rage for generations. Kidnapping and murder were mountain sports. Many of the inhabitants were Muslim, some were Orthodox Christians. Across the mountains, the Georgian and Armenian churches followed their own suffering-inflected heritages. And pagan habits lingered, insinuating themselves into the religions of Paul or the Prophet. The Muslims of the High Caucasus prided themselves on the purity of their faith, but many of the less rigorous clans and tribes clung to practices whose roots stretched below the reach of history's spade.

Guided by a cheerful, uncertain local, we climbed the lower ridges in our Lada. It was a wonderfully tough little car, willing to take trails that would have broken the front axle on an American sport utility vehicle. The paved roads turned to gravel, the gravel to rutted dirt and extraordinary puddles. By the time we reached the first back-country plateau, my coal-town background had been called into service. After teenage romps on old mining roads (where I once bent a car's frame while trying to impress a girl), I could get our sedan through just about anything. But it was slow going. At each of the ponds that passed for puddles, I had to race forward, splash through with the gas pedal pressed to the floorboard, then let the car cough itself to death on the far side. After five minutes or so, the simple mechanism would be dry enough to repeat the process.

The hidden world was ravishing. Were it not torn by wars, the Caucasus could live well off tourist dollars. Haunting vistas opened one after the other, literally breathtaking as we gained altitude. Each prominent hillock bore a timeless guard tower. Many were ruined, but others were kept in service by mountain families. Fortified hamlets nestled in the glens. Elsewhere, the ancient walls had broken down, but not the wariness of the inhabitants. Despite the brutal incursion of Soviet power, the Caucasus remained the realm of both the *ghazi*, the proud Islamic warrior, and the *abrek*, the bandit who has turned from the laws of Allah. Both archetypes were poised for a vivid comeback.

Although confused about the route—which was intricate and long—the guide paid off. An encounter with a wedding party at a cluster of huts might have turned ugly had we not had a companion who knew the dialect. (Russian, even when understood, was an outright liability.) A group of swarthy men pressed down toward us. Dressed in a rough combination of tribal costumes and ill-made Soviet suits, they looked convincingly unpleasant. And armed. We expected that, at the very least, we would have to pay a depleting toll in Marlboros to break free. Instead, we were invited to a goat roast.

But we had to press on. Despite intermittent failures of judgment on both our parts (at times I thought my comrade's secret motto must be "Caution is for the weak"), Peter and I were graced with good instincts about the presence of danger. Not the petty risks of flirting with borders or playing hide-and-seek with incompetent security agents, but the no-nonsense, those-fuckers-will-kill-you mood that some of us can sniff at a distance while the rest of the pack keeps going. And we both sensed that it would have been unwise to remain in those high valleys after dark.

As we traveled deeper into the mountains, the guide was just plain scared. That always tells you something.

We found it. We bounced around a corner and there it was: the City of the Dead. Folded into a hillside and wrapped around a pond that served as the River Styx. There was no smell. Only the piercing mountain air in our nostrils. We looked down over a panorama of 100 or more one-room huts. With their mottled whitewash and small, high, open windows, they might have been the homes of African tribesmen.

Every single hut was stuffed with corpses.

This wasn't an Indiana Jones discovery. Other travelers had been there before us. As ancient as the huts appeared, some were still in use. It was sacred ground and we trod respectfully, peering in through the openings in the walls. Some of the structures were in good repair; others not. Each mausoleum belonged to an Ossetian family—although the site dated back to the days of the Alan tribespeople. For an unknown number of centuries, the mountain people had brought their dead to the glen, laying fresh corpses atop those already faded to leather and bone, offering them to the mountains. The bodies dried and shriveled, and their festive burial garments paled until all you found were skulls with clotted hair and long bones with fused tendons. A pelvis wore a pink scrap of fabric that once had been scarlet. The bodies toward the bottom—what could be seen of them—had been mashed together in a unity beyond death.

Doubtless, there were rules for the burials that we could not understand. Rituals are essential to those left behind by the dead, whether the Indians of the American plains or the eccentric Christians of up-country Sulawesi, the Hindus arriving in Varanasi with shrouded corpses tied atop their automobiles or the decorous prayer-book chants of Episcopalians. When science has unraveled all of the other mysteries, the borderline of death will still enchant us.

I wondered at their lives, not at their deaths. Each hut contained histories that had gone unrecorded, realities we could no longer reach. From the cautionary tower of Serb skulls erected by the Turks at Nis, to a monastery lined with bones in Lima, I've felt no *frisson* of dread within such places. I find them compelling.

The fickle mountain weather had gone gray and stray raindrops made us blink. We left. It was time to put aside any vanity about my driving skills and just get out of there as quickly as possible. A sudden downpour could have stranded us. We had to reach the paved road—and Soviet civilization—before dark.

We soon saw a modern settlement far below, evidence that the guide had been befuddled about our route. Still, the road wound like a snake, bizarre in its contortions. And needless risks are stupid risks. It was time to go back where Moscow's law pertained. The mountain people were already more dangerous than the state, a sure sign of the Soviet demise coming later that year.

We reached the main road. The overcast lifted, revealing a peacock twilight. Drained, our guide asked Peter a parting question. "Explain to me, please, why a person wishes to visit such a place?"

The Georgian Military Highway is an engineering masterpiece connecting Vladikavkaz to Tbilisi, on the far side of the Great Caucasus. Built at an extravagant cost—in rubles and in lives—it permitted the armies of the czar to shift forces over alpine terrain to crush rebellious tribesmen. Later, the commissars in the ranks of the Red Cavalry crossed it to shoot their poison into Georgia's veins. Thirsty for the oilfields of Baku and the Middle East beyond, the Nazis wanted the road desperately, but could not quite reach it. In peacetime, it was open to civilian traffic, although heavy cargoes traveled the rail lines that hugged the coasts to the west and east. A scenic wonder and a strategic prize, by the time we drove it the road was a crumbling mess.

Today, it's militarized again and infernally dangerous for any civilians who gain permission to use it. But on the day we drove across the Caucasus, the greatest danger we faced came from the herds of sheep that clogged the narrow, broken-up roadway. Or from inattention, as sheer drops stunned us or cloud-veiled peaks called our eyes from the turns ahead.

At first, the "highway" follows the Terek, a mountain torrent. Then it climbs. Dutiful, our Lada never boiled over, but the going was slow, due to the steepness of the grades, the ferocity of the switchbacks, and the need to pay attention to potholes whose dimensions exceeded the richest dreams of American tow-truck operators. Rusting World War II–vintage artillery pieces sat in the high saddles, winter warriors whose last mission was to precipitate avalanches before the snow build-up became too great a danger. Thin old men in cloth caps or gnarly *shapkas* made their way along the road with staves. *Aouls*, alpine pueblos, gripped the flanks of mountains. Fewer and fewer women appeared, even though most villages were Christian. This was a closed, secluded world, alert to intruders. The coming years would prove that wariness as apt as it was fruitless.

We drove through clouds, imagining Mt. Kazbek soaring above us, with the Darial Gorge below. A black-shut ski hotel marred a slope. We crossed the Devil's Bridge, entering Georgia to the utter disinterest of the hung-over guards at the checkpoint. For the Romans, peering up from the south, the spot had marked the end of the reasoning world and the start of realms beyond the reach of treaties. Obscured by ghosts of fog, the legendary Queen Tamara's castle—rocks and ruins—hid from view. Tamara was either a patriotic heroine or a temptress given to flinging drained men from her battlements. It depended on which party told the story. Some Georgians insist there were two Queen Tamaras, one virtuous, one profane, just as religions pare the devil from their god's hide to keep things tidy. Perhaps Tamara was both good and evil, part history and part legend, true to the spirit of the mountains. And we had passed into the historic bounds of Georgia. Medea was a nice, little Georgian girl.

Flower-speckled meadows eased the harshness of the Krestovy Pereval, the Pass of the Cross. The highway's summit at 7,858 feet above the sea was meager in altitude compared to the wild peaks that flanked it. Beginning the hours of descent that would torture the car's brakes, we took turns driving, both to share the chance to admire the wild landscape—the driver had to pay strict attention—and because the serpentine road soon dizzied the man behind the wheel. Broken watchtowers, some reduced to their foundations, marked the turns where the czar's engineers had judged the risk of ambush to be mortal.

We paused at an icy spring to wash our faces. Waking ourselves from a noonday dream. Neither words nor photographs communicate the majesty of the Caucasus. And there is more. Perhaps it's the weight of so much death upon them, but those mountains hold a sense of mystery that neither the Alps nor the Rockies, not the Andes nor even the Himalayas hold for me. The Caucasus range is haunted. And you needn't believe in spooks to understand. You have only to go there.

Sun broke through the clouds as the road fell, revealing drops of several thousand feet—there were no guardrails to interfere with our view. Tiny villages clustered in deep valleys, wedged between mountainsides so steep and close that the inhabitants must have lived most of their lives—even the summer days—in the shade. Goat bells chimed. Now and then, a strong-legged shepherd ambled across a field a brutal climb away from the rest of humanity. We hardly saw a car or truck all day.

If you pay attention as you descend into Georgia, you spot no end of ruined castles and lesser fortifications. Now and again, a spoiled church or the broken wall of a monastery testifies to the tribulations of faith. You wind down from the chill of the clouds and the warmth of the south sneaks up to embrace you. Abruptly, the air tastes hot in your throat. The hilltop churches—each defensible against yesterday's weapons—appear active now. You have a sense of crossing a primal frontier, of returning to civilization.

Georgia is oriental. But it's European, too. It's Christian. But haunted by djinns. And its survival is cause for astonishment. In the course of one of the last Ottoman invasions, the Turks who sacked Tbilisi didn't kill the women they raped. Instead, they severed the Achilles tendon on one leg of each of their victims, young and old, hamstringing them. For decades thereafter, limping women reminded the Georgians of Turkish might and cruelty.

The Bolsheviks were worse. As are all men and movements who swear that their abuses will lead to a perfect world.

Yet, Tbilisi—Tiflis to yesteryear's visitors—retained an alluring grace. Some of its beauty would be scarred by street battles later that year as a neophyte tyrant fell, but the city's character had out-lasted the Soviets, just as it had endured and outlasted the Turks. Did I mention the Mongols? Or the Timurids? Or, for that matter, medieval Armenian kings, ancient Hittites, expansionist Persian shahs, and the raiding tribes down from the mountains? The Christian kingdom of Georgia endured them all. And if it no longer had a king, nationality remained as a monument to humankind's genius for survival. In May, 2005, it seduced an American president into performing a jig in public. No matter how many times Georgia loses, it somehow seems to win.

Pastel facades, fading gracefully, colored the hillsides of the old town. The city had grown around a promontory topped by a mas-sive fortress above the Kura River gorge. From shattered battle-ments you looked down on mosques and Turkish baths, on myriad churches—many profaned under Soviet rule—and on galleries decorated with wrought-iron arabesques that echoed New Orleans as much as they did the domestic architecture of the Per-sian and Ottoman empires. Houses leaned out over rushing water. Parks climbed slopes. Nothing seemed flat, not even the boule-vards slashed across the mountainside.

Our days in Tbilisi were full of unexpected encounters, of sur-prises around each corner, of slow glasses of tea and scrambles through stony meadows where besieging armies had raged. One morning, a spry old man adopted us for a day (without asking our permission), dragging us across the city with a vivacity and energy embarrassing to two military officers half his age. In the course of a tour of private rooms where the clock had stopped forty, sixty, or even eighty years before, we, the exotic foreigners, were exhibited to a "famous" sculptor whose extravagant opinion of himself needed no corroborating evidence. He was bear-pawed and swollen, and his work was awful but large: the visual equivalent of those bands of the acid-rock era whose massive amplifiers substituted for talent. His bas reliefs were Grand Funk Railroad in bronze.

In torrents of sour breath, he lectured us on the cosmos.

Next, we were presented, with wonderful formality, to "Tamara the Great," who had been "the most famous Georgian singer of the 1930s, the most beautiful woman in Tbilisi." The diva had been as pleasing to Comrade Stalin as she was to the glass-mannered noblemen awaiting the secret policeman's belated knock.

An invalid trapped in a tiny walk-up flat in the old quarter, Tamara appeared to lie on the edge of death. She could not have been less than ninety years old. Her not-much-younger sister had tossed down the keys from a balcony, unwilling to face the stairs to unlock the front door. The sister was the caretaker and official greeter, hovering, excusing, and interpreting the broken language of illness while Tamara moaned on a worn divan, draped in a mottled sheet and asking for medicine. Assaulted by the sickroom smell—intensified by splashes of perfume—Peter and I immediately wished ourselves elsewhere. Although painted with old-fashioned makeup, the near-corpse before us could barely open her eyes. We assumed we were unwanted intruders, that our guide had let his enthusiasm get the better of his judgment.

We were wrong. Ever so slowly, Tamara roused herself, mastering old flesh accustomed to having its pains indulged. At first, the belle of bygone Tbilisi could do no more than offer a skeletal claw, lifting it a few inches from her bed. But a new smile quivered, letting us glimpse her few, brown teeth. She needed fifteen minutes to muster the strength to rise to a sitting position—assisted by her sister and our escort. Yet, it soon became clear that visits were a cherished ritual, a last joy. Space was made and chairs were found. I began to see the cluttered room's details: photographs whose contrasts had been diluted by time, a few concert posters, framed newspaper clippings posted on the walls for long-ago visitors to admire, holiday junk and empty medicine bottles. The sister shambled off to find refreshments, while our guide cooed to Tamara as a mother does to a child.

As she straightened, the diva's sheet fell away, revealing a soiled housecoat—not dirty, but stained beyond scrubbing. Withered to a caricature of her strong-featured countrywomen, Tamara's face hid behind a tyrant's nose. Sunken eyes strained to see beneath a forehead heightened by her scalp's retreat. Her brittle hair was the gray of cigarette ashes. She wheezed and began excusing her reduced circumstances, a queen still baffled by the loss of her throne.

Confronted with this talcumed diva, Peter's manners were instantly at their best. You could almost hear heels crack together. When he threw his society switch to "on," it was like watching a champagne *menage à trois* of manners involving the Duke of Windsor, Maurice Chevalier, and Bluebeard. The faint lisp in his speech strengthened and his fingers seemed to grow longer. His courtliness, without mean vanity, had the natural grace that royalty has lost. Gallant, in the high sense of that word, Peter's heart was transparently kind. Ever patient with the weak, the interest he took in the slightest soul marked him as a gentleman more surely than a coronet could have done.

Beaten into me by a Teutonic aunt, my own more somber courtesies sufficed. I might have served as Peter's Hessian aide. The sister, bent and humble, served us fruit liqueur and wafers as delicate as Tamara's wrists. After an essential prelude of banter, the shriveled diva coquettishly allowed herself to be persuaded to sing one song, then another, from her heyday. An ill-tuned guitar made an orchestra. Her voice was no more than a croak.

But her eyes flamed.

Magic seeped into the world as she sang. Her faulty pitch and stumbling memory for lyrics meant less with each refrain. Another pair of verses and she reveled in the dignity of remembrance. As she entertained foreigners again after half a century—we might have been ambassadors in gala uniforms—her spine grew more erect with every chord, until she was an imperious Queen Tamara. Her cawing no longer seemed laughable. Startlingly musky and low, another voice emerged, a rasp fit for lamplight, garters, and private booths.

We saw a lustrous girl imprisoned in a breathing corpse. A vixen disguised by time, she was determined to impress upon us the glories of Georgian womanhood. Her eyes traced down over our shoulders, flirting, as if she might make a haughty selection between us—and the one she favored would have no choice but to bend to her will when summoned. Her ancient fingers snaked with startling grace. The world held still to listen.

At last, she closed her eyes and sang not to us, but to herself, to the past. Yesterday became more real than Peter or I could be. Even her bearing dismissed us. Untried by life, we couldn't be taken seriously, with our white teeth and boyish complexions. Not compared to the lions she had known. The heroes who had held her and whispered were gone, the age of giants was over. The mountain torrents were dry. The men who remained were froth on trickling streams. No matter the tempo, each song was a lament.

We sipped sharp orange liqueur in the stillness her music made. Careful, as if the air itself might break. I didn't dare to eat a sugared wafer. The noise would have seemed a roar.

Amid odors of decay in a tiny room, she sang for better, prouder lovers than us.

———————————

We strolled along Rustaveli Prospekt, a boulevard lined with government buildings destined to be shelled by tanks, looted, and burned when winter came. But freedom had not yet arrived, so life was quiet and pleasant. Passing by a shop window, Peter noticed a pair of antique *kindjali*, the ornate daggers of the Caucasus. We went inside to browse and found ourselves in a not-quite-free-market shop that sold everything from old costumes to new art.

And I stopped cold. Good painting grips me. The artist's challenge and the intelligence officer's dilemmas are remarkably similar: Both must develop an eye for the telling detail and the ability to reduce the complexity of the world to a manageable coherence. Then both need to communicate their vision convincingly. The way in which the finest artists *see* more acutely than others mirrors a top-of-the-game intelligence analyst's ability to block out humanity's white-noise and listen to the revealing undertones.

Ultimately, it comes down to talent, instinct, the unlearnable. Training is essential, but it only takes you so far. Some men and women can paint, others can't. Art schools make students, not artists. Similarly, no combination of graduate degrees, dedication, and hard work can make a stellar analyst of someone who wasn't born with the right mental quirk. I learned more about intelligence work from Cezanne and Hopper than I did from government manuals.

I saw brilliance on the walls of that Tbilisi shop. Among our other ambitions, Peter, Henry Nowak, our erstwhile travel comrade, and I had resolved to loot the Soviet Union of the finest art we could scavenge as our old enemy failed. But I had never seen anything on offer as fine as the paintings hanging through an archway in a room used as a gallery.

There were subtle abstracts and clever representational paintings, all unmistakably from the same hand. Big canvases of conches—photo-realist in their precision—were pungently erotic. Color experiments, disciplined and unerring, put me in mind of what Whistler might have painted had he lived at the end of the twentieth century. The nudes on display were melancholy—reveries amid crumpled sheets, superbly human, flesh you could smell.

In our postmodern world, two types of painting are especially difficult to bring off. Abstract art—or call it by the vogue name of the moment—usually amounts to nothing more than pretentious slops on the walls of Manhattan galleries. Nudes are tougher still—most painted today are either purposely revolting, immature attempts at profundity or look as if they were meant to hang above a jacuzzi in the Playboy Mansion.

Leonid Semeiko was a master of both forms. And of others. His combination of versatility and depth fused in a personal style as distinctive as it was disciplined. There was nothing superficial or hurried about the least of his paintings, no sense of impatience or of a hustler on the con. Every work looked inevitable. I've met a few painters I thought had significant talents. But only Semeiko possessed a dash of genius.

I *had* to meet him before we left the city. Fortunately, Tbilisi's a small town when it comes to who knows whom. The woman who commanded the shop knew Leonid well—his studio was a few blocks up the hill.

Handsome and young looking, Semeiko was an ethnic Russian married to a woman from Mingrelia, in Georgia's western reaches. One moment, he looked wiry, the next almost tubercular. His hair was pale brown. His paintings, too, relied on pale tones, on muted greens and grays, on hazy yellows and the pink of sun-deprived skin. I would meet him again, in Moscow, where the winter cold would rip into his faltering health and his pride would refuse the gift of medicines. I hope to live out my life surrounded by the paintings I stretched to buy from Leonid. Should my eyesight fail, I will trace my fingers over the texture of their surfaces, remembering.

But what does art matter? As Bruce Springsteen remarked, it doesn't mean anything if there isn't a girl.

In this case, there was a princess.

Delighted by our enthusiasm—and our hard-currency purchases—Leonid invited us to his home across the city for a "true Georgian meal." Always on the lookout for anything edible, we agreed without hesitation. Wearing clean shirts rummaged from our bags and bearing minor gifts through the evening dust, we found his apartment. The solid building predated the worst Soviet mediocrity. The artist's teenage son opened the door. He was a well-mannered boy, whose interest in the West proved thoughtful, not faddish. Leonid's wife, Manana, appeared in the narrow hallway at the boy's shoulder. Dark-haired and light of movement, she retained the physical poise of the ballerina she had been. She struck me at once as kind and strong. And there was no mistaking her uncommon beauty.

Leonid had not yet come home from his studio. But we were expected. And there was another guest, as well.

The young woman was handsome, not beautiful. Not quite discreetly, we were informed that she was descended from a Georgian princely house (of which there had been many). Her family had intermarried with Russian nobility. "Of course, none of that matters now," the princess said in a flush of shyness, unsure of what the American guests might think. But it *did* matter. She possessed an unmistakable grace that almost made me believe that bloodlines *should* command respect. Her cheekbones suggested the sort of intelligence unsuited to the commonplace. Neatly and modestly dressed, her hair rebelled against her will, instantly winning my sympathy. She looked easy to hurt.

Already worn by the stresses of Soviet life, the princess lacked repose. Perhaps twenty-five, she seemed cornered by life. She was still single. Unwilling—perhaps unable—to settle for the life she saw around her. Her teeth were even, but gray.

It was instantly, painfully clear that she was intended for Peter (who said nothing of his own lineage). In a rambling conversation with Leonid amid his quarry of canvases, I had mentioned that I was spoken for. But Peter had been reticent, in one of his else-where moods. So the Semeikos decided to do a dear friend a favor. We both sensed, with some embarrassment, that Peter was meant to fall in love with her, to lift her away from the morass in which she had been stranded, to break the evil Soviet spell enmeshing her.

The Peter Zwack I had known as a lieutenant at Fort Huachuca would have annihilated the poor girl—then left her smiling through the taste of tears. But Peter had been smitten at last. Womanhood's vengeance was a lively *mam'sell* from Louisiana, whom he would wed the next year, to his own astonishment.

Incredibly, Peter behaved himself. It was like watching Don Giovanni pass up a duchess to play checkers. Leonid came in at last, and we fled into a discussion of painting, politics, Georgia, and all the world.

The dinner was abundant to the point of obvious sacrifice. Georgian cooking is famous—treasured in old St. Petersburg and even in Soviet Moscow. And Manana could cook. We plunged into a banquet of chicken in a smoky sauce with walnuts, fish fresh from mountain lakes, marinated lamb, no end of bright vegetables, and hot stuffed breads. The pastries that followed surpassed those of Greece or Turkey. Only the wine, once famous, from Tsinandali, could not keep pace with the splendor of the meal. The Soviets measured the production of wine solely in terms of volume and perverted a culture thousands of years old.

It was a lovely, laughing, wistful evening, slipping into night as the bottles emptied. Peter flirted gently, just enough to be man-nerly and kind, but did no more than that. Manana smiled, proud of her husband. As Leonid was proud of her. If their friend was a princess, Manana was a queen. Their son watched which sweets I favored and took none of them, ensuring there would be enough for me. No one wanted the evening to reach its end.

As the hours passed, the princess seemed to lose physical substance, as if she became a ghost when the dark came down. The lamplight showed fine lines starting from her eyes and her skin grew translucent. At first sight, I had thought her decorously athletic, perhaps a tennis player. Now she appeared frail. Unreasonably, I felt as if I could see her heart beating.

Her goodbye handshake was as light as breath. As Peter and I walked down the street, I saw her watching from a window.

I met no end of sad cases in the Soviet Union and its chaotic aftermath. But the memory of that "princess" stays with me. It's not that I was drawn to her myself—some women reach you, others don't, and why remains a mystery. Rather, I *liked* her, although we had said little to each other. There are some fellow human beings you wish well upon a brief encounter. She seemed good. And lost. I hope her handsome prince arrived—they sometimes do. I hope she's happy and thriving, with a healthy brood, in belatedly democratic Georgia. But so many dreams vanished into the Soviet twilight and its savage aftermath that it's hard to have confidence.

In the comfort and clarity of my American home, I stare at Leonid Semeiko's paintings and wonder.

Peter and I would go on to Gori, the aptly named birthplace of Stalin, skirting the armored vehicles that blocked the roads into truculent South Ossetia and heading west toward the Black Sea coast. We would transit Mingrelia and touch Adjaria—soon to insist on a gangsterish autonomy—then turn north through Abkhazia, with its tea plantations, orchards, and coming civil war. The roads were scabbed, the ports rotten, the beaches narrow and vile. The green hills seemed sloppy drunk in their lushness, as if the local motto was the shrug-shouldered Russian expression, "*Xhozhiana nyet*." The usual English translation is "No one's in charge," but the true meaning is closer to "Nobody's responsible for anything, so screw everything, fart, and get drunk."

We would end our trip by the Black Sea, back on soil claimed by Russia for Russians. We listened to the fantastic dreams of earnest young vacationers at Sochi, lying on a stony beach and swimming in dirty water. After the heat broke, we drank beer in an odoriferous disco as hard girls tried to out-Western each other, sad as bleached hair. We slept in a brand new, already-broken hotel and woke to the standard brown bread and pink jam, with margarine that smelled like a by-product of an oil refinery. Sorriest of all, our spaceship-atop-a-blockhouse hotel wasn't even open to average Soviets, who had to cram into rented rooms down in a gulch. Without connections, hard currency, or a Western passport, the fruits of Communism, meager as they were, remained out of bounds to the proletariat.

The USSR was a hopeless case, in need of a mercy killing. We sensed that its hour was coming, perhaps in months, certainly in a year. Later that summer, as I sat in a staff-college classroom in Kansas, tanks would fire into the Russian parliament and the face of the tall white building would burn black. The Soviet Union would die overnight and Boris Yeltsin would begin his reign in a fit of exhilaration that ended, as things Russian so often do, in drunken exhaustion.

The new Russia was about to be born, however misshapen, and Peter and I had seen more of the gestation than any of our contemporaries. But when we got back, no one in the U.S. intelligence community was interested. If the data didn't come from a satellite, it didn't count. The human factor was messy and unpredictable. Better to count tanks and ships and wait for a revival of the Cold War.

Intelligence failure is as old as it is willful.

Our trip was far from wasted, though. Peter and I had learned far more than we could put into words for years afterward. We often returned to the region after Yeltsin stood on that tank, but our road trip had an incomparable impact on the way we saw the world. We had absorbed what no academic texts or intelligence documents can give you: the scent of daily life, the temper of the people, the taste of the land. Traveling, you take in far more than you understand, calories of knowledge waiting to fuel some future intellectual labor. For an intelligence officer, especially, what seems meaningful at first often proves useless, while casual details sum to understanding.

We had passed through the Soviet sickroom just before the hour of death. Our inheritance was a grasp of reality that informed Peter's work for years and put my views of Moscow on a collision course with the optimists who learned what little they knew of Russia from books or brief delegation visits. In the Clinton years, Washington was a lonely place for anyone who refused to join the chants about Russia as our democratic twin—a peculiar echo of the Left's 1930s insistence, against all evidence, that Stalin's Soviet Union was the promised land.

As we walked back to our hotel, bellies swollen after our dinner with the Semeikos, our journey was drifting into its final stage. But I didn't want to head west to the Black Sea until I had at least tried to reach Armenia, despite lacking the proper papers. And Peter wanted to take a spin in Azerbaijan, another place we had no right to be.

It was a formula for trouble.

We never had a real argument, but we came close on the morning I had picked to dash into Armenia. I had it all planned out. But Peter wanted to alter the route, to drive into Azerbaijan then swing west, returning through Armenia.

I argued that we should take one risk at a time, that we could slip into Armenia on a back road, while the only way into Azerbaijan was along the main route that led over the Red Bridge. We'd have to cross at a major internal border post, where our lack of the appropriate visas would be all too evident. Finally, I was convinced that the Azeri-Armenian border would be closed, leaving us stranded. On top of their local upheavals, Baku and Yerevan had already begun the bickering that would lead them to full-scale war. The problem of Nagorno-Karabakh loomed, although the killing had subsided to the level of clan feuds while Russian provocateurs auctioned arms to both sides. To me, an attempt to enter Azerbaijan looked like a losing proposition in itself. To try to reach Armenia that way seemed crazy.

But Peter was confident we could pull it off. After all, we'd bluffed our way through plenty of tough spots, not only that year but on previous trips ranging from the Baltic states through Central Asia.

I grudgingly agreed to give it a shot. One thing you can count on in a military officer is that he'll sign up for utterly stupid ideas to avoid seeming weak or afraid.

So off we went, with the windows down, the speed-punched air encouraging us, and a foolish plan we both would have mocked had we been in our right minds. We had begun to feel invulnerable, and there are few conditions more dangerous.

The road was clear all the way to the Azeri border. With a glance at our passports, the Georgians waved us through. There wasn't even a line on the Azeri side.

And then it all went wrong.

An Azeri officer, surrounded by armed subordinates, decided he ought to scrutinize our passports. He began by asking for Peter's. Testing it in his hand as if for weight, he smiled, then leafed through the pages. Taking his time.

I laid a pack of Marlboros on the dashboard. Casually. Just in his line of sight.

"No visa," the officer snapped.

Peter went into his charm mode. This time, it didn't work.

"We just want to visit Azerbaijan. Just for the day," he said. "We've heard so many wonderful things about your homeland. We just thought we'd drive around a bit, then cross into Armenia and go back to—"

My heart plunged through the floorboards. "Armenia" was *not* the magic word. I've made plenty of my own whopping mistakes, but that morning Peter pegged out the meter. He began arguing with the customs officer.

His passport disappeared. Orders fell like blades. The guards closed around the car.

"We must inspect your vehicle. And your luggage," the officer said. "You must get out of your car." He gave commands in dialect to his underlings. We hadn't packed much for the day, but the car got a thorough going over. The officer watched with a snicker as a recruit showed him a half-empty carton of Marlboros, our cameras, and a packet of crumbling biscuits.

I tried my hand. "I've always heard wonderful things about Azeri hospitality. All we wanted to do was see the land of Nizami Gandjevi."

The name had no effect. Even though Azerbaijan was the only country in the world that had a national museum dedicated to the poets it claimed.

"You are smugglers?" His face was amused, mean, confident.

"No. We just wanted to visit Azerbaijan."

"But why do you want to go to Armenia? The Armenians are bad people. They cut the throats of women. Of little boys."

"We weren't really going to Armenia. My friend's Russian isn't so good. It was a mistake. He didn't mean—"

"Armenians are vermin. Filth. But Americans like Armenians. Is this not true?"

"Americans like everybody. We're friendly people."

"Why do you try to enter Azerbaijan without a visa?"

"We thought we could get one at the border."

"This is forbidden. You are here without the law. You have done a criminal act."

He was right.

An unshaven sergeant, young and eager, stepped up and gave his report. Our vehicle held no packages of heroin, no automatic weapons or other munitions, and no gold ingots.

If the customs officer was disappointed, he didn't show it. All of it was a game. *His* game.

I had begun to sweat. And it wasn't only from the morning sun. Peter's forehead shone with moisture.

"Look," Peter said. "We're sorry we made a mistake. We'll just go back to Georgia."

The officer looked at him with a cat's smile. Abruptly, he shrugged and surprised us. "All right, then. Go. Get out of here. Turn your car around and go."

Trying not to show the extent of our relief, we turned to our car. Instinctively—blessedly—Peter patted down his pockets.

He stopped cold. "I need my passport," he called after the officer.

"What passport?"

"You took my passport. You need to give it back."

"I gave it to you."

"You have my passport."

The three of us stood staring each other down—a scene from a spaghetti western. The enlisted men watched, uncertain.

At last, the officer put his hands on his hips. "I don't have your passport. I gave it back to you. You should be glad. You're criminals because of the thing you have done. And I'm letting you go. You should thank me."

Peter's face reddened. I just wanted him to keep his temper. It was easier for me, of course. I still had my own passport buttoned in my shirt pocket.

Nonetheless, this looked like the end of the line. We either created an incident on the spot, or Peter had to report the loss of his passport to the embassy in Moscow, a hen-house of bureaucrats who loved to peck their own kind. End of trip, end of career. Of both our careers. And the damnable thing was that we both loved the Army. We each could have done a thousand other things—Peter's family pestered him to take over their expanding list of distilleries—but nothing else seemed remotely as satisfying, or as much fun as being a soldier. And intelligence work was a bonus.

"You must go now," the officer said, gesturing back toward Georgia. "Or I will have to call my superiors." He crossed one wrist over another. "And they will arrest you."

I had an inspiration, just short of a golden light descending from the heavens.

"All right," I said. "Call them. Call your bosses. And call the KGB. Tell them how you stole an American passport." I stared at him hard and he stared back. "Or I can call them, if you want. We're American officers. The KGB knows we're here. It's no secret. Or do you think the KGB's stupid?"

He folded instantly. I could see it in his eyes seconds before his body-language changed.

"I didn't take his passport," he said grumpily, a bad child caught out. "Why would I take his passport?"

"American passports are valuable. On the left, on the black market."

"I'm a policeman."

"And you took his passport," I said. Then I added, "Unless it was all a mistake. Mistakes happen."

Peter watched and listened with growing amusement. And relief.

"Come inside," the officer said, turning toward his office. "Let's drink a glass of tea."

"First, we need to find my friend's passport."

"I don't have it. It's probably in your car. It probably fell out of his pocket. That's probably what happened."

"Your men searched the car."

"Stay here. Sometimes they don't search very well. I'm still training them."

He barked another order in dialect, moving toward our car. I moved to follow him, but Peter touched my arm. He had it figured out. Then I got it, too.

The officer formed a football huddle with his subordinates. Murmurs, hand and arm movements, too much for the eye to follow.

Our tormenter turned back toward us with a smile, showing a gold front tooth. His men swarmed over the car.

The pretended search hardly lasted thirty seconds. A sergeant rose from behind my seat, holding up a blue passport.

"You see? It was there all the time. Under your seat," the officer said.

"I do apologize," Peter told him, as the sergeant handed over the passport. "I was wrong. My mistake."

Don't overdo it, I thought. But it was hard not to grin.

"Next time you come, you come with a visa. We will show you true hospitality. Not like the Armenians." He made a sour face and flicked a look across the border. "Or those Georgians."

"We'll be back," I said. "Count on it. And we won't make such a foolish mistake next time."

"Thanks," Peter told him, "for all your help."

Before we left, we gave him one pack of Marlboros. To pledge undying friendship between the people of America and the people of Azerbaijan. And to make sure he didn't change his mind before we crossed back into Georgia. We were still entirely in his power and it was only a matter of time before he remembered it.

A few years later, I did return to Azerbaijan. By then, it was a war-torn country with the saddest refugee camps outside of Africa. The streets were rich in history and poor in spirit, the residents dejected by the past year's losses at the front and fearful of the future. Baku, with its electoral dictatorship and its Caspian oil, was a global capital of intrigue and corporate piracy. The shoreline was an environmental catastrophe. Like all bleeding lands, Azerbaijan fascinated me. I would even write a novel, *The Devil's Garden*, about its wretchedness, conspiracies, and weird beauty. But that morning I was glad to put the place behind me.

"Jesus," Peter said, after the Georgian border guards waved us past again, this time in the other direction. He stared straight through the windshield and gnawed on a fingernail—something he did only after a serious ordeal.

"All right," I said with perfect confidence, "now let's go to Armenia."

THE
TEMPTING FORTRESS

IT BEGAN WITH TWO PRINTS ON MY PARENTS' BEDROOM WALL. SMALL, hand-tinted, and gilt-framed, one showed the fortress of Dowlatabad on India's Deccan plateau, while the other's caption read "The ruins of old Delhi." They enthralled me.

Impossibly exotic, those prints spoke of a world far grander than Pennsylvania's coal towns. Black-and-white films on television intensified the allure: *Gunga Din, Lives of a Bengal Lancer, The Charge of the Light Brigade, Kim*. The trail led on to Kipling and John Masters, to tidbits on Robert Clive, Tipoo Sultan, and Cawnpore. I learned that there had been much more to Cornwallis and Wellington than Yorktown and Waterloo. During a holiday excursion to John Wanamaker's in Philadelphia, I wasted my meager funds on a bottle of "camp coffee concentrate" because it showed a British officer, wonderfully pukka sahib, on the label. I knew that the Sikhs, once conquered, had served nearly as loyally as the Gurkhas, and that there was no higher honor for a subaltern than to be mentioned in dispatches . . . although it was the "political officers" who won the Great Game.

I wanted to climb the Khyber Pass and enter the Burmese jungle, to prowl the alleys of Peshawar and penetrate the citadel within the walls of Dowlatabad.

I would.

But I could not know that then. The world sprawled out of reach. We have already lost our sense of how far away things were less than a half century ago. My first journey that didn't involve the backseat of a car occurred when I was six. It began with a flight to Arizona on a series of TWA propeller aircraft (I remember because I was given a model airplane). My ears hurt miserably. I cried.

Arizona was already sacred to our family: my father, at fifty-one, had eloped to Phoenix with my twenty-year-old mother. Dad was a lion who looked like a bear. She wielded a conquering smile and a starlet's haircut. My father wanted my younger brother and me to see Tombstone, saloons with sawdust floors, the saguaros, the vastness. After a life spent in coal mines and the miasma of collieries, the western skies bedazzled him. I remember the Silver Dollar Saloon and a brown and yellow badge I wore on my cowboy vest. A stewardess, as those glamorous women were proud to be called, gave me two Chicklets for my ears on the descent into Chicago, where even then all humankind changed planes.

We went to Miami and stayed at a middling hotel, the Safari, where the plaster giraffe seemed far less foreign than the savage tribal accents from New York City. My brother nearly drowned. *I* saw him at the bottom of the pool, and he was saved. St. Augustine was better, with the Castillo de San Marco to prove that history was fierce and wonderful. Some of my earliest memories—predating

our expedition to Arizona—are of driving down old U.S. 1 to
DeLand. My father's trotters wintered and trained nearby. (Later, we
would struggle to hang on to a battered old car and dinner might
consist of fried potatoes, but my earliest days were ruinously privileged.) I recall the chill and the heavy mist as we stood by the track
on winter mornings, listening to the hoof chop of a favorite horse,
Prince Eton or Queen's Joy, invisible on the back stretch. The
ghostly hooves rounded the last turn of the track, urged on by an
aging jockey. Suddenly, with the force of a surprise attack, the horse
thrust through a gray wall, huge, swift, wonderful.

That was in the 1950s, the age between the hejira described in
The Grapes of Wrath and the mass tourism of the jet age. Super-
highways had not yet changed our lives, and the Boeing 707 had
not flown a single passenger. Stuckey's stands, not resort spas, were
the epitome of travel for our kind, and the serial signs promoting
Burma Shave delighted us as no technology ever could have done.

We knew the world was out there, though. History still mattered in school curriculae; uncles had seen Paris during the war;
and draftees came home with war brides who, it strikes me now,
had not always married for love. When the age of JFK arrived at
the dawn of the 1960s, my class spent an entire year studying our
Latin American "neighbors." Yet, there wasn't a single Latin in our
town, and I once mistook a tawny Italian girl—she was splendid—
for a negress. Inspired by an earnest teacher, I wrote a play about
Bolivar and San Martin through which my classmates suffered.
Ahead of my time with narrative compression, I began and ended
South America's revolutionary era in just under five minutes.

And there was always a subscription, from my Aunt Clara, to
National Geographic Magazine.

Imaging myself as made of the stuff of heroes, I was a sticky romantic, lamed by imagination. Daydreams didn't help in backyard football matches. But I couldn't stop myself. Even the Dutchie towns to the south and the anthracite valleys around us concealed a new mystery over every hill. Glimpsed from a distant crest, Tamaqua, Pennsylvania, might have been Samarkand.

In the days before 24/7 sensationalism terrified parents, we covered thirty back-road miles on our bikes in a day. You could walk the railroad tracks to the county seat. Pocked stripping roads led to abandoned collieries, the castles of our feudal world. If you watched out for the copperheads, you could thrash through the brush to the bed of the Schuylkill Canal, a superhighway of the nineteenth century. I wanted to know what hid around the corner.

Then came David Lean's film, *Lawrence of Arabia*. And James Bond. I had a belted raincoat and tried to smoke French cigarettes, but couldn't stand them. I prowled the Irish flats by the railroad tracks, imagining foreign women in my future and praying my adolescent dandruff wasn't permanent.

Our family fortunes turned downward. Sharply. I recall vignettes I could never bear to write down. There was no more travel, except short drives to ask my father's old business partners—men to whom he had been imperially generous—if they would give us money for his insulin. It was *always* those who had been less fortunate themselves who came up with a few dollars.

I lived in books and took up the guitar.

My first trip abroad came in 1970. Eighteen years old, I arrived in London with $300, a gold Les Paul Gibson, and a remarkable lack of talent. I jammed around, living on chips, bottled milk with the cream separate on top, and pints of beer. I loved the idea of being a musician more than I loved music. What swept me away weren't the nights in Soho clubs or concerts with one vivid band after another, but the names: Piccadilly, Belgravia, Westminster, the Strand, Drury Lane, Baker Street, Paddington Station, Victoria Station, Covent Garden. The places in the books and songs were real. I was probably the only rock guitarist in London that year who spent more time in the National Gallery than practicing.

Grimy and shabby though it was before Margaret Thatcher spanked it and gave it a scrub, London was good to me. It helped me begin to accept that I would never play as well as my ego demanded, that I would always be, at best, a second-rate musician. I had my fun with six metal strings and plenty of wattage. But my destiny lay elsewhere. If I had one.

Travel *does* help us see what we cannot see otherwise. As we discover the world, we uncover ourselves.

My real career as a traveler began two years later, when I had my first of many confrontations while crossing a border—a life-long habit I cannot seem to shake.

I had decided to return to my childhood dream of being a writer—in a few more years I would also revive the twin dream of being a soldier. And writers had to travel, didn't they? Charter flights had grown cheaper and life had already taught me that you can get by on very little. With a light suitcase in lieu of a back-pack, I began to make my way across Europe, pausing first in Zurich to visit an unsuspecting girl I had met in London. Her widowed mother welcomed me to the jaw-dropper family home, where I horrified the neighborhood by practicing knife-throwing in the garden.

I got a Yugoslav visa at the consulate in Zurich. I was headed for Greece, by train.

In 1972, Belgrade was dusty and squalid, about as European as a water pipe. To save money, I shared a three-dollar room with a wanderer from New Zealand. The imaginatively unsanitary hotel sat two blocks from the train station. We found ourselves on the same floor as a Russian delegation. Noisy, ever-drunk, and wary of contact—whether with us or the Yugoslavs—the Russians hardly looked like the vanguard of a superpower. Stuck in an armpit hotel, they crowded into their rooms to drink. The bottles that littered the hallway in the morning often remained throughout the day and beyond.

My true introduction to Soviet culture came when I walked down the hall to the men's toilet. The instant I opened the door to the little closet, the stench mugged me. Soviet marksmanship was, to say the least, deficient. I had never seen an animal's pen so vile.

I shut the door. Since it seemed to be all males on the floor, I decided to try the second cabin, the one for women.

The Russians had gotten there first.

Over the years, I found much to like and a bit to admire about the Russian people. But their sanitary standards would make a sergeant-major cower.

Of course, there was more to Belgrade than drunken Russians. I had read about Tito's success in blazing an alternative path to a socialist future. While Marx was often invoked on university campuses, I actually had read the sage of Trier and Hampstead—

although I already found his prescriptions suspect. Still, I was prepared to find a flourishing realm, with flower maidens in folk costumes and a welcome for the guests of a happy people.

Belgrade was a pit. It made the poorest coal patch back home look like millionaire's row. In a city of leaks, splices, and faulty telephones, the third-rate goods on offer were still unaffordable to the slumping public. The people I met were surly and fearful—unless they were drunk, in which case moods could go a number of ways. But you could at least buy a block of cheese, a bun, and a bottle of cheap Dalmatian wine, which made for a far better meal than anything the flypaper restaurants offered. I befriended a group of students and we played their guitars on a street corner deep into the night, serenading scruffy apartment blocks. To my dismay, the young Yugoslavs had accepted Neil Diamond as their musical god and they howled "Song Sung Blue" with Serbo-Croatian accents. The neighbors hurled bottles down from their windows.

There was nothing like firsthand exposure to dialectical materialism to teach you that the dialectic rarely delivered the material. Leftist rhetoric is wonderfully seductive. The tragedy is that those stirring promises are worthless.

What Belgrade lacked, above all, was human dignity. True to the icy calculus of Marx, it treated human beings as mere integers. It was a pattern I would see repeated countless times in the years to come.

If capitalism occasionally picks your pocket, socialist slight-of-hand will steal your soul. All of the lofty claims were just a gussied-up version of the old something-for-nothing con that rabble-rousers and saints have worked through the millennia.

Marx and his followers simply timed the market, working a grift that left tens of millions dead and over a billion lives stunted. The least savory human being is the "man of ideas."

I found an empty second-class compartment on the train leaving the classless society. July grimed the air. The six-passenger box stank of old sweat, spoiled food, and crushed-out cigarettes. I bullied the window until it stuttered down and looked south, as if I might spy Greece just past the signal lamps.

Glancing back into the depths of the station, I saw a black man sprinting for the train. Lofting a dufflebag, he looked intensely fit and distinctly out of place. As the last whistle sounded and the train creaked into motion, he hurled his bag aboard and followed after, leaping for the grips and hauling himself inside.

Exploding into my compartment, he smiled hugely, with polished ivory teeth and skin burned black.

"How is it, mon? How are you, my friend?" he asked in Caribbean English. He had judged me in a blink.

The train crawled, hardly stirring the air in the cabin. The heat had weight. But to keep the window open, we both had to sit with our backs to the coal-burning locomotive. Soot and cinders dusted the opposite bench.

We gained speed, but not much. Serbia receded in slow motion. Gregarious as the announcer in a tourism commercial, my unexpected companion talked and talked.

He was a professional soccer player. From either Jamaica or Trinidad, I can't remember with certainty.

"These Yugoslavian people," he said. "They are stingy men. They ask me to play for them, but they offer me peanuts. I will not play for nothing, mon. Not for these peanuts. I am not a monkey."

"So you're going to Greece?"

"To Thessalonica. I'm going to audition for their team. These Yugoslavians," he clucked and shook his head, "they want me to play for them very badly. So badly, mon. But you cannot have something for nothing. They look at me and think, 'This black fellow must be stupid.' But I know my value. That is the truth of the matter. I call them out of bounds."

A cart came by with refreshments, most of which were alcoholic. The footballer bought himself a mini-bottle of raki. When I shook my head at the vendor, my traveling companion stopped him. Then he glanced at me again.

I must have looked pathetic. With my money running low, my weathered jeans, and the long hair stuck to my temples.

"I am such a rude boy," the footballer told me. "You must join me, be my guest."

He bought three more small bottles, handing two to me.

I never was a man to turn down a free drink.

Waving off my thanks, he said, "These Yugoslavians think I have no money. But I have money. I am not a poor man, a beggar."

We drank. Later on, we drank some more. He was a kind and pleasant man, the sort who brightens a journey. We talked about the United States and its disinterest in soccer, then about European girls, of whom my companion was fond. We shared our similar impressions of socialism's shortcomings.

When the train stopped in Pristina, my new friend bought us cheese pies from a granny on the platform. What I saw of the city in passing made me instantly nostalgic for Belgrade. We rode through poor country in the evening light, throbbing over the rails. Stretches passed in silence while we pondered the future and past as travelers do. But the quiet was always vulnerable to the footballer's mighty laugh. He possessed an endless arsenal of stories.

We drowsed. There were mountains, another curl of the Balkans, a region I knew only from the fiction of Ivo Andric and Milovan Djilas. We paused again in Skopje, with a reek of scorched brakes. Groggy, I leaned out of the window, hoping to clear my head—several more rakis burned in my stomach. But I was gone. As the train snapped into motion again, I sat down and gave in to sleep.

We emerged from black night into a yard scoured by spotlights. The glare yanked my eyes open.

The border. Fine with me. I was more than ready to put Yugoslavia behind me. Deep into *The Odyssey*, I was primed for my first swim in that wine-dark sea.

Men in uniform paced the yard, some with dogs, others with submachine guns. It looked like a scene from a spy film. I had never seen anything like it in my sheltered American life—the northern border with Austria had been nothing like this. Although I knew I had nothing to fear, I felt a pleasant little pulse of dread.

Men barked orders. Doors opened with a wheeze and slammed shut again. Nothing seemed to be happening very quickly.

We waited.

After several minutes, the footballer grew impatient. "Mon, I'm hungry. This is not enough for me to eat." He slapped his belly. "I will burn up all this fat. Watch my bag for me."

"Don't you think you should wait?"

"I'll be back in a jiff. I'll bring something for you, too."

And he was gone. I hoped the train wouldn't leave without him. I felt indebted and protective.

Bleary, with the good effects of the alcohol gone and only the sourness left, I sat listening to the border guards work their way down the corridor. Wishing, for his sake, that the footballer would make it back to his seat in time.

New footsteps thumped down the corridor, more purposeful than those of the passport inspectors. They did not pause at any of the compartments.

Until they got to mine. An officer ripped the door open, looked around with a glimmer of confusion, then settled his eyes on me and started shouting. In Serbo-Croatian, a language that had not been taught in Schuylkill Haven High School.

I didn't have a clue what he was saying. But he wasn't happy.

"I'm an American," I said lamely. I couldn't come up with anything better. Barely twenty, scruffy, and thin, I didn't exactly have a commanding presence. Nor did my voice sound confident.

I stood up to get my passport from my bag on the overhead rack.

The officer shoved me back into my seat. Furious. Then he changed his mind, grabbed me by the upper arm and pulled me to my feet. Still shouting.

His breath smelled of onions.

The officer, a Slav, turned to his darker subordinates. Giving orders in a furious voice.

Seconds later, I was marching down the corridor with a submachine gun's muzzle tapping the small of my back.

Schoolboy fistfights—which I routinely lost—and bottles flying across barrooms as my rock band hammered away had not prepared me for this midnight reality of uniforms, an obscure language, and guns.

With the officer striding ahead of us, I was guarded as if I were a deadly criminal. Or, at the least, an Enemy of the People. We dismounted from the train and headed for a building beside the station. Squat and pocked, it looked as if it dated to the last days of the Ottomans.

Inside, I was a sensation. And something of a bewilderment. There was more barking. Plenty of it. In a struggling voice, I repeated that I was an American. It made no impression. My captors' English was as limited as my Serbo-Croation.

They hustled me into a cement-walled room at the back. With a single lightbulb dangling from the ceiling, a bare table, and a few unmatched wooden chairs, it aped the interrogation room from a black-and-white spy film.

The officer had not given up on getting answers from me. He had only been catching his breath. His expression was so maddened that I thought he was going to punch me. Oddly enough, that didn't frighten me much. I'd been punched before. What froze my guts was the sound of a whistle, followed by shuttling cars. My passport was in my bag in the compartment. Without it, I was nobody. I imagined the train crossing the border into Greece without me.

I tried to speak reasonably to the officer. Asking if anyone spoke English. Telling him that I hadn't done anything, that I had no idea what they wanted from me. My voice quivered and I only made him angrier.

The door opened. My interrogator straightened, the gesture of a subordinate. Another officer, no older but with a recognizable sense of privilege, stared at me. Utterly befuddled.

Stepping closer, as if to be certain of what he saw, he spoke, at last, in English.

"But . . . you are not a black man." He shook his head, pondering. "You cannot be the black man."

That was my first introduction to the lethargy of the Serb mind.

"Do you *know* a black man?" he asked. "Was there a negro man on the train today? Does he travel with you, this fellow?"

Nurtured on the silliness of literature and films, I wondered if I should remain silent, protecting the footballer. He had been kind to me.

"Come with me," the senior officer said before I could answer. Perhaps he read my face. As he had read a thousand faces before mine. "We will find him. You will point to him for me."

I didn't have to play the Judas, after all. Although I do not doubt that I would have done so. Just as we left the building, another detachment marched the footballer toward the door.

He smiled at me—that wonderful smile—and shook his head. As if to say, "These Yugoslavians . . ."

They put me back on the train. The footballer's bag was gone, but mine was still there. Urgently, I rummaged for my passport.

When I drew it out, my hands were shaking.

The train began to shunt across to the Greek side of the border.

I never learned what happened to the footballer or what accusations he faced. Perhaps he was a marked smuggler and I had confused the ambush planned by the customs police. Or maybe the Belgrade soccer team *really* wanted him to wear their colors. Since then I have learned that such affairs happen at border crossings every day. Hundreds of times. Thousands. But we, the privileged, do not see that underside of travel, unless we glimpse an exchange over a shabby man's expired passport or pass a few Latinos surrounded by our authorities as we stroll into Tijuana or Juarez. You can't say that such people disappear. They're invisible from the start, at least to us. It was as if I had traveled with a ghost.

Before the day was out I was in Athens, exhilarated. As soon as I found a place to flop, I headed for the Acropolis. The sight of it pierced me. Childish it may have been, but I could have leapt in delight. I wandered in the rubble and stared through the haze at the sea beyond Piraeus.

Back then, you could crawl all over the Parthenon. There were no ropes or guards to warn you off. You could even take a nap against one of the pillars, which I did. Then I went down to the Plaka, amid the din, where I drank retsina because it was cheap and ate what I could afford.

That journey ended on Mykonos, where I slept under the open sky, read Homer on topless beaches, and survived on honey, yogurt, bread, and wine. Some Aussies working at a beach club let me slip in to shower, flirt with the tourists, and cadge drinks. A bemused tavern owner kept my bag safe. I lived in surfer shorts, adding a t-shirt at dusk. Conflating freedom with carnality, my fellow travelers made things lively. There were yachts offshore and ambitious beauties dockside. Rich divorcees, their flesh scorched to jerky, prowled down from hillside villas and immaculate old queers begged smiles from the waiters in the tavernas. You could sit at an outdoor table and watch the sun sink, nursing wine that was cheaper than a cola. I fell in with a blond refugee from Prague who deserved better companionship. Much too late, she cursed me. It wasn't a bad life at all and I can see how people fall into the rhythm of it, letting their lives meander.

The junta was in power then, and the young Greeks I met were unhappy. But none of us cared. Foreigners were allowed the run of the house, as long as they paid up. Mykonos, not yet bleakly gay, was a playpen for Westerners no Greek would invite to his home. And we played.

When my money ran out, I went home to a clinging girl-friend, beautiful, brilliant, and monstrous.

Among the many reasons I joined the Army, one was the chance to travel. And I got it. Beginning with Fort Leonard Wood, Missouri, or, as Army wags put it, "Fort Lost-in-the-Woods, in the State of Misery." There were gorgeous sunrises, of which I saw an abundance. I enjoyed basic training, with the vibrant obscenity of its cadence calls and the surprising ease of a regimented life. The characters were boundlessly entertaining, from the theatrical drill sergeants to the bizarre assortment of recruits who volunteered for the military in the mid-1970s. I befriended the toughest guy in my platoon and the rest went smoothly.

I'll never forget one drill sergeant, a southerner. Confronted with a recruit's genius for inane mistakes, he'd slap his hands on his hips, cock his spine like a rising cobra, shake his head in wonder and declare, "Well, fuck me dead with a reindeer dick . . ."

Now, of course, we train young men and women together, so the poetry is gone.

Packed off for a specialized course at Fort Huachuca, Arizona, historic home of the buffalo soldiers and a base for the Apache wars, I fell in love with the high mountain desert, once and forever. A busload of us arrived near midnight on a Friday. Liberated from basic training, my comrades rejoiced to find a beer dispenser in the barracks. A spoilsport, I made my bunk and climbed into it.

I had my reward in the morning. The only survivor of the Battle of the Beer Machine, I walked down the slope to the mess hall in brisk October air. Across a misted plain, the Dragoon Mountains rose like ghostly islands. The Chiricahua range purpled in the distance. The landscape was visual cocaine.

Something made me turn around. And I saw the Huachuca Mountains rising directly behind the barracks: stark, stern, weathered. If I didn't gasp outwardly, I did inwardly. The bare majesty of that morning gripped me and never let go.

Fort Huachuca was home to the U.S. Army Intelligence Center and School, but no real intelligence work was done there, only training, testing, and the thoroughly incompetent formulation of doctrine. USAICS prepared Military Intelligence officers and the enlisted soldiers who would become analysts, interrogators, image interpreters, counterintelligence agents, and radar crews. Dusty and inert, the town outside the main gate sprawled across the desert like an old dog in a coma. Sierra Vista might better have been named "Siesta Vista" in those days, when its excitements were limited to a biker bar and the Saber Lounge, a carnivorous strip joint.

The desert and the mountains were what mattered. I ran alone up the canyons, startling sunbathing rattlesnakes, and climbed above the gulches and arroyos in air as sharp as cold gin. My personal life had been in disarray and those first, few months in Arizona as an enlisted man were exhilaratingly lonely. In the Army, I felt free. Later, when I returned to Fort Huachuca as a lieutenant, I discovered Nogales, Mexico, and the beaches along the Sea of Cortez, which had not yet been developed. There were always women then, few of good character. We gripped each other on summer evenings that excused desire and lies, betraying lovers, spouses, and friends with vigor. The wages of sin were, at most, brief discomfort. Resilient flesh trumps conscience in the young.

That came later. And I have resolved not to exhume the corpses littering my private life. May they rest in peace, for many deserved a better death.

Assigned to the 8th Infantry Division in Germany, I was stationed in Bad Kreuznach, a spa town on the Nahe River with good local wine and the house of the late-medieval Dr. Faustus tarted up as a restaurant. The town offered Roman mosaics, a castle blasted during a Swedish siege, the church in which Marx married an unsuspecting girl from the bourgeoisie, an embarrassed plaque where a synagogue stood until Kristallnacht, and best of all, a 17:04 train to Paris on Fridays—which I boarded whenever I was in funds and a weekend pass permitted.

Although their government's posturing can resemble a bad striptease show, I enjoy the French—who can only be shamed by a disappointing meal. Even in the 1970s, the aging farmers you met in country taverns near Chateau Thierry would not let you pay for your own beer, once they learned that you were an American soldier. And Paris . . . in Germany, I didn't have a car or a telephone even as a sergeant. My rented attic rooms by the river had no radiators against the German winters, only a feeble heating unit under the kitchen stove. But frost on the inside of the bedroom window seemed a bargain in trade for weekends in a simple hotel off the not-yet-sanitized Rue St. Denis.

Late one Friday evening, I checked into a particularly cheap hotel, snagging a giveaway-priced garret room. It even had a private bathroom with a dim light and working plumbing. I felt as if I were beginning to master the city and, although it was nearing midnight, I strolled off to have a stand-up supper in the Quartier Latin.

When I returned and opened the door to my room, dust billowed around me. I groped for the light switch and flicked it.

The ceiling of the bathroom had fallen in. A mammoth chunk of masonry and tile had crushed the commode.

It would have been a nasty way to go.

I still like Paris best in March, when the gray rain drives you to sit over a glass of wine behind a café window. The rain stops and radiant light fills the air, painting the facades across the street. You see what Monet saw.

Back in Bad Kreznach, the early morning walk to the *Kaserne* led through wet streets that shimmered under the lamps. It was always March there, too, and the streets were always empty. I wore an unauthorized sweater under my field jacket, but all defenses were vain against the damp. My boots tapped over the cobblestones as I marched from the old quarter where I lived through a business district bombed flat and rebuilt badly. Then I crossed black rail yards on a footbridge and passed rows of workers' houses, prim and dreary. Just before the barracks, there was a small bordello (which I was too vain ever to enter). The light outside was blue, not red. Twice along my route the air thickened with the fragrance of local bakeries, as rich and seductive as flesh.

After our morning calisthenics and a dull company run, a hot shower in the barracks warmed me for the first time since I had left work the evening before.

The Army was incalculably good to me. I would spend a total of ten years in Europe, but none were as precious as those first three when I was an enlisted man. And it was thanks to the Army that I missed most of the disco era back home, the lowest point of culture in humankind's history.

Instead, I hiked through golden vineyards with my friends and marched across snow-swept fields high in the Hunsrueck, determined to make it on foot from the Mosel to the Nahe before the Monday-morning formation. I knew where I could get a good, cheap meal of *Sauerbraten* near the university in Mainz—where it always rained—and where a soldier's pay bought the best dry Riesling. I walked everywhere I could, but took a train to Munich and visited Dachau. In the photographs on display in the concentration camp museum, you cannot tell who's more astonished by what they see, the prisoners or the GIs.

A German woman, a decade my senior, invited me to Florence, where she lost her patience when I spent too much time before paintings her guidebook didn't mention. I endured her longer than I should have done, in love with her Schwabing apartment.

But the European heartlands were too tame. I wanted to get back to Greece, and to go beyond it. When our Cold War mission struck a lull, a comrade, Jerry Marish, and I persuaded our superiors to let us take a full month of leave. Joe Woodall joined us. He was a resourceful combat engineer and a good man on the road, always grinning.

We descended the east coast of Italy in a baggage car, with the door rolled back to welcome the May weather. Sitting on our backpacks, we opened one bottle of wine after another as glimpses of the glittering sea teased by. South of Ravenna, the conductor joined us, perching on a mail sack to share our lunch of bread, ripe cheese, and grapes. He told us we might have chosen better wine.

From Brindisi, we sailed for Corfu, crossing the Adriatic under velvet clouds and moonglow. I met an unforgettable American girl who promptly forgot me. But Greece was what mattered: Durrell's Corfu, where we raced motorbikes like madmen and got beach tar on our feet. We took the ferry to Patras and a bus to Athens, followed by a deck-ticket voyage to Crete.

We climbed in the Lefka Ori, where I hurt my knees, and bunked in a Greek friend's ancestral village. The hospitality bewildered us until it emerged that I was intended for Evtichios's spinster sister. That wouldn't have done, and after a few more tales of popping German paratroopers told by an elder who had lost five brothers in the war, we escaped and met a brace of German girls as we hiked to the southern coast. There were always German girls in Greece, determined to get their money's worth from their vacations. They did not display their trousseaus—although they were apt to display a great deal else.

Matala was leprous with backpackers who only wanted cheap hashish. We island hopped. After clambering over Crusader ruins on Rhodes, I banged up a motorcycle in the wake of a wine-sodden lunch. Given that I wore only a swimsuit and running shoes (I have a snapshot taken minutes before the wreck), I cannot fathom how I walked away with just a few scrapes. The rental bike was returned well after dark. But Rhodes is one of those islands where Scandinavians pack in like sardines and boil themselves like lobsters. The evenings in town were vile with boisterous drunkards—not the amiable sort who know roughly when to stop, but the determined drunks bred north of the Alps. To this day I feel no need to visit Rhodes again.

We boarded another ferry and put into Patmos, climbing up to the cave where John the Not-So-Divine wrote the Book of Revelation in the blood of generations yet unborn. I had to see the lair of the most destructive madman our civilization produced until the twentieth century. The keeper from the hilltop monastery stretched out his paw for money.

With its unwashed monks and perversion of the Gospels, Patmos repelled me. Josef thought I was mad to leave an arrangement we had with a pair of Bavarian blonds, but their end-of-holiday passion could not hold me. Jerry went along with me to a few other islands—I recall a noseless old syphilitic sipping ouzo in a café on Lesbos; his eyes were as cloudy as the watered liquor. We made our way to Turkey in a fishing boat.

Impoverished though it was in 1979, Istanbul made it clear to me that I could never settle for the good order of Germany or for all the red wine in Beaune.

My eyes were fixed on the east.

But it was time to get serious about my life. I realized I loved the Army. And I was good at my work. But if I remained an enlisted man, I couldn't do a quarter of the things I hoped to do. It had been a great lark, but it was past time to grow up. I applied for Officer Candidate School in 1980.

At Fort Benning, Georgia, I broke my wrist playing football halfway through the course. The orthopedic surgeon who pushed the mosaic of bone chips back into place botched the job and the arm had to be rebroken a few weeks later. A second doctor warned me that I might not be able to continue in the Army. But that was nonsense. I put my sergeant's stripes back on to supervise punitive work details, ran road races with my cast in the summer heat, and peeled off the plaster early. I had to start OCS from the beginning again, which meant a repeat of the harassment of the first half-dozen weeks. But the only problem I had was keeping a straight face. I understood the game, and the verbal abuse made sense (some of it was admirably inventive). If a training officer can break you down by barking at you in a chow line, how on earth could you lead troops while enduring the strains of war?

I was impatient to get done with all of the nonsense, though, to get back to the field. My taste of intelligence work had hooked me. I wanted to get at the Soviet empire, to take it on single-handedly.

That had to wait until my officer's apprenticeship was over. After more lackadaisical training at Fort Huachuca, I was sent back to Germany, assigned to the 1st Battalion of the 46th Infantry in Erlangen, a wealthy city that disdained the lingering presence of American troops.

As a soldier, it was the best thing that ever happened to me. Surrounded by aggressive, talented peers—several of whom were destined for generals' stars—and serving under a succession of hard-edged commanders, my years at 1-46 were a better school for an officer than any formal training course. I loved it, and came within a day of transferring from Military Intelligence branch to the Infantry. Two things stopped me: First, the realization that, while Infantry branch had plenty of first-rate leaders, MI was in pathetic shape and needed officers who weren't afraid to kick over the trash cans. Second, I had enough of a sense of myself to realize that my talents and desires were better suited to intelligence work. In the Infantry, I would have been one more cap-buster in the pack. In MI, I might make a difference. Anyway, I was too self-absorbed to be a first-rate Infantry officer, and I recognized that, too.

I traveled whenever I could, climbing in the Dolomites and cross-country skiing in the Fichtelgebirge, eating my way through Alsace and imposing on English hospitality, but my position didn't allow me to stray too far or stay away longer than a week—I had to be able to get back to the *Kaserne* overnight, if necessary. That ruled out the Congo or Nepal.

The battalion worked six days a week in garrison, with drawn-out motor pool inspections on Saturdays. Lt. Col. Ralph Hagler, a red-haired Special Forces veteran, was an inspiring, merciless commander who got out of bed each day looking for a fight. His successor in command, Werner Wolfgang Banisch, was a stern but secretly goodhearted officer born in Beuthen, Silesia. His father had been a German NCO—lost at Stalingrad—and his family had to flee westward in 1945. "The Wolfgang" served first in the Canadian military as an enlisted infantryman, then in the U.S. Army in Vietnam. His face looked carved of bone with a dull knife. Their standards must have been the highest in any line unit and our aging combat vehicles rarely measured up. Thanks to Master Sergeant Pomeroy, my M-577 track was always spotless and never broke down. But headquarters vehicles were, rightly, inspected last, so the first half of our weekends burned away. I read Thomas Mann and Joseph Roth while waiting.

I prospered in 1-46 for two incidental reasons: First, both Hagler and Banisch had been commissioned through OCS, so we all were members of the anti–West Point club; second, when Hagler tried to spook me upon my arrival in the battalion I stood up to him—which bewildered him for a moment, then gave me a head start in credibility. The finest commanders under whom I've served all shared an absolute intolerance for weakness in subordinate officers. Aggressive errors could be forgiven—timidity, hesitation, or evasiveness, never.

Then there were the frequent trips to fire our gunnery tables at Grafenwoehr, ARTEP maneuvers at Hohenfels, and field exercises to master the terrain we had been assigned to defend if the world blundered into war. I had a good eye for ground, which meant more work. I kept count: in 1982, I spent 163 days in the field. In the German winters we slept on the ground. No tents, since we had to be ready, at least in theory, to rise from the snow and fight. Or from the mud, which was in truth more frequent. It rained viciously, penetratingly, and we curled up in sodden sleeping bags, night after night, for weeks. "Infantry weather" we told each other, rueful but pretending we were immune to all discomforts. The Army destroyed my love of camping out.

I took soldiering seriously, staying fit to the point of vanity and marching through Clausewitz in German. And I was game for anything. On a chill September day, our brigade commander wondered aloud if the river beside which we stood was too deep for his tanks to ford. The engineer officer with us had no idea, so I stripped and dove into the Tauber's poisoned waters. It *was* too deep for tanks, with a bottom too unstable, although the current was not too swift for leeches. In our aged headquarters building, inherited from the *Wehrmacht*, I drafted war plans as well as intelligence estimates for my battalion before being dragged up to the division staff. Absurdly earnest, I studied old battlefields and new weapons, working incessantly on foreign languages all the while. There was also a well-intended, ill-fated marriage along the way.

I began writing for professional magazines and journals, to more acclaim than my novice insights—often wrong—deserved. I attended another required training course at Fort Huachuca and hoped for an assignment farther afield, perhaps to Turkey or to some exotic niche. I craved the narcotic of distance.

Instead, I was diverted at a general's request and sent to Fort Hood, Texas—a great place to be a soldier and a worse place to live than Albania in a plague year. In nearly twenty-two years in the military, that was the only time the Army assigned me to a post that was utterly wretched. Even Austin, just over an hour away and rich with music, could not redeem years lost in Killeen, Texas.

Damned to Fort Hood, I began to write fiction again. I had finished my first novel, *Bravo Romeo*, while still a sergeant in Bad Kreuznach (in contrast to its intolerant image, the Army was always supportive of my publishing), but then my life had been consumed by the military calling. At Fort Hood, I needed an outlet to keep me sane, so in the evenings I assembled another novel, *Red Army*, which, to my shock, would become a bestseller.

During my exile in Texas, I realized that Military Intelligence was headed in precisely the wrong direction, relying ever more upon technology and ignoring the essential human factor. The technocrats had the budget in their hands, and those who command the purse-strings rule any bureaucracy. They had convinced themselves that all the intelligence that mattered could be processed by the computers at Fort Meade, Maryland. Meanwhile, across the ocean, Mikhail Gorbachev was scrambling to keep the fading Soviet Union alive with desperate reforms. A world was cracking, the intelligence community denied it, and I was playing with maps in Fort Hood, Texas.

I *had* to get to Russia, to get into the thick of things. A captain with the first gray hairs on my temples, I had to make a change before it was too late. I didn't want to become another dreary staff officer who judges his success in life solely by the timeliness of his promotions.

Warned that I was ruining my career, I applied for the Army's Foreign Area Officer specialty. Each year, the FAO program selects a small number of officers for intensive language courses, advanced degrees (I already had mine, snatched along the way) and training in target countries. I wanted to focus on the Soviet Union and concealed the fact that my master's degree in international relations had involved a concentration on Latin American affairs.

Accepted, I got a year of Russian-language training on the Monterey Peninsula—Eden for grown-ups—and arrived at the U.S. Army Russian Institute in Germany in midsummer.

It was 1989.

FROM MUSTAPHA,
TO NATASHA, WITH LOVE

WHEN SADDAM HUSSEIN INVADED KUWAIT IN AUGUST 1990, I KNEW we could easily overpower his military. I had seen the best of his officer corps that spring. In Riga, Latvia. Drunk and whoring.

I sat in a disco bar with Henry Nowak, a fellow officer and my closest friend. Dutiful, generous, and morbidly funny, Henry combined the temperaments of Galahad, St. Francis Xavier, and Johnny Rotten. Neither of us found discos of any sort appealing, but beer, like love, is where you find it. The club was better supplied than our foul hotel.

Late northern light probed the windows. The room was far from full and we soon realized why no young Latvians were present. The disco had been taken over by Iraqi pilots brought to the wheezing USSR for training. No respectable Latvian girl would get within spitting range of them.

But Latvia was not populated solely by tall blonds redolent of Viking raids. Their ranks swollen by Stalinist imperialism, Russians haunted the cities. Muscovite womanhood supplied the flesh for the disco.

The club was a down-market hooker bar, where the husky girls were realists. Pleased with their captive Iraqi clientele—who possessed *valuta*, cherished hard currency—they didn't bother hustling us beyond perfunctory smiles. To the Iraqis, who measured lust by the pound and admired gold front teeth, those chubby chemical blonds were the stuff of dreams.

The girls worked them over. Flirting, pouting, insisting on being won. The Iraqis were a bedraggled bunch with slender forearms, unable to sit still. Tightly sheathed in colors unknown to nature, the prostitutes looked as top heavy as triple-scoop ice-cream cones.

The DJ played sing-song Europop and guttural Russian rock. Few patrons danced, none well. While Henry and I sipped beers, the Iraqis downed hard liquor. We briefly intrigued a few of the pilots, but American officers in mufti could not compete with a harem.

Underdeveloped countries send three kinds of officers abroad for training. Many are well-connected mediocrities for whom the program is a perk, a vacation not to be taken seriously. (Even the U.S. military is loathe to fail foreign students, and word gets around.) A few are selected on merit. The third sort are the watchers, intelligence operatives tagging along to ensure the party line is never crossed: social hi-jinks are okay, but don't criticize the regime. Having recently ended its grim war with Iran and with ripening plans for Kuwait, the Iraqi military might have been expected to take such training more seriously than most. But you learn to read your fellow officers, whether they're in uniform or not, on duty or at play. And those Iraqi pilots didn't have grit. There was no crispness, no sense of vocation, no rigor about them. They were the sort who do what they're told until they spot a chance to run away.

The Iraqis splurging on imported whisky that night were the pilots who would fly their planes to Iran a few months later, rather than face the U.S. Air Force in combat.

An Iraqi made a wrong move. A rotund woman rose from his table, face the color of salmon on a plate. Equally ready to cry or curse, she fled across the dance floor to impale herself on a barstool. Sweeping thin blond hair back from black roots, she focused on the array of bottles. Refusing to look back. After fumbling through her bag, she lit a cigarette.

Half her size, her Iraqi suitor rose from his chair to follow. His companions spread their mustaches in amusement, but feigned sympathy. The other girls smoked with their jaws on their fists, too bored to choose a side.

The Iraqi hurried to the alcove by the entrance. An array of sweets, cigarettes, and oddities climbed the racks behind the counter. He spoke to the barman in loud English that quickly failed him, then pointed at a large pink box of chocolates.

Money changed hands.

The Iraqi marched up to his paramour, holding out the chocolates and smiling. She ignored him. Theatrically. His pleading and cajoling made no apparent difference. But it was all a ritual, haggling for a carpet in a bazaar. At last, he laid the box on the bar by her ashtray.

The pilot walked to the stage and gestured for the DJ to bring his ear closer. More bills changed hands. The DJ stopped an upbeat tune in mid-play and flipped on a slow number. The loudspeakers told us, in Russian, that "This song is from Mustapha, to Nastasha, with love. . . ."

The public display of devotion cracked her defenses. Natasha looked over her shoulder. Delicately. With a wistful smile. As if recovering from a lifetime's wounds. The Iraqi officer rushed to her side and extended a hand, inviting her to dance. It was a mating ritual from junior high—not innocent, but naïve.

They danced like eighth-graders, too. Unsure and uncomfortable, shy of their evident wanting. Finally, the Iraqi clasped her to him.

His comrades called out their encouragement.

"I can't watch any more of this," Henry said. "No beer's worth it."

Riga was much better than its guests. Tourists were drawn to its medieval heart, but beyond the park where battlements once stood, the city had an art nouveau soul. One of Europe's loveliest streets, a fantasy of curved facades and oval windows, ended at a single tasteless building, which the KGB had taken as its headquarters. Not long before, walking by those doors would have raised the pulse of any man or woman. But the world had changed. The Soviet Union's death certificate would not be signed for another year, but it was obvious that Latvia had seceded. The people ignored the outposts of Moscow's empire. The KGB were nothing but *svolotch*. Scum.

Ethnic Balts preferred to speak scraps of German or Radio Liberty English rather than the tongue of their oppressor. Nationalist demonstrations packed the squares and boulevards, their defiance expressed in folk costumes and scorching complaints about all things Soviet. Old, forbidden flags appeared. Russians who complained were scorned. The fear was gone. And once the fear is gone, no dictatorship long survives.

Along with Lithuania and Estonia, the neighbors on its flanks, Latvia had served as a plaything of greater powers. Conquered by the Teutonic Knights, the indigenous population had been reduced to serfdom on its own lands. Riga became a prosperous port and a member of the Hanseatic League, a rehearsal for globalization. Lithuania expanded, then contracted. Gustavus Adolphus, the insatiable military tourist, passed through during his Polish wars. (A window in the Lutheran church commemorates the Lion of the North.) Eventually, the Russian knout replaced the Prussian fist, but the German-speaking nobles remained in place, favored by the czars for their baffling diligence. The revolutionary wake of the Great War brutalized Latvia, yet the territory escaped the Bolshevik claw. For a time. From 1920 until the Red Army crossed the border again two decades later, the country experienced a renaissance of art, design, and vivacity.

By the time Henry and I arrived in 1990, with visas bought through a German tourist agency, the Soviet biliousness had been purged from Riga's museums. In its place, the Latvians assembled exhibitions celebrating their interwar culture. I was stunned. The intelligence, taste, and craftsmanship surpassed the better-known achievements of Scandinavia during the same fertile period. From coffee pots to films, from etchings to architecture, products told of a people who had been storing up talent for centuries. In their years of freedom the Latvians built an admirable nation.

Then the Russians came back. With red stars on their caps and helmets. Another new museum documented Communist atrocities. Arrests. Torture. Summary executions. Deportations. Anyone suspected of being a bourgeois—dressed too neatly for a commissar's taste—disappeared into the mass graves in the birch woods, into the river, into basement execution chambers. Those who didn't receive a bullet in the back of the skull were packed into trains headed east beyond the Urals.

The Soviets were not merely trying to cow a population, but to exterminate a culture. The Latvians didn't give up easily. A woman proudly told me her mother's tale of how the wives of Stalin's generals, *nyekulturniye* straight from the collective farm, expected to lord it over the Latvians at Riga's opera house. When they visited the shops to buy gowns for the performance, the Latvians sold them negligees—in which they marched down to their seats on the arms of their husbands.

The Nazis invaded. In a year, the Soviets had made themselves so hated that the Latvians welcomed Hitler's legions as liberators. Setting aside old grudges, Balts volunteered to join the *Wehrmacht*'s foreign auxiliaries. Local Jews paid a gruesome price for their purported sympathy with the Bolsheviks.

Everyone would have a turn at suffering. After three years the Soviets came back. This time, they meant to complete the purge their commissars had begun in 1940. Anyone suspected of German, capitalist, anti-Soviet, or faintly imperfect sympathies of any kind found himself in a cell. If he was lucky. Politics settled personal scores. Families died to empty desired apartments. Even wartime service behind the lines on behalf of the Soviets raised the suspicion of a partisan's independent mentality. Conformity was everything, and even that wasn't enough. Whispered words cost lives. Lies killed. Between the war, the Nazis, and the GULag, a quarter of Latvia's population perished.

Russian colonists filled the vacant rooms. The worst lodging in Latvia was better than communal barracks in remote industrial settlements or the poverty of collective farms. Hacks refashioned history. Street names were Russianized. The USSR felt permanent, a new and merciless incarnation of the empire of the czars. Dreary decades passed. The persecutions tapered off, but life stagnated.

Then, in one of those rare blessings on humankind, the Soviet Union withered into senility. By 1990, Latvia had been reborn in the public mind, if not yet on the map. The quickest way to make yourself unwelcome was to greet a Balt in Russian. As I found out.

It was a heady place to be that spring. Even on the quietest day, you sensed passion on every side, a resurrection. The Russians grumbled into their vodka bottles, shocked by their own powerlessness. In Lithuania, impatience with the pace of the Soviet retreat turned violent, but the Latvians simply marched forward, bringing their history down from the attic and laying it out for all the world to see. Hope enchanted the streets.

In Riga, I befriended a German surgeon who longed to take a scalpel to her past. It was a time of personal revolutions, too.

Each life includes days whose richness cannot be shared. One of my perfect days involved nothing more dramatic than a bus ride from Riga to Tallinn. The route traced the Amber Coast, a stretch of cold, white sand as beautiful as Heaven on a holiday. Dark blue waves lapped a coastline of low dunes adorned with stunted trees, worn rocks, and golden reeds. Birds rose broad-winged from marshes, black against the blue-enamel sky. No end of books praise the palette of the south, the lemon light of Italy, or the hues of an Arab souk. But there are no colors so true and piercing as those of an early summer day in the north, when white clouds temper the brightness, lulling your eyes before the sun reappears. The world grows deep and detailed: the gnarl of driftwood, talcum sand, the vast, competing blues of sea and sky. A walk on the shore becomes a stroll with God.

The amber that washes in might symbolize the lost world of the Baltics. The sensibility inherited from my father's family gave the landscape resonance. For all my cheering-on of the new Baltic freedoms, the sandy fields outlined by supple trees evoked a vanished *German* world, a culture that survived conquest and plague only to disappear in Hitler's inferno.

I have no sympathy with Germans claiming property rights in the east. No restitution of any kind is due. The war-spawned migrations that rid Baltic registries of their German names did not sweep out millions of innocents. From Kaiserslautern to Koenigsberg, Germans *loved* Hitler. They embraced his madness and backed him with their lives. *Every* German soldier guarded Auschwitz.

Yet, the heart can feel empathy with the ghosts that walk the land bewildered. How could their world end so suddenly, so entirely? The Germans on the Baltic shore were poor relations to those on the Rhine or Elbe. Far from the Hollywood image of the imperious *Junker*, those counts, barons, and *Freiherrn* were more apt to rent a seaside cottage than to own one. They were the indebted landowners in the novels of Eduard von Keyserling, a writer overdue for revival in the English-speaking world. The rest of the Germans were shopkeepers or professors, country doctors, Lutheran ministers, or government functionaries. Within the borders of czarist Russia and *Ostpreussen* alike, the Baltic Germans had to count their coins and the errors of an elder son could ruin a family's fortunes. Marrying off daughters was a worry. Many a woman with an impressive coat of arms and no dowry withered away in the family *Landhaus* reading novels borrowed from a neighbor. A summons to St. Petersburg or Berlin for the paterfamilias meant a hasty visit to the tailor for a new coat—purchased on credit—and concern over the length and cost of the stay. The growing season was short, the land poor, and the harvests never abundant. The hope was ever that the next generation would put things right. It was a life of fragile gentility and isolation, Germans according to Chekhov.

Of course, the native people lived far harder lives. Perhaps it's best that Keyserling's world was annihilated. Perhaps it had outlived any purpose it ever had. (An aging and childless aristo in one of Keyserling's novels remarks that "*Aussterben ist vornehm*," dying out is distinguished.) Yet, the dunes I passed were populated by his characters, even if only I saw them.

They were far more vivid than my drowsy bus-mates.

Our destination, Tallinn, was *still* Reval. And Tartu was still Dorpat. That lost world lived on in my blood and bones.

The curling streets of Tallinn, with their medieval gables and brand-new basement bars, were resolutely German. And Estonian, too. But, despite the proximity of Russia, there was no trace of

Moscow or even St. Petersburg in the old quarter, unless one counted bits of cyrillic lettering and the trash in the alleys. Tallinn was an outpost of Europe, on the edge of a barbarous world. The city's walls had been a necessity.

Finnish drunks pissed on those walls that June, weekend tourists roaring with cheap vodka. But Tallinn's towers once had marked the reach of civilization. As I write in 2006 and consider the paranoid Russia of Vladimir Putin, it's easy to believe that they still do.

Henry had no patience with my reveries. He saw history from the other side of the battlefield. In 1939, his father had been a Polish infantry officer. Bronislaw Nowak fought the Germans. And the Russians. Escaping from Mauthausen concentration camp, he fought the Germans again as a partisan. After the war's end, with Poland clamped between Stalin's jaws, he served as an officer with the auxiliary troops the U.S. military hired to guard its support installations in occupied Germany. Eventually, Capt. Bronislaw Nowak made his way to Cleveland. The officer became an auto worker. Through mutual friends, he found a wife, a woman of the Polish aristocracy who had taken refuge from Communism in Argentina. Together, they built a new life—the classic immigrant story. Rather than indulging in nostalgia for a lost world, the Nowaks embraced America with discipline and pride. (It took eighteen years of friendship for me to learn that Henry's mother descended from the Dzieduszyckich line of the House of Sas, whose military traditions date to the early fifteenth century.)

Fiercely American, both Nowak sons became career officers in the U.S. Army. The elder Nowaks still live in a Cleveland suburb, where Bronislaw, in his nineties, grows incomparable tomatoes.

Shortly before we traveled to the Baltics, Henry had been promoted to major. (As this book goes to press he's still in uniform—as a brigadier general.) An Infantry officer turned Russia hand, he resembled Peter Zwack not only in being the son of an immigrant, but in the ease with which he exploded the myths of the Left about the brute nature of military men. If you hankered to discuss Steiner, Gombrowicz, Camus, or Borges, Henry would humble you with his ability to recall long passages and his grasp of an author's subtleties. He could quote Poland's greatest poet, Adam Mieskiewicz, for hours without stopping and knew more about European cinema than any Manhattan critic. He would scramble up mountains without losing his breath then give you a lecture about the sins of John Foster Dulles, St. Augustine, or Keith Richards.

Tall, lean, and hawk-faced, with black hair thick as a pelt and fond of a leather trenchcoat when off-duty, he looked like a dangerous secret policeman. Until he smiled. Then you learned that Henry revered every note The Clash ever recorded, could cite obscure discographies from the bebop era, and off-handedly recognized obscure Brazilian pop recordings. Dour at first impression and guarded with strangers, he danced maniacally when the mood came over him. I never knew him willingly to miss mass on a Sunday morning and the only time he ever gave me a killing look was when I made an ill-tempered remark about Catholicism. He had the mind of a Jesuit and the heart of a Franciscan.

As an officer, Henry was rigorous to a degree that would have humbled a Prussian. He took notes in the tiniest handwriting I have ever seen and displayed the largest heart I have ever known. Personally austere—he refused to butter his bread—he was inexhaustibly generous with others. Shy with women, despite the attractive figure he cut, he was as chivalrous as the heroes in the novels of Henrik Sienkiewicz. A friend could trust him with anything, from a fortune to a woman, and even the worst enemy might count upon his word. With a dark Slavic sense of humor—turned most often upon himself—and a romantic spirit he imagined that he concealed, he was brave, stoic, and wonderful to tease.

With his Polish heritage, Henry took rather a different view of the Baltic Germans than I did. But we shared an identical grasp of the Russian genius for making the worst of every opportunity. Traveling through the Soviet Union with Henry was like riding at the side of a Polish prince of the Golden Age—you could view the hapless Russians through his knowing eyes and he had a sixth sense for their fatalistic indolence. He could bully them, too, in better grammar than educated Russians spoke. A provincial waiter who claimed the kitchen had no eggs soon buckled under the wrath of Henry Nowak.

After we left Tartu for the old Russian heartlands of Pskov and Novgorod, Henry was spared further elegies of mine. We sat on the bus eating vodka-filled chocolates for breakfast and admired the Russian ability to present us with squalor the moment we left Estonia. In a blink, we had entered the world of Gogol's scheming peasants, corrupt bureaucrats, and hapless victims. The Soviets may have killed Mother Russia's intellectual culture, but they couldn't temper her self-destructive soul.

Rolling past clusters of grubby cottages strewn along deteriorating roads, we didn't need to exchange a word. We understood this world down in our guts. Our German and Polish ancestors might have fought each other—our friendship was a testament to the transformative genius of America—but our grasp of Russia was a testament to old blood.

———————

St. Petersburg is a syphilitic beauty. Beloved by tourists who rarely remain long enough to sense the sickness beneath her painted face, that city is the invalid sibling of robust, rambunctious Moscow. St. Petersburg feels unnatural, and she is. Built on a marsh at a cost of uncounted Russian lives, the city began as Peter the Great's attempt to shift his eastern country to the west. He feared and disliked Moscow, with its reek of incense and treachery, its purdah-like women's quarters, Byzantine robes, and the rats of Kitai Gorod. The Stalin of his day, Peter could not bear the human failings of his subjects. He wanted them to rise up to his vision and whipped them to death to encourage them, lacking the self-awareness to see that his goal of outdoing Europe was as vain as a peasant's dream of magical wealth. He wanted to make Russia stop being Russian, and used force willfully and vainly.

The Winter Palace stretches along the Neva River, as tacky as a long white limousine, the ultimate trophy of the nouveau riche. The contents of the over-praised Hermitage betray an equal disregard of taste. The Romanovs didn't buy great paintings—they bought great names signed at the bottom of third-rate paintings. One can almost imagine a Wall Street magnate snapping at his agent, "What part of 'Buy me a Rembrandt!' don't you understand?"

Everything in czarist St. Petersburg was built for show. The palaces had to be bigger, the boulevards wider, straighter, longer. Lice gripped the hair of countesses, but the chandeliers glittered. As flamboyant and careless as their owners, the in-town mansions of the aristocracy dumped shit from their windows into canals where cholera stewed. For all of the public opulence, St. Petersburg remained bitterly poor, a human stable for 99 percent of her inhabitants. Tolstoy was a Moscow writer, but Dostoevsky remains St. Petersburg's literary saint and father-confessor. Gogol understood the city's darkness, too. Perhaps Vladimir Putin sensed it before he took himself off to Moscow.

St. Petersburg is proud of her culture, of her laundry lists of composers and writers, her art collections and concerts, her opera and ballet. But just as the city's ideas have been imported, so has her talent: she's sterile. Valery Gergiev of the Kirov, perhaps the greatest conductor of our time, hails from the Caucasus. The great paintings that hang in the Russian Museum (by far the best collection in the city) wasted little oil on St. Petersburg. The memorable canvases are landscapes from the heartland or character studies, tableaux of oppression, or scenes from myth that anticipate photorealism—all culminating in color fantasies so rich their frames barely contain them. Kramskoi, Shishkin, Repin . . . Levitan, Serov, Vrubel . . . who among those ardent geniuses loved that consumptive northern fraud of a city? Their paintings feel imprisoned, as if hanging on the walls of the Peter and Paul Fortress across the river.

St. Petersburg seems weirdly inhumane for a city, that greatest collective achievement of humankind. It lies in the natural order of things that men rebelled against her contempt for the individual, for flesh and blood. Decembrists, anarchists, Bolsheviks—all were driven to violence by the ominous winter nights.

The St. Petersburg we saw on that trip (and on others that would follow) was still Leningrad, a city of miserable industries and uniform tenements, of Disneyland country palaces, laughable Soviet monuments, and illegal concerts in cellars that stank of piss. Human beings were bluntly for sale, as was the little they had. Even the white nights could not glamorize those quays and boulevards, although the half-light softened the decay. (Treated to another layer of cosmetics now, St. Petersburg remains a city of rotten teeth behind her painted lips.)

Chekhov knew. His three sisters didn't pine for "St. Petersburg, St. Petersburg, St. Petersburg," but for "Moscow, Moscow, Moscow. . . ."

Calcutta isn't the "city of dreadful night." It's St. Petersburg. Calcutta is warm and human. St. Petersburg has a soul colder than her winters—her side streets feel the way Vladimir Putin looks. From the megalomania of the city's founding through a revolutionary incarnation as "Petrograd," from "Leningrad's" sufferings in the Great Patriotic War to the bright veneer and corruption of today, that cursed city has always been the home of fear and sorrow.

We were eager to fly off to Moscow, where Peter Zwack would join us for a trip to Central Asia—long terra incognita for American officers. Henry and I had walked along the embankment deep into the mauve night, taking our conversation far too seriously. We felt blown as we sat down in our second row seats on a small Aeroflot jet. My leather jacket was worn white at the elbows and Henry had been growing a beard for the duration of our trip. To nervous Western eyes, we might have passed for Soviet citizens, although the locals were not fooled for an instant.

We were cranky, too, a penalty of far too little sleep. When the plane failed to start its engines on time, we grew sarcastic, mocking the endemic inefficiency. Two dark-complected gangsters sat in front of us, their big-shouldered suits a fantasy from the era of Bugsy Siegel. It wasn't their day. With the incomparable rudeness Aeroflot had perfected, a flight attendant ordered the Chechens out of their seats, telling them to find places at the rear of the aircraft, if they could. Conditioned to respond meekly to authority in public, men who might have killed over such a slight on their home ground gathered up their belongings without grumbling.

Switching facial expressions with terrifying speed, the flight attendant smiled brightly at us, the Westerners, and explained, "*Ozhidaiem ochen vazhnevo cheloveka.*"

We were waiting for someone very important.

Henry and I looked at each other. I do not recall which of us said snidely to the other, "Yeah, like Boris Yeltsin, right?"

A black limousine zipped up to the boarding stairs. Boris Yeltsin got out.

At the time, he was in exile from Moscow, polishing his reputation in St. Petersburg. Everyone sensed that he was the coming man. I had finished his autobiography a few weeks before. It wasn't the typical Soviet (or American) everything-was-perfect political memoir.

Accompanied by a single aide, he leapt up the stairs and paused at the head of the aisle, letting the passengers admire him. He grinned and waved, the perfect politician. Everyone applauded.

Yeltsin was a striking man in 1990. Not yet bloated by alcohol, his face had the even skin of a man who has regular facials. His blue suit was of good cloth and well-tailored—distinctly un-Soviet. His shirt shone true white and his tie was neat. The winning new model of the Russian bear, he projected even more size than he possessed. The only feature that did not suit a classic pol was his grin. He didn't only smile with his mouth, as party men do from Washington to Beijing. His eyes smiled, too.

He *enjoyed* being Boris Yeltsin.

As soon as he and his aide were buckled in and the flight attendant had finished fawning over Boris Nikolaievich, the engines growled to life. Without the customary Western pause, we rolled down the tarmac.

I waited until we were airborne, then leaned forward to introduce myself and Henry. It was wonderful to watch Yeltsin react. For a moment, the fact that he had been seated with two Russian-speaking U.S. Army officers took him aback. But he was a pol, after all. He mastered himself and answered with aplomb. I mentioned his autobiography, wishing him well. Henry, who could barely contain his laughter, produced a metal crest from the U.S. Army Russian Institute, the notorious "Garmisch spy school" we attended. It displayed the institute's motto, "For a better future," in Russian.

Yeltsin accepted the gift, examined it in the palm of a thick hand, furrowed his brow, nodded, and then pocketed it. We chatted briefly, with Yeltsin as gracious as if we might provide the deciding votes at a Politburo meeting. Then we left him in peace, savoring the thought that the KGB's control of affairs was not what it once had been.

Wildly different one from the other in temperament, Gorbachev, Yeltsin, and Putin met identical tragedies: each man did things that needed to be done but overstayed his purpose. There was no gracious way to leave—it was still a land for czars. After changing the world, Gorbachev would be humiliated and dismissed like a schoolboy. Yeltsin's bravery and lust for life would degenerate into drunkenness as his newly "free" people celebrated corruption and his government grew aimless. Putin would provide the rigor a chaotic society craved, but succumbed to the paranoia and despotism beaten into the Russian soul. Far from democracy, Russia has never even mastered the art of an orderly transfer of power.

Even deprived of its empire, Russia is too vast and conniving for a single man to rule. From Peter the Great to Putin, the illusion has been the same: the notion that an individual's strength of will could command the rain to stop and stay the winds.

In Moscow we found Peter Zwack surrounded by new friends in a hotel bar.

THE GREAT KHAN'S MORNING AFTER

DUST. WHEN YOU SCOOPED UP THE MOUSE-GRAY SOIL IT FELT startlingly light. With the texture of talcum powder, it ran through your fingers like silk broken down to microscopic grains. That earth was dead.

Our bus had stopped with a shiver and grunt midway between Bukhara and Samarkand. A platoon of German tourists stumbled from the torrid interior. They smelled of socks worn a week and looked as bedraggled as refugees. Having signed up for A Thousand and One Arabian Nights, they'd gotten thirty days in the hole. Had they whined just a bit less, I might have sympathized.

The men lined up by the roadside, a firing squad of tormented kidneys. Their women disappeared from the shoulders down, squatting in an irrigation ditch across the blacktop. A touchdown pass away, black-haired boys splashed in a collecting tank, larking in stagnant water surfaced with chemical rainbows. They roiled the algae and made the gray weeds shiver. Some of the kids wore hand-me-down underpants, others nothing. All looked jaundiced and happy. One boy lifted his face toward the sun.

Fields stretched into a distant haze that hid Afghanistan. All around us, cotton struggled to grow in the murdered soil. One of the world's thirstiest crops, its planting had been decreed decades before by bureaucrats in Moscow. They did to the earth what the GULag did to humans.

The invisible border to the south was demarcated by the Amu Darya, Alexander's Oxus, whose tributaries rallied in the Pamirs and Hindu Kush. The fabled river was not meant to irrigate thousands of square miles of desert. But nothing was impossible for the bureaucracies of Stalin or that bear-pawed bumpkin, Nikita Khruschev. No apparatchik dared to say, "We can't."

Cotton came. The waters seeped away. The earth grew cancered and died. Now the stunted cotton plants drooped like neglected geraniums, withered and brittle. They were parasites growing on a corpse.

"Grim," Peter muttered, shaking his head. Henry looked down the highway toward Samarkand. With an expression of disgust.

There were no birds—the power lines tracing the road hung bare. Nothing crawled over the earth, no movement excited the eye. The summer insects hummed feebly. Landing on your forearm or your shirt, they seemed too weak to carry on. You imagined them gasping for breath, and when you brushed them off, they didn't cling.

Shrieking, a dun-colored boy leapt back in the pool of chemicals.

The bus grunted to life again. Our minder called for everyone to reboard. With her department-store-model looks and super-model vanity, she had grown used to extracting gifts from Western men. Our indifference turned her venomous, her spite exacerbated by our habit of disappearing from the approved itinerary. In the spring of 1990, a confused era between the Soviet Union's hospitalization and its death, the only way we could get visas for the Central Asian "republics" had been to sign on with a German company offering educational tours. ("Educational" meant grubby, cheap, and sordid.)

The minder narrowed her viper's eyes, furious because we had her nailed: as long as we rejoined the group at key points, she didn't dare make a fuss when we disappeared—which we did frequently. Reporting us would have suggested that she was too weak to control her charges. And she would have done anything to preserve her position, which granted her routine contact with foreign businessmen of the sort who give finer presents to teases than they ever bring home to their wives. With chestnut hair cut like Lauren Bacall's in *To Have and Have Not* and a sailor-boy blouse of the sort children once wore, she was alert, deft, and as poisonous as the dust that stung my hand.

That dust was poisonous, indeed. When the waters of the Amu Darya did not suffice to turn great deserts into gardens, Soviet scientists waged chemical warfare against the earth with fertilizers, pesticides, and magic potions.

Nature took her revenge.

Earlier in the week, we had flown into Urgench, the launching pad for visits to Khiva, whose antique heart had been preserved by the city's inconsequence. Its walls were Khiva's bell jar, separating a specimen from a world that had moved on. Even the squalor was authentic, a pungent retort to those inclined to romanticize the past. I remember ornate columns and turquoise tiles, doors carved to show up the neighbors, pocked children, and sewage in the lanes. A girl sat on a stoop picking lice from an infant's scalp.

We stopped at a general store deep in the desert and found not only cold cans of Stella Artois—an inexplicable miracle second only to that of the loaves and fishes—but two Hungarian engineers working on a project a few hours deeper into the Kizyl-Kum. They reacted to Peter's family name as if they had just shaken hands with a fairy-tale prince. Our beers were free.

Urgench displayed a few ancient tombs and high-rise graves for the living. Everything threatened infection: the air, the water, the earth. Just to the north, the Aral Sea was dying—thanks to the diversion of the waters of the Amu Darya and the Syr Darya (the ancient Jaxartes). In thirty years, the shoreline had receded 40 percent, leaving salt flats swept by the seasonal winds. The blowing sands were, literally, diseased. The Soviets had built biological-warfare laboratories and test ranges on the Aral Sea's islands. Now some were so close to shore a rodent could splash over to them. Others, the worst, would soon join the dry land.

As the Soviet Union came apart, so did its secret laboratories. Ranges were abandoned, facilities went untended. Gates were locked, as if that might keep the pathogens in or thieves and animals out. When those winds blew down from the Polar waters and out of western Siberia they swept up death: plague, tularemia, anthrax, hemorrhagic fevers . . . viruses and bacteria lurked on those islands like caged animals anxious to escape. Local epidemics were not reported to the World Health Organization. Some were never reported as far as Moscow.

And then there were the toxins in the water supply that caused spectacular birth defects.

Even so, Urgench didn't have it as bad as parts of Kazakhstan to the northeast. Towns and villages adjacent to nuclear test sites—adjacent meant anywhere within hundreds of miles—bred masses of congenital deformities that trumped anything a horror-film make-up artist could imagine. It was a freak show multiplied by thousands.

Anyone who imagines a shred of humanity in Communism or militant Socialism need only study the Soviet treatment of the workers of the world. When the masses are raised above the individual, individuals suffer *en masse*. In a perverse way, the derelict behavior of the bureaucracy was more frightful than the intentional exterminations. When a tyrant kills, we have someone to hate. But what can we make of a system that murders millions through neglect and inattention? The planned murders were only a fraction of Soviet suffering. Poor planning killed as many, if not more, from the scheme to produce a wealth of cotton in the desert, to the Virgin Lands project that dumped city slickers in the Kazakh steppes bare-handed—then ordered them to produce absurd quotas of grain for the state that exiled them. Millions died.

But what do those "millions" mean to us? Figures on a page. Accounts of their suffering don't even spoil our appetite for lunch. The media lure us with tales of kidnapped girls, while genocide rates a few paragraphs on page nine.

And yet. Listing the Soviet Union's sins does not excuse those of its predecessors. For all the damage they eventually did, the czar's white-coats and, later, the Red Cavalry initially improved the lot of the people in the emirates and khanates now seated in world bodies as Uzbekistan, Turkmenistan, Tajikistan, Kyrgyzstan, and Kazakhstan. Nowhere was Islam more backward and oppressive, the tyranny more willful and gore-slopped, than in nineteenth-century Bukhara or Merv.

The Russians *did* bring progress, and not only of the material kind. The worst tormenting of women eased, at least in the cities. Law prevailed, if of a rough and ready sort. The Bolsheviks brought schools and public health programs—prior to the Red Cavalry's arrival in its streets, up to half of the population of Bukhara suffered from the local variant of Guinea Worm Disease, a water-borne infection that spawns long, thin parasites under the human skin; when the worm's head finally emerges into the open air, it must be trained, ever so carefully, around a stick until it exits the body completely, since a break and the remnant's death would lead to mortal infection. The affliction is as agonizing as it is grotesque.

Forever an invasion route, the region always suffered. It had its golden ages, from Alexander forward a few centuries, then again in the great age of Islam, the era of Omar Khayyam and Ibn Sina (Avicenna to us). But the last grandeur ended almost 600 years ago, in Samarkand, with the murder of Ulugh Beg, Islam's last renaissance man and the grandson of Tamerlane. Assassinated by the mad mullahs of his day, who found his speculations on science disturbing, he prefigured Galileo by almost 200 years. Thereafter, Central Asia faded from view, its trade routes withering under competition from Europeans sailing east in deepwater ships, its culture hardening, and its prejudices deepening. By the time the armies of the czar arrived in the nineteenth century, cities that had once bejeweled civilization harbored only the colorful savages captured in Verashchagin's canvases.

The conquest of Central Asia is a chronicle of valor, dash, and cruelty known to few Westerners. Beginning with grisly failures, it proceeded through forced marches across "impassable" deserts, Turcoman ambushes and stormed citadels, past mounds of severed Slavic heads and into ancient cities swept of life—as they had been countless times down the centuries, by countless invaders. Some of the tribesman fought on through the 1920s, until the Bolsheviks broke the Naqshbandi order with machine guns, heavy artillery, and brutality that outdid "Eastern barbarism."

It's as if every civilization that ever possessed those vast, barren lands and rare oases competed with its predecessors to see just how much damage could be done. For now, the Soviets are the champs. Their forerunners contented themselves with torturing human beings. The Soviet Union tortured the earth itself.

Melons. Dark green and round as cannonballs. Or pale, mottled, and oblong. Halved with a knife, their exposed pulp showed intimate and moist. In the summer heat, those melons looked as enticing as Delilah's daughter on payday.

We never bought one, never bit into a single cool, sweet slice. Risking plague or radiation is one thing, but dysentery is something else again.

In the old Soviet Union, watermelons were a valued treat, sold by the pound. To increase their weight, vendors hawking them in the bazaars and markets commonly injected extra water—badly polluted—with an old syringe. Melons were the quickest ticket to misery in the Soviet empire—swifter by far than annoying the KGB.

Rebuilt after a devastating earthquake a quarter-century earlier, Tashkent rose from the steppes on a slapdash foundation, its concrete walls fissured and uneven. The height of an apartment building or hotel inspired fear, not awe. (Anyway, the water pressure faltered before reaching the upper floors.) The boulevards were broad, the lives narrow. Upon arrival, we had been warned to stick to the Slav areas, since the spirit of universal brotherhood didn't extend into the Uzbek quarter. Above all, we were to avoid the native market.

Of course, we headed directly for the marketplace, leaving the wide sidewalks to hunt down unpaved alleys draining muck. You smelled the bazaar before you saw it. The stink of discarded offal (not that much was discarded) mingled with the scent of hot, ripe fruit and the aroma of spices sold from burlap sacks. The seasonings were as colorful as the silken dresses worn by the Uzbek women.

We got our share of looks—no smiles. But it was midday, we were three, and fear was beneath us.

We moved in a bubble of quiet amid the bustle. Nobody insulted us or moved to block us, but no one called to us to buy their wares. Stubbled in a manner that would later become fashionable in Hollywood, the men looked at—not into—our faces, while the women behind the piles of carrots and aubergines inspected us from top to bottom, taking special interest in our shoes. Once, I caught the gold-toothed smile of a girl with midnight eyes.

A teenage boy leaped at Peter, raising a maroon lump from a torn newspaper. He thrust the blob toward Peter's face before Zwackie could sidestep him.

It wasn't a weapon. It was a heart, perhaps a sheep's. So fresh it steamed and seemed still to be beating.

"*Russki?*" the punk demanded. Are you Russian?

"*Amerikanetz, ya Amerikanetz,*" Peter told him. "*Mi Amerikantsi.*"

"*Amerika?*" The boy looked as befuddled as if we'd told him we came from outer space.

"*Da. Iz Ameriki.*"

The boy shook his head. Hard. As if wishing a fly out of his ear. Then he recovered and held up the heart again, although in a friendlier manner.

"*Kupitye?*" You buy?

Peter didn't think he would. We picked up some apricots, though. And pistachios. As word spread that we were Americans, the tension eased. We still were not quite welcome, but we were tolerated. Hashish was available, but we declined, to an eager seller's dismay.

I wasn't sure the place had a trouble-free future.

Tashkent was, and is, the capital of Uzbekistan. The corrupt lived well then, and live even better now. For the average, put-upon citizen, little has changed and little ever will.

Until you penetrate private lives, there's not much to Tashkent, despite its size: a bad museum or two, a moldy officers' club from czarist days, and worn-down people, Slav or Uzbek, making what they can of limited lives. My fondest memory of the city comes from a later visit, when I joined a delegation whose purpose eluded me then and eludes me still. I was strolling alone in the evening, in the hour when the sunset burns the pollution dusky pink. Turning from an avenue toward a stretch of dilapidated quarters, a young couple caught my eye. You knew at a glance that they were not yet married, but would be. Already slightly stooped, the boy looked earnest and just handsome enough not to shame a girl. The young woman on his arm was plain and thin, but her cotton dress swayed gracefully and there was no ghost of malice in her face. She seemed the sort of girl who makes the best bargain she can in life and then expects no more.

Between us, at the sidewalk's edge, an old woman sold flowers. As the couple approached, she held up a bouquet. The crone knew her business, for she didn't offer the most elaborate arrangement, but exactly the one she judged the young man could afford.

The boy stopped. His date curled around his arm as she stopped, too—a second after he did. The woman held up the flowers, saying nothing. She looked at the boy, then smiled at his girl. Finally, she settled her eyes back on the boy.

I slowed my pace amid the homeward rush. I wanted to hear what might be said. But that wasn't necessary. A silent-movie scene played out. The boy's face—good-natured and a tad weak—said that he was calculating. How much money did he have on him? How much could he afford to spend? Clearly, he wanted to buy his girl that bouquet.

For an agonized moment, he wavered. Wondering if he should be sensible and save his rubles for some looming necessity.

The old woman just smiled behind the flowers. And waited.

The girl tugged at her beau. Gently. *Come on. I don't need flowers.* She put on the brave smile such girls keep ready for disappointments. *Come on, now. We'll be sensible.* Her left hand joined her right upon his forearm. Leading him away.

The boy shook her off. And reached into his pocket. He waved away the middling bouquet and pointed at a larger one in a bucket.

The old woman raised three fingers.

Dripping water, the bouquet rose. The old woman took the money, dried the stems on her over-skirt, and handed over the flowers to the boy.

Without a word, without meeting her eyes, he laid them in his girl's arms.

She parted her lips to speak, but didn't. Her teeth were even, but gray. Then she closed her mouth and looked down at the pavement, not at the flowers.

When she raised her eyes again she wore the most beautiful smile I've ever seen. For that one moment—perhaps for that whole evening—she was a beauty to break immortal hearts.

Cradling the bouquet in the crook of an elbow, the girl returned her hand to her lover's forearm. She passed me with her face tilted heavenward, proud as a queen and crying.

Blake's "dark, Satanic mills" still belch—on the outskirts of Chimkent, a city stamped from the earth to exploit what lay beneath it. It was near to nothing and offered nothing, yet someone in the Chimkent *nomenklatura* had sufficient pull to force Inturist to divert foreign visitors his way. We were told it was the birthplace of Nellie Kim, the Olympic gymnast. And then we were told nothing else.

Our hotel was skid row as reimagined for a Jim Jarmusch film. No one even tried to keep it clean. Squashed bugs gripped the walls where drunken fists had slain them. There was no air-conditioning, nor did the windows open. We drenched our bed-clothes with DEET and still woke with red welts.

Our treatment was the finest the city could offer, and you make the best of things. We strolled the nondescript streets, looking for anything of interest and finding nothing until we reached a park in the early evening.

It was Saturday and the workers of the world had come out to rest under the dusty trees. The city's concrete harshness softened before our eyes. Children ran—but did not shout as Western children would. The little girls wore bows like great white butterflies at the back of their heads, affixed to coiled buns or clipped between golden pigtails. The blood here was Slavic, Russian, and Ukrainian. More forced resettlements. And as the generations changed the wretched place became home.

Old men played chess, oblivious to the teenage boys swaggering down the green arcades in slow motion. Packs of girls laughed at the lot of them.

A diagonal path led to a square where a white-haired veteran fingered an accordion. Rows of medals weighed down one breast of his suit coat. Open-mouthed and toothless, he nodded his head in time to a brisk polka. A middle-aged woman danced out, laughing her head off. She looked like Khrushchev's twin sister, right down to the girth and facial moles.

She wasn't drunk. Her laughter was pure joy.

The crowd clapped along, but her dance needed no encouragement. She was having a splendid time, spinning on her fat legs, and the devil could kiss her ass.

I don't doubt for an instant that some human beings found moments of joy even in concentration camps. Our sorrows fill the pages of the history books, but it's that inextinguishable human capacity for joy—eruptions of bliss too pure to be called defiant—

that should astonish us. I still recall her gray dress, the big mole on her left cheek, and the way she lofted a handkerchief above her head while her other hand lifted her hem to tempt the world and give herself some air. She grinned and wiggled her butt.

Things wiggled back in our hotel room, too. Congealed heat settled on our cots like winter blankets. I was bunking with Peter that night, with Henry off on his own, and it was painful to watch as Zwackie inspected his surroundings. He didn't even want to sit on the mattress. As fastidious as he is otherwise brave, our room's squalor appalled him. Creatures scurried across the floor, ignoring us. We had a private bathroom—a privilege only for foreigners and party bosses—but it would have been better had we been denied one, since it only meant backed-up sewer gases and more wildlife from the drains.

We washed our faces in brown water and went down to dinner.

Chaos. We had no choice but to join the Germans if we wanted to eat, and they were in high complaint. The hotel restaurant had no bottled water, no soda, and no beer. Nothing refrigerated at all. Only warm Crimean champagne, pink and sweet as syrup, and warmer vodka. (That morning we had visited a state farm, the Mitchurin Sovkhoz that produced wine quite drinkable by Soviet standards, but the manager was forbidden to sell any to visitors—everything had to be shipped off and he had never seen a bottle of his wine for sale in a shop.)

Adding to the excitement of outraged Germans, the restaurant—the only one in the city—doubled as a disco. The Lambada had reached the Soviet provinces that season, invading the world's farthest reaches like a medieval plague. Like so much else that reached Central Asia, it mutated. On liberty from a nearby base, brown-faced Kazakh and Uzbek recruits in brown-wool uniforms danced together, ignoring the few girls at the edge of the room. The boys held hands above their shoulders as they boogied down. They had no idea how to dance the Lambada, but they were having a grand time.

The same could not be said of us. When the gristle that passed for meat on our platters had been chewed out, a German divorcee with an air of entitlement grasped Peter. When he put her off, she grew insistent, fueled by the champagne. Too worn to be as gentlemanly as usual, Peter let her know firmly that he wasn't having any—upon which she tore into the guide as if chastising a pimp who hadn't delivered.

There was no ventilation, and neither hygiene nor laundry had been part of the training regimen for the soldiers who packed the room. As the music swelled and the air thickened, the Germans wilted and left, bypassing the forlorn whores who had put on their best duds for us. We closed the place down, drinking what we could stomach and chatting with the locals. Our Russian was far better than that of the young soldiers, but they all were anxious to hear about America. And we had to drink enough to face our rooms.

In the morning, we were roused earlier than scheduled to visit the pride of Chimkent before breakfast. It wasn't Nellie Kim, but a sheep-pelt museum. Since the elevator in the high-rise government building housing the shrine was *na remont*, we had to climb seven or eight flights of stairs.

More than a bit hung over, we smelled the pelts before we reached the right floor. They were shut in a sweltering room and not all had been well-cured. After locking us in to insure that no one could make off with a pelt or two, the curator—unshaven and unsteady—pulled down a succession of shaggy dust-collectors from the shelves that climbed the walls. The stench rose, grim as a third-world dump. The Germans who had made it up the stairs wouldn't have passed muster as a master race that morning. Nor am I certain that Peter, Henry, and I were looking our best.

Gold pelts and gray, russet pelts and black. I should have paid attention to the various grades of *karakul*, the tightness of the black curls, the particular sheen. But all I could do was to scratch my bites and ponder how my life had reached such a low point.

Catching the mutinous mood around her, our minder clapped her hands.

"We will go now. You have seen the wonderful attractions of the city. Now you will have your wonderful breakfast at your wonderful hotel."

"Fuck her," Peter said, his mood robbed of all gallantry. Sleeplessness laced his eyes with red and his mouth must have tasted as sour as my own.

We came from another world, one of such privilege that it didn't translate here. Supermarkets, not missiles, beat the Soviets. The grave of the Unknown Soviet Citizen should read "Died of neglect."

In another hour we would leave Chimkent. On the bus heading back to our "wonderful breakfast," I thought of the dancing woman in the park. Who would never leave.

Thank God for that capacity for joy.

There was little joy in Bukhara in recent centuries. Bukhara is where Islam turned dark as midnight and the sternness of faith prefigured that of today's fiercest extremists. Its last emirs were men who ruled without mercy and killed for amusement. Their religion and their hands were soaked in blood.

It was not always so. A thousand years ago, in its age of grandeur, Bukhara was renowned as "the city of books." Firdausi, the poet and chronicler, graced it with his epic *Book of Kings*, the *Shahnama*. Avicenna, the physician who shook medicine from its stupor, was born in a nearby village. Under the spell of Persian culture, the city competed with Samarkand in splendor.

Genghiz Khan leveled it, preserving only the Qarakhanid minaret. Legend claims that the tower disarmed the Great Khan with its intricacy and beauty, but he probably left it standing as a testament to his wrath—as if an invader flattened every structure in Manhattan except the Empire State Building, preserving one memorial to his power.

After the Mongols faded back into the steppes, the city rose again. But it never regained its cultural preeminence. Its great fortress, the Ark, loomed over a city where time atrophied until it lay inert below the painted *mihrabs* of a hundred mosques. A religious center, Bukhara reached its theological apogee as a refuge for Sufi mystics, the radiant hope and later shame of Islam. As Sufism collapsed from ecstasy into morbidity, the city declined into rigor disguised as faith, its soul as barren as stone.

The heads of the emirs' enemies crowned a forest of stakes in the *maidan* below the Ark. War parties brought back loot and slaves, but closed the gates against all new ideas. The city lived from trade and theft, until trade withered, leaving only robbery. The people hammered away at minor crafts, their skills imitative and second-rate. Even the famous Bukhara carpets were knotted by tribeswomen in the Afghan hills. The city's merchants were middlemen, nothing more. (A cultural brake at work from the Red Sea through Central Asia is that wealth always came from the value added in trade, not from native production, an economic model unsustainable in the industrial and post-industrial ages; Islamic societies continue to suffer from a deadening lack of creativity in the twenty-first century.)

By the nineteenth century, Bukhara had become a gnarled, grim barracks where even traders watched their steps and infidels were doomed. At the city's moral nadir, two particular infidels appeared: a pair of British officers, Col. Charles Stoddart and Capt. Arthur Connolly. Each played one hand too many in the Great Game. First one, then the other, they found themselves shut in underground cells below the Ark. A religious zealot, the emir entertained himself by watching his jailors drop flesh-eating vermin and serpents atop them. When the British Empire failed to do him homage, the emir had the half-dead officers dragged out for a public execution. During his lengthy imprisonment, Stoddart had been forcibly converted to Islam, but he used his brief return to the sunlight to denounce the emir as a despot. The axe fell. As devout as Chinese Gordon, Connolly refused to bow to the faith of the Prophet and died beside his brother officer.

When my own brother officers and I reached Bukhara, we found a city drab as a mouse, despite its turquoise tiles and historic architecture. History's equivalent of a reptile house, the place repelled me, but fascinated me, too. In his own notes on our visit, Peter recalls a squad of elderly veterans, pranksters bedecked with medals and crowned with square Uzbek caps, drunk and singing by one of the inner reservoirs that watered the population during sieges. (No matter how little else its subject peoples learned from Moscow, they acquired a taste for vodka.) We sat on rope beds in the shade of a teahouse, a *chaikhana*, watching the veterans celebrate themselves. Striking up lazy conversations, we let the world go by.

We had intended to visit the tourist-trap chamber of horrors in the forecourt of the Ark, where crude mannequins filled in for Connolly and Stoddart in their old cells, but the display was, of course, *na remont*. Peter and Henry were in a mischievous mood and decided they'd break in. They weren't going to leave Bukhara without paying homage to our predecessors.

I wasn't interested. I had gone cranky—in one of my metaphysical funks—and preferred to sit in a madrassah, listening to a mullah's broken Russian as he gave me the official line on Islam. His eyes were dead and his right hand crept back and forth like a lobster's claw.

For as long as I can remember, I've been fascinated by the endless variety of ways in which local populations channel the universal impulse toward a godhead. As for Islam, I admired many of its professed tenets, but despised its long degeneration and social practices. Conversations such as the exchange in that Bukharan Koranic school convinced me that the world's troubles would not end with the Soviet Union's decline. Faith is unkillable, untame-able. Oppressed, it coils until it finds the means to strike back with all its amassed venom. Communism proved a weak tourniquet in the end.

Whenever I could, on that trip and many others, I sought out mullahs, mystics, priests, faith healers, fortune-tellers, and simple believers, trying to *understand*. At most, our souls catch glimmers of illumination that evade us moments later. To understand the psychological particulars of another man's faith is perhaps the hardest mental task we can put to ourselves, and the mind always fails us in the end, requiring the (risky) engagement of the soul. What I did take away from the hours spent cross-legged in madrassahs and mosques over the years is that civilizations falter when the question mark disappears.

While I was mulling over God and man at Bukhara, Peter and Henry were having fun. Ignoring the closed sign below the Ark, they climbed over the gatehouse wall in a public square in broad daylight. The action was so extraordinary that the locals just walked by, determined not to believe their eyes. But luck and daring take you only so far. Reaching the notorious cells, my comrades soon alarmed a caretaker—who conjured a mob resembling the peasants on their ornery way to Dr. Frankenstein's castle.

And Peter and Henry *looked* suspicious. On the road for a month, Henry had grown a dense black beard. It bristled between his gambler's straw hat and the denim shirt of a convict. Tall and outwardly somber, he might have been Clint Eastwood's understudy in *The Good, the Bad and the Ugly*. Naturally, Peter looked dashing. A bit too dashing. He wore a baby-blue tank top that showed off his swimmer's physique—and offended the sensibilities of the more devout locals. Besides, it's always awkward to explain how you popped up in a locked compound with high halls and keep out signs in an ill-tempered police state.

Peter charmed their way out of the fuss. In those lost, golden days, Americans could get away with almost anything. The Zwack flair did the rest.

Peter's family saga was undergoing a remarkable upturn just then: Hungary had slipped the socialist leash and, intent on developing a market economy, invited Peter's father—Peter the Elder—to return and take back the distilleries the Communists hadn't modernized since 1948. In short order, Peter's father was designated as the free Hungarian government's first ambassador to the United States. It was all swift, complex, and heady, involving a State Department dispensation for the elder Zwack to return his U.S. citizenship in order to become an ambassador *to* Washington. For all the turmoil they brought to a family settled over two continents, the sudden developments were a long-awaited vindication.

Later, Peter's father would become an influential—and incorruptible—voice in the Budapest parliament (and the recipient of death threats). Along the way, he not only rebuilt the family's beverage empire, but presented the Pentagon with a situation in which the Hungarian ambassador's son was a rising U.S. Army intelligence officer with clearances so restricted their nomenclature was classified. (At any given moment, Peter's mother, a timelessly handsome woman and the most adventurous of the lot, might have been walking across China or pursuing rare tigers.) It was all madly contrary to diplomatic practice, government regulations, and military grumpiness. The Zwack family brought it off with élan.

You couldn't say the same for the Soviets or their Central Asian clients. That journey and subsequent trips to the region convinced me that none of the "newly independent states" were going to become model democracies. As we delved deeper into Central Asia, the Soviet veneer—it was no more than that—cracked to reveal the grain of cultures not much changed by the Communist interval. Once you broke free of the official brotherhood nonsense, the native populations could be as otherworldly—and unreachable—as the Indians of the Andes.

The views I formed were unpopular in the subsequent orgy of naivety. President Clinton salted the upper reaches of the State Department with amateurs convinced that the former Soviet empire would turn into Iowa overnight. Reality was irrelevant, chummy feelings were in. The Clinton administration was run by intolerant dreamers formed by the campus radicalism of their youth. With neither self-critical faculties nor experience of the world beyond their privileged domains, they never lacked self-confidence. My forecast that Central Asia would remain Central Asia was dismissed as Cold War obstinacy.

But you didn't have to wait too long to see an old reality emerge as the new reality. The emirs and khans returned. Men who had posed successfully as good Communists morphed back into beghs, emirs, and pashas overnight. This time around, they called themselves "presidents."

The most disappointing of them all—the only man who had given any reason for hope—was Nursultan Nazarbayev of Kazakhstan. He was a master at saying the right thing and had a real chance to spur his country forward. Instead, he yanked back on the reins—even as he assured credulous Westerners that their agenda was his agenda: when the time was right for change, he'd get to it, but not yet. . . . Today, Kazakhstan remains fervently underdeveloped, despite its new-found wealth from natural gas, and creeping oppression has turned it into one more Central Asian emirate.

On later visits, I would listen as panels of Kazakh officers made excuses, as round tables of businessmen made excuses, and as unctuous government officials made excuses. And I always repeated to myself the military law that "the maximum effective range of an excuse is zero meters."

Nazarbayev might have broken the long, grim thrall of the region's history, since his Soviet-manufactured country suffered neither a killing weight of historical baggage nor a developed appetite for Islam's more-backward forms. Many ethnic Kazakhs had continued as nomads into the mid-twentieth century and much remained unsettled in the social order. The Kazakh turn to Islam had come late and remained tangled with shamanism. The people had no seductive tribal memories of empire. And their new country had the highest proportion of educated, Slavic citizens of any of the region's instant states—and those Slavs were not, initially, anxious to return to Mother Russia, where housing and jobs didn't exist. Foreign good will abounded. Western corporations were anxious to pour in money—which they did for a time, turning Alma Ata (now Almaty) into an almost-livable city.

Nazarbayev found the development and consumer tinsel in Almaty too threatening, too Western, too subversive. In the grand tradition of Asian despots, he designated a site in the remote steppes as Kazakhstan's new capital (to the despair of diplomats grateful for Almaty's influx of consumer goods and scraps of nightlife). A dictator after all, he towed his country into the Central-Asian mainstream. And there it will stay.

It's impossible to think back on the heady, early days of the Soviet rout without a peculiar sense of loss—history ground up more lives than it should have done. Yet, memory is shaped by all that we digested in the interim, and nostalgia has ingredients secret even from ourselves. Ordering from the menu of the past, I'll take the vignettes and skip the epic.

More encounters were whimsical than ominous back then. To the urban elite, the West was glamorous, desirable, and vague. We sat on a verandah in then–Alma Ata, with the sun-struck mountains in the distance. A shining teenager confessed—largely to Peter—that her dream was to go to Paris and meet her idol, George Michael, a pretty-boy English pop singer briefly in vogue. She really believed it might happen. One only hopes she was not too discouraged by the subsequent news of the singer's arrest for misbehavior in a public men's room.

Islam Karimov, the sultan of twenty-first-century Uzbekistan, should rule from Bukhara, not Tashkent. His imperious style is squarely in the regional tradition. (He's a two-bit Tamerlane, without the vision, valor, or taste.) For strategic reasons and from sheer lethargy, our government gave him a pass as political opponents disappeared and his crackdown on Islam (despite his forename) only provoked greater extremism. At last, his brutality became too excessive even for our State Department when, in 2005, his goons cut down hundreds of demonstrators in Andijan, a city whose bleakness would have driven Francis of Assisi to violent rebellion.

Tajikistan is chronically broken, while Kyrgyzstan's chronically bumbling. But if your taste in dictators runs to the flamboyant and Marxist (Groucho, not Karl), Turkmenistan was your place and the late (as of 2006) Saparmurad Niyazov was your man. A blustering, smiling murderer, Niyazov renamed himself "Turkmenbashi," or "Head of all Turkmen." With his lacquered hair swept back, his silk suits and bull's torso, he was a dictator as imagined by Mel Brooks.

The wealth brought in by natural-gas deposits went overwhelmingly to the construction of monuments to—care to guess?—Turkmenbashi. The commoner's standard of living remains lower today than it was under the Soviets, but Ashkabat, the capital city, gleams like Las Vegas remodeled by Albert Speer. Turkmenbashi enforced a cult of personality the Kim dynasty of North Korea could only envy, while his appetite for loot embarrassed even his fellow despots. And the world said nothing as long as he sold gas cheap. Kept down by no-nonsense security forces and bullied to spy on each other, the locals survived by hustling, stealing (from the state, whenever possible), and relying on family connections. They also maintained a sardonic sense of humor.

Another friend of mine, Col. Tom Wilhelm, whose sense of adventure puts my own to shame, was riding through Ashkabat in a cab in the late 1990s. Hideous government buildings lined the boulevards and all of the grand avenues led, inevitably, to a column topped by a gilded statue of Turkmenbashi. Hidden mechanical works had been synchronized so the leader's face moved precisely with the sun. His features gleamed from sunrise to sunset.

Tom had seen the statue before. Making conversation, he said to the taxi driver, "I see that Turkmenbashi turns with the sun."

Pretending mortification—which dissolved into a mischievous smile—the driver replied, "No, no! You are wrong, sir! The sun turns with Turkmenbashi . . ."

And at the end of it all lay Samarkand, the city of wonders. If I found Bukhara repellent, Samarkand was magnetic. A well-intentioned exaggeration common to travelers is to say that we sat and stared at a wonder for hours. Well, I sat for hours before the Registan, with its three luminous madrassahs. The evening sound-and-light show was trashy and silly, but in the morning light the Registan seemed to me one of the most alluring places created by humankind. You needed no sympathy with Islam to grasp its sacred nature. I returned at least once each day.

The high facades of the madrassahs are a mish-mosh of high Islam, Sufi symbolism, astrology, and Persia's Zoroastrian hangover. Despite the ban on human or animal likenesses, lions striped like tigers prowl the Shir Dar's high arch, with Mongol-faced sunbursts peeping over their backs. Dull-witted deer await the big cats' jaws. The standard geometric patterns and flowers are there, too, but elevated to a level of uncommon beauty. The calligraphy above the madrassah's inner arch is a dignified signpost along a divine path. With its minarets and turquoise dome, the Shir Dar seems a fairy-tale castle of faith, as do its two brethren bordering the square. But words don't do. The Registan must be seen. And *felt*.

Soviet restorers have been criticized for using replacement tiles produced with the "wrong" techniques and for hotting up the effect, but that's all nonsense. Photographs taken before the Bolsheviks arrived show tumble-down piles destined for oblivion. Godless Soviet archaeologists lovingly saved the city's monuments—not only the Registan complex, but the enormous, earthquake-bothered Bibi Hanum mosque, Tamerlane's tomb, the time-hallowed mausoleums of the Shah-e Zinda strewn between the Timurid city and its ancient parent. Beyond the graves of dubious saints lies Ulug Begh's hilltop observatory, where calculations pierced Heaven a half-century before Columbus sailed.

If Bukhara's alleys remained oppressive, Samarkand's quiet lanes drew you on to walk just one more block, then another, despite the heat. Not all was grand—carbuncles of Soviet architecture plagued Samarkand, too. But the back streets held homes that, but for electricity, had changed little down the centuries. In the poorer quarters, women still drew water from public fountains. As they lugged it away, their multihued, ankle-length dresses shimmered and their black hair glistened under their caps. On other streets, low, thick houses, fortresses besieged by the heat, lingered on from the czarist era. As always in Soviet cities, there was a tinny amusement park with delicious, bacterial ice cream. And the bazaar was good for an unfettered conversation. But you came back to the Registan. For its sublime grandeur.

Sitting there, I tried to understand how a civilization that created such a wonder could have fallen so far. I already knew the technical answer: Islam froze by the mid-fifteenth century, when science-fearing zealots knifed Ulug Begh to death. He had been an astronomer and mathematician, a botanist and poet, a soldier and, as the cliché goes, a scholar. He was a ruler, as well, the grandson of Tamerlane the Conqueror, Marlowe's Tamburlaine. Despite his fearsome reputation, Tamerlane sought to turn Samarkand, his capital, into a center of learning, science, and the arts. Until his untimely death, Ulug Begh fulfilled his grandfather's dream.

I knew that Islam went into lock-down thereafter. The building continued, but the thinking stopped. *Why?* How had a civilization whose learning had exceeded all others shut itself down so swiftly and so thoroughly? How did the bigots—the hard, old men—win? Where did the poetry go? And the wine? The various cultures that summed to Islamic civilization in its heyday had been capable of breathtaking cruelty, but they also built societies without peer in their sophistication. What happened?

There are no end of alleged turning points, all ominous in retrospect, and as many excuses for failure as there are stars in the firmament. But we still can't quite say *why* the Islamic heartlands suffered their cultural collapse.

Whatever the cause, Islam tried to stand still. And it couldn't work. A civilization either continues to evolve, change, grow—or it begins to decay. The gangrene we began to smell in the late twentieth century had appalled British nostrils a full century earlier. Why didn't Muslims themselves attempt to stem the deterioration?

Why did it take Soviet atheists to restore the Registan, a treasure Muslim rulers ignored for centuries? Elsewhere, the situation was worse, with the Saudis purposely obliterating monuments from the Ottoman era because to preserve them would have been to show them a deference due to Allah alone. It was hard not to despair.

The Muslim world I encountered over the years stumbled between lethargy and outbursts of messianic nihilism. It had no innate steadiness, no coherent purpose, only extremes of discipline and delusion. It was as suited to the modern world as the codpiece and the crossbow.

And yet there was no end to the devotion. Women, to whom Islam offered least, crowded the old steps to the tomb of a Naqsh-bandi saint, some climbing the weathered stones on their knees as medieval Christians entered the shrines of Rome (or devout Mexican Catholics approach the Virgin of Guadalupe today). Part picnic, part pilgrimage, the Shah-e Zinda's hillside swarmed with radiant silk dresses and their synthetic imitators. Of course, Uzbek Muslims are Sunnis. And, of course, Sunnis don't worship tombs, no matter how holy the occupant. But the women—and a few crippled men—who had come to beg for the intercession of their saints knew little and cared less about what the graybeards in Mecca or Cairo decreed as proper forms of worship. They were doing what their ancestors did, making offerings and pledges at the graves of emirs and their concubines, their tombs sanctified only by time, custom, and error. Soviet might could not persuade these people to give up Islam, today's Salafist fanatics will not persuade them to give up their cherished saints. I was supposed to be admiring the architecture, but the vibrant faith of the living beings around me tugged my attention away from the tiles and stones. That day I got my first inkling of how powerful local traditions could be in the face of oppression. Later, I saw the phenomenon everywhere, from Indonesian and West African Islam, to the evergreen-bough Christianity of northern Europe. Belief is ineradicable.

I've written elsewhere of Samarkand, in a book on strategy and in a novel, *Flames of Heaven*, the plot of which I bent to include the city. So instead of returning yet again to Ulug Begh's observatory, I'll leave Samarkand by recalling the way the three of us left it that June.

The afternoon was infernally hot. Drained, the Germans leaned forward in the bus to the airport, as if that might get them home a split-second sooner. Peter, Henry, and I were headed back to Germany, too, to Garmisch, which would serve as a base for future trips, some official and packed with activities, others far more useful. For us, the wrapped-up journey had been marvelous, and we tipped our snarling minder with Texan extravagance. We were not so much anxious to leave, as reconciled to our return to classrooms, research papers, and the intricacies of Russian grammar (which Henry mastered, I managed, and Peter mangled).

At the ratty airport, the three of us were culled abruptly from the boarding line just as the Germans proceeded out to the plane—which was due to take off as soon as everyone boarded. We had no idea what we'd done. Perhaps our she-wolf minder had gotten her revenge—which hardly seemed fair, since we'd tipped her a great deal better than she deserved. Maybe the KGB still had teeth out here and had been compiling dossiers on us. Perhaps all those horror stories at which we'd scoffed were true. Charges, lies (and some truths): a diplomatic incident. Yet, they'd stamped our passports and handed them back to us without any bother.

A youngish man in a white shirt with aviation shoulder boards walked up to us. Smiling. A companion stepped up behind him, eager as a drunkard in a strip joint.

"You are Americans?"

Yes.

"Then we must have a drink together! Before you travel away."

"But our plane, it's about to take off and—"

He waved away our concerns. "No, it isn't. I'm the flight controller. Anyway, it won't be so long. Only a drink or two."

We lodged a feeble protest, but it didn't wash. So we agreed to join him. For one beer.

Delighted, he led us back out of the terminal, across the parking lot, and into a ramshackle café. We all sat down.

No beer. Only vodka.

"Then we will drink vodka! To friendship!"

Perhaps it's the German blood, but of the three of us I'm the most sensitive to schedules. Henry rushes madly at the last minute, arriving just three-and-a-half minutes late, angry at himself and scattering apologies. Peter gets there when he gets there, and everyone's delighted to see him. I'm chronically early.

So I was the one glancing at my watch as we were treated to warm vodka and a big, sugary, half-melted chocolate bar. I hinted that, just maybe, we should be thinking about getting on the plane and letting it take off. Even Aeroflot must have *some* pride.

"*Vipit do kontza!*" Bottoms up. And the glasses were topped up again.

After about forty-five minutes of very serious drinking, we staggered back to the terminal. I hoped that the air-traffic controller wouldn't have to juggle too many other planes as we were taking off.

The Soviet Union was a colossal sham: *Pokazuka*, one huge Potemkin village. The KGB passport gals and the customs inspectors, all of whom had put on a great show of diligence while they were on stage an hour before, didn't blink as our new friends walked us straight through the departure hall, across the tarmac, and up to the aircraft stairs.

"I'd better get back now," the controller told us. "You will tell America hello from me, please!"

Climbing the stairs to the aircraft, Peter rolled his eyes. The stewardesses plastered on their baby-doll smiles, but their eyes were malignant. The instant we stepped inside the fuselage, we understood why.

It must've been 135 degrees in there. And I'm resisting the temptation to write "140" only because I might not be believed. Up front, where the best seats were reserved for foreigners and bigwigs, the Germans were whining and snapping and making impossible threats. The Aeroflot crew ignored them. But it wasn't our travel mates for whom we felt sorry. We'd had enough of them. The real victim was some poor bugger who'd been carried aboard on a gurney and lodged in the aisle. He was swathed from scalp to foot in bandages, with an intravenous feed. Unable to protest, he was covered in blankets, to boot. Headed to Moscow for medical treatment, he must have been cooking.

We would have been delighted to take off immediately. But our new friend seemed to have detoured on his way to the control tower. We weren't worried about him, since he'd told us he also served as the airport's manager, but the natives were getting restless. And the heat truly was miserable.

We waited. And waited. Up front, the flight attendants helped themselves to drinks. The passengers were invisible. But that was just the way Aeroflot was in the good old days, and those painted gals weren't having a good time, either. They were sweating like Oklahoma hogs in August.

At last, the aircraft jerked to life, shivering the glasses in the galley. We started rolling across the apron as fast as the pilot could go, as if he feared being stopped before he could lift off. We made a quick pivot onto the runway and, without a pause for final clearance, the engines roared and the Ilyushin shot into the sky. It was a pin-you-to-the-seat military take-off, with every part of the airplane groaning and shaking.

By the time we leveled off, the stewardesses had started to flirt with Peter.

BLOOD IN THE BLACK GARDEN

WHILE STUDYING AT THE U.S. ARMY RUSSIAN INSTITUTE, I WAS
selected for early promotion to major and attendance at the Command and General Staff College at Fort Leavenworth. I was surprised, since I had shunned the guaranteed-promotion jobs in
favor of those I believed vital to Military Intelligence. But as I left
Bavaria for Kansas in the summer of 1991, I lost my front-row seat
for the Soviet drama's last act. For a year, I would fade back into
the abstractions of field manuals and staff procedures as history
moved on without me.

Shortly after my arrival at Fort Leavenworth—where history
is literally imprinted on the soil in the wagon ruts marking the
start of the Santa Fe Trail—the Communists in Moscow staged
their last, inept attempt at retrieving power. Yeltsin climbed atop a
tank and the Communists climbed down. Gray careers ended in
suicide or surrender. It galled me not to be there, to be scouring
logistics tables on a bluff above the Missouri River while the
world changed on the banks of the Moskva.

But contrary to generations of complaints, the Army generally knows best. My year at C&GSC was valuable, if sometimes exasperating, dragging me back into my profession after three years immersed in the long pageant of Russian brilliance and brutality, sentimentality and drunkenness, incomparable art and mass murder. The worth of staff college isn't what you learn behind your desk, since a good officer already knows most of what's taught. The greater purpose is to gather in the tribes, introducing those tentatively anointed as future leaders to each other, tossing Infantry and Military Police officers, Ordnance majors and Medical Service Corps captains together in small staff groups where each soon learns that he or she is not the only star in the military firmament. The curriculum is structured so that the collective (ah, I knew *that* concept!) only succeeds if everyone contributes his or her discipline-specific knowledge. The goal is for the students to teach each other. Groaning, they do.

I remember every member of my staff group with respect—if wryly, in a few cases—but we suffered a loss toward the end of the course that shaped my later beliefs on personnel policy. One of our "dirty dozen" was a superb Military Police major, capable, fit, conscientious, and generous in helping others when we stumbled. Although discreet, she also was a lesbian. A spurned lover turned on her, luridly detailing the major's private life through official channels so the charges could not be ignored. I testified on the major's behalf at her court-martial, but her qualities as an officer could not protect her. Broken-hearted, she was expelled from the Army. She stayed in touch for a little while thereafter, but I think she reached a point where she could no longer bear to be reminded of the vocation she had lost. She was good and honorable and brave, and our country and the Army suffered when we cast her out.

Otherwise, the year was far from gloomy. The chain-of-command overlooked yet another of my periodic idiocies. Friends flew in to visit and we fled to Kansas City, an hour away. I love KC, with its robust restaurants, miles of craftsman-era homes, and a boosterish cultural life that, despite its wealth, evokes Chekhov's provincials. Thomas Hart Benton's corn-fed nudes entice the unsuspecting guest and you easily imagine Harry Truman stepping out of a downtown chop house with his bowtie and Midwestern grin—or Charlie Parker pawning his saxophone again. Kansas City's made-in-the-USA vigor felt marvelous after years of German fastidiousness and Russian neglect.

Beyond lay the prairie, at once the most American of landscapes and the twin of the Russian steppes.

I received a follow-on assignment to the Army Staff in the Pentagon, but encountered chutes and ladders along the way. I had hoped to stay at Fort Leavenworth for a second year to attend the School of Advanced Military Studies, a program that trains operational planners—fickle, I'd fallen back in love with the "real" military. The SAMS director, Col. Jim McDonough, placed me atop his list of selectees, but the Army personnel system said, "No." I'd been in various schools for four straight years and it was time for me to earn my pay again. I was disappointed, but once again the Army knew best: I needed to get back to work. And there were plenty of potentially good war planners, but fewer officers with the knack—and eccentricities—necessary to be a strategic scout. The only compromise Jim McDonough, who also was charged to write doctrine, cajoled from the personnel system was a few extra months at Fort Leavenworth for me to work on the latest edition of the Army's capstone field manual, FM 100-5, OPERATIONS. The drafting was well underway, but Jim had been reading my out-of-step scribbling on military affairs and wanted a fresh perspective.

So I stayed on for the summer months, when the heat clubs Kansas to the ground. The converted stables in which we worked weren't air-conditioned and the writing team, which had been hard at work for a year, naturally resented the intrusion of an officer lower in rank who had the ear of the boss. I had no influence on the manual. Facing the sudden end of the Cold War, the Army found it difficult to move beyond its vision of massive tank encounters, while my own exposure to the fracturing Soviet Union had convinced me that much of the service's future lay in the scrap-heap conflicts no general wanted to fight.

By mid-July, I realized I was superfluous, although Jim wasn't ready to give me up. My ideas about the future of war were anathema to the establishment, but the enduring benefit of my stint on the drafting team was getting to know Jim McDonough. Our paths would cross repeatedly in the coming years, always at some policy juncture where those in power wanted problems to go away. We sensed, correctly, that we could trust each other. Later on, we had to.

As I write, Jim is reforming the penal system in Florida, which had become criminally corrupt. The system's directorship is a dangerous job even for a retired Infantry officer and veteran of multiple wars. Jim's thriving.

He came up from the New York streets and the term "pugnacious" is precisely right. He boxed his way through West Point. Square-shouldered and erect, he projects so much meat-eater energy that you perceive him as leaning forward like a fighter in the ring. To Jim, a desk was a cage, but in combat boots and in command he gave his subordinates a sense that losing was impossible, that, if necessary, he would take on the world by himself and win. Standing at attention, he seemed to be punching the air around him.

A lieutenant during the last years of the Vietnam War, Jim had written a memoir of infantry combat at the platoon level, as well as a novel about Waterloo. He came across as get-out-of-my-way tough, but his vestigial on-the-block accent masked a well-developed mind and a genial private side. Jim got hard things done.

Unfortunately, one of the things we got done that summer remains the greatest regret of my years in uniform. Jim got the call on one of those summer mornings when Kansas turns your uniform into a hot, wet towel. The Balkans were erupting and neither the Army Staff nor the Joint Staff back in the Pentagon had anyone on hand who could offer a useful analysis of the region. Jim turned to me.

I had revisited the Balkans and kept up with developments, but I wasn't an expert on Yugoslavia.

"This is a fire mission," Jim said, dismissing my protest. "Give it your best shot. I need it before the end of the duty day."

I drove to my quarters off-post so I wouldn't be disturbed by office chatter. Over the next several hours, I typed up a summary of what I knew about Yugoslavia and an analysis of what we could expect as the situation worsened.

I predicted the coming brutality with an accuracy that time for reflection would have diluted. But I also made the worst analytical error of my career. With the Cold War over, the European powers—led by the French—had been arguing that the presence of American troops on the continent was no longer necessary, that Europe could handle its own security problems. My mistake was twofold: first, I took the French at their word and, second, I looked at the raw numbers of European troops available to resolve the Yugoslav crisis and forgot the elementary law that what matters in any conflict is strength of will. I recommended that the United States stay out and let the Europeans handle the matter.

The paper—fifteen single-spaced pages—went all the way to the White House and, in its small way, helped shape our choice to remain aloof.

Of course, the Europeans failed to act resolutely. Yes, they had plenty of troops—on paper. Instead of engaging decisively, Berlin, Paris, and London resurrected dormant rivalries that stank of 1914: The Germans tilted toward their old allies, the Croats, so, naturally, the French leaned toward Belgrade. The British tried to have it both ways, but found their sense of justice corroded by nostalgia for their cooperation with Tito's Serb partisans against Croat fascists.

NATO be damned, Europe had learned nothing—while I learned never to trust what European powers say. Had I had the common sense to recognize that Europeans could not act effectively without American leadership, that dashed-off paper would have suggested a pre-emptive approach to the atrocities inevitable to any outbreak of violence in the Balkans. Our military leaders might have taken a different position in the Washington debate and we might have engaged three years earlier, instead of passively watching a series of massacres. Tens of thousands of lives might have been saved.

I reasoned badly, and they died.

––––––––––––

The Balkans weren't the world's only trouble spot. That July, a vicious backwoods war of the sort that lay in our future ravaged Nagorno-Karabagh, a historically Armenian cluster of mountains marooned in Azerbaijan. It was the first major conflict in the series of breaking-up-is-hard-to-do wars that punctuated the USSR's collapse.

The U.S. Government had opened an embassy in newly independent Armenia a few months before, but at the State Department's insistence, no military attaché had been assigned to it. State was convinced that the Age of Aquarius had begun and that military officers were not only unneeded in the new embassies opening up in the wake of the retreat to Moscow, but that those in uniform were a dangerous impediment to Foggy Bottom's vision of peace in our time. The new ambassadors learned the hard way over the next few years, but a great deal of time was lost and damage done by then.

Meanwhile, the lack of a U.S. officer in Yerevan meant that we had no trained eyes on a vicious little war with strategic ramifications. The Russian security services and military had engaged in arming and egging on both parties, even permitting active-service officers to serve as mercenaries on the Azeri side to keep the conflict stoked. The Soviet state was dead, but the KGB's heirs were determined to preserve Russian influence over the "near abroad" until a new government coalesced in Moscow and came to its imperial senses. Doing all they could to excite old hatreds, the Russians took a classic divide-and-conquer approach: they now had Muslim (if hardly strict) Azeris and devoutly Christian Armenians killing each other over barren mountains both believed had been given to them by history, blood, and God.

The Pentagon showed no interest in sending anyone to watch this seminal fight. We didn't "do" little wars, and the generals were absorbed in vain attempts to stave off reductions in our standing forces, in budget battles and arguments over the lessons of Desert Storm—a seductive war whose anomalous nature obscured more than it revealed. As the killers with rusty Kalashnikovs loomed on the horizon, Beltway insiders searched for technological solutions to yesteryear's problems.

I asked Jim to let me take a few weeks of leave so I could go to Armenia at my own expense. He understood and agreed. Together, we worked the system to get the necessary permission slips as swiftly as possible and Jim had the sense not to alert a single general officer that I was going.

Soon I was on my way back to history's junkyard.

———

Memoirists of the Eastern Front claim that scouts could distinguish between German and Russian bunkers by their odors. German positions reeked of urine, while Russian trenches stank of sweat and strong tobacco. Yerevan airport combined the three scents to greet the stampede from the plane. Lip-scorcher cigarette butts speckled the floor and the uniforms of besieged officials didn't fit at the collar. The noise level in the arrival hall suggested a nineteenth-century foundry.

My flight from Moscow had been delayed for ten hours, depositing me in Armenia after midnight. There were no lines for passport control—affable barbarism reigned. Encamped families overwhelmed the security cubicles as hysterical relatives engulfed the arriving passengers. Women wept. Awakened, children howled and sat down hard in the middle of the floor. Unshaven men passed envelopes between them as an impossible number of people stormed the struggling baggage conveyor. Wrapped in plastic and bound with rope, huge parcels clogged the belt. Patched vinyl suitcases tumbled over one another. Splintered wooden crates cut grabbing hands. My bag would have stood out instantly.

Except that it hadn't arrived. There had been no flight connections to explain it, since I'd collected my luggage at Sheremetovo airport upon my arrival in Moscow, stayed downtown overnight, and checked in again at Domodedovo to fly directly to Yerevan. (We touched down briefly in Vladikavkaz, but only to take on fuel.) Assuming my bag had been stolen, all I could do was shrug.

I always packed emergency supplies in a small carry-on, so I had my essential toiletries, a change of underwear and socks, and an extra shirt. I could make do. But the checked bag held my emergency medical supplies—in those days of pervasive shortages, when regional medical care was itself in trauma, we always took along emergency syringes and a few basic medications. In the event of an injury, I would have to go native. (Whether picking over the USSR's corpse or shambling through African graveyards a decade later, tainted syringes worried me more than bullets ever did.)

I filled out a form for a bored girl with a ripe mole and returned to the dwindling crowd. I had been overconfident about another matter, too: Dollars still worked wonders in those days and I had assumed that, despite a well-known fuel shortage, hard currency and a thriving black market would transport me the dozen kilometers into the city. But there were no taxis or buses in sight. Packed cars sputtered off, suspensions grinding. Even a huddle of *na levo* boys with contraband couldn't help me. They were stranded, too.

Tired, grubby and not especially good-humored, I went back into the terminal to search for anyone who might be able to help me. And I spotted a potential savior lingering near the baggage belt, standing between two stuffed green duffel bags. He might have been just another stranded passenger but for one critical detail: he fingered a set of car keys as if they were worry beads.

When you bum a ride in a conflict zone, there is an ironclad rule: seek out someone who's smaller and weaker than you are. The man with the duffel bags looked perfect: he was an encouraging six inches shorter than me and his face hid behind black-rimmed eyeglasses wider than his shoulders. (Those shoulders curved in toward a shrunken chest.) He might have been Woody Allen's Armenian cousin.

He never looked in my direction, but kept his eyes on the gloom of the passport-control corridor. Waiting for a wife? Or for a relative who worked the open-air markets in Moscow to feed an extended family?

I startled him when I spoke. Finding me close, his eyes registered an instant's fear, then eased into curiosity. I started my spiel in high-flown Russian.

"Excuse me, Citizen . . . I'm an American and I've come to Armenia because all my Armenian friends in America have told me what a wonderful—"

"You need a ride?" he asked hopefully.

"*Da, eto tak. A kak vi—*"

"Please, I will give you a ride. I am sure it is all right, but I must ask, of course. Soon my boss will be coming. I must ask him, but I am certain he will provide for you a ride. He is very curious about Americans."

"Thanks very much. I—"

"Perhaps you will help me? While I am waiting for him?"

I shrugged. Sure. I'm here to help you.

"If you could take these bags," he said, "and place them in the boot of the car, I would be grateful. They're very heavy."

He held out the keys and described his vehicle.

I expected to lug both bags at once, but when I jerked up the first one, it pulled me back toward the floor. It might have been a pillar of cement. The muscles in my groin telegraphed a warning.

"You must be careful," the driver said. "They are very heavy."

Awkward as a new recruit, I got one of the bags up on a shoulder. Through the canvas, I thought I felt tin cans.

With shoulder, spine, crotch, and knees complaining, I lugged the bag into the parking lot and found the car, a dented Lada. I had to rearrange two ragged tires, a slop of tools, and a fuel can to make things fit. When I tipped in the duffel bag, the rear of the vehicle sagged.

Nobody was running off with that piece of luggage, but I locked up the vehicle carefully and went back inside for the second bag. My benefactor still stood by himself. The lights—never bright—had dimmed. Closing time.

When I flipped over the second bag to reach the carrying straps, I noticed what I should have spotted on the first one: The bag was a sealed diplomatic pouch. Property of the Iranian embassy.

This, I thought, is going to be interesting.

The second bag was lighter—no cans. I loaded it up then waited by the car as the driver had asked. Beyond the weak lamps of the terminal, the night hung so black it seemed to have texture, as if you would have to push aside layers of curtains in order to pass. You would not have guessed that a capital city lay eight miles away.

The Russian-induced energy crisis had bitten harder than the press reported. But, then, few Western journalists had time to spare for a place as remote and uncomfortable as wartime Yerevan. Those who covered the situation generally did so from Moscow.

After another ten minutes, the driver emerged to hold the door for his boss, a classic new-school Iranian official with close-cropped hair, a precise beard, a colorless suit, and a shirt buttoned at the neck. He smiled wonderfully.

The driver introduced us, assuring me that his boss, Tehran's charge d'affaires in Yerevan, was delighted to offer me the hospitality of his car. The diplomat spoke no Russian and I spoke no Farsi, but the driver translated between us, explaining along the way that he had been a professor of foreign languages at Yerevan's university for many years, but had taken the chauffeuring job to feed his family. It was the sort of story I would hear again and again in the hardscrabble country.

Most of the drive was taken up by the Iranian's questions about America. He showed no interest in our security posture, but had a boundless curiosity about California, where he had relatives. He leaned toward me in the backseat, his tone yearning for Orange County.

I told him, not quite honestly, that it had been my lifelong dream to contemplate the rose gardens of Shiraz and to visit the great mosques of Esfahan. I laid it on thick as peanut butter about my respect for Persian civilization and the importance of overcoming the differences between our two countries. He nodded as eagerly as a child and, by the time we entered the lightless city, I had him near tears. (In dealing with anyone from the Middle East, no talent is as important as the ability to lie with more grandeur than your conversational partner.)

I had asked to be dropped at an old hotel where a faded telex promised me a room, but the Iranian begged me to join him for a glass of tea at his embassy first. It would have been the right thing to do to accept, but my body was still on Kansas time and utterly out of juice.

"Then you must come tomorrow to visit us! You will find us most easily: Your embassy is in the same hotel, by the presidential compound. It is only one floor away! Come, my friend! The guards will let you in, there will not be a problem. But you must come!"

The car chugged up to a bleak scrap of Soviet architecture. Glass doors threw back the flash of our headlights and went dark again. Puttering through the streets, I had not seen a human being beyond the car windows. And I could not see one now.

"You must make a powerful noise at the door to awaken them," the professor explained.

The diplomat got out of the car to say goodnight, giving the professor an order that sent him scurrying to the car's trunk. I made the standard Persian gesture signifying that "I would give my eye for you, my brother," and the diplomat seemed about to embrace me.

A can of beans came between us. The cement-heavy duffel bag was crammed full of cans of stewed beans. If that was what the diplomats ate in Yerevan, it did not bode well for my own dining experience.

I should have taken the can, but just could not bring myself to do it. It all seemed too pathetic.

"My brother," I told the Persian, "keep these for me and we will eat them together, when I visit you. Insh'Allah."

The diplomat laid his hand over his heart.

The next day I dropped by our infant embassy to let the staffers know I was in the country. They were startled and miffed, but since I had come as a tourist and had all of the correct permission slips, they could not order me to leave. But they had their small revenge: when I told them about my encounter with the ayatollah's godson, every diplomat in the room stiffened.

"You are *not* to speak to or have *any* contact with the Iranians here," the ranking diplomat told me. "Absolutely no contact!" He shook his head and waved his hand, in case I had difficulty understanding English. "They're always trying to initiate conversations in the stairwell, you know. But," he continued with a superior smile, "we don't let them engage us."

And there you had our diplomats: Unwilling to talk to our enemies on the stairs. Unwilling to learn. And utterly unwilling to embrace the world as it is, rather than as their fine educations had convinced them it must be. The only worthwhile piece of information I got from them was the address of a nearby restaurant that would feed me well for hard currency.

Repeated thumps on the hotel's front door roused an unbuttoned uniform with an unhappy old man inside it. Smelling of sleep and brandy, the doorman let me in, muttered, relocked the door, then shuffled back into the shadows. The only light in the lobby was a hurricane lamp atop the reception desk. There was no electricity at the moment.

A skeletal young man of the sort employed universally by poor hotels found my reservation and guided me upstairs with his flashlight. The floor matron snapped out of a drowse into full alertness—no drinker she—and lit her candle. After palming a dollar bill, the clerk let the matron guide me to my room.

"*K'sozhaleniyu, vodi seechaz nyet.*"

There was no running water, either. But a full bucket waited in my bathroom. A candle and matches on the nightstand would see me through until morning. It wasn't the Four Seasons, but military service puts things into perspective and a bug-free bed under a roof was better than a sleeping bag in the mud.

The matron was cheerier than her Russian counterparts. "Tomorrow," she told me, "there will be water for one hour. It is this way each day. I will tell the day girl she must fill your tub with water. But is this your first time in Armenia? You are most welcome, sir."

She told the truth. Armenia did welcome me. Each of the major populations of the Caucasus displays a distinct national temperament. The Azeris welcome foreigners eagerly, wondering what they can gain from the acquaintance. Erratic Muslims, they then get drunk and forget to ask for the favor. Georgians are hearty, but lapse visibly into their calculations when they think you aren't watching. Their schemes grow so elaborate they topple over of their own weight. Less effusive than their neighbors, Armenians possess the stern dignity that suffering polishes to a gleam. They, too, would gladly profit from knowing you—such is human nature—but they're too proud to beg. For all of their fabled slyness in business, the Armenians I met were poor, yet generous to the point of shaming me.

I went to sleep that night to the sound of a gunshot.

In the high-summer afternoons, the city held still. Its shops empty and offices starved of purpose, Yerevan ticked off the hours until the heat loosened its grip. Refugees stranded in front of a government hall on a central plaza (no longer Lenin Place) shifted with the sun to gain what shade they could, then settled down into despair. Even the children lacked the energy to rise from the bundles of dark clothing that composed a family. Country folk from Karabagh, the city's hardness bewildered them—they knew how to survive in a forest, but not on a concrete sidewalk. They lived off one meal a day delivered by a truck with suffering gears. You caught their fetid scent across the square.

Decades of pollution had stained the pink stone preferred by Stalin's architects, but the buildings from those terrible years still suggested rectitude and pride. All that came after was rotten, though, the slapdash apartment towers and dirty-glass arts complexes, the leprous stadiums and each "Palace of the People" with its soul-pulverizing modernism. Stalin's taste was heavy, but it was nonetheless a form of taste. He sought to awe the workers of the world, and did. The gray men who succeeded him did the minimum necessary to placate those they ruled. Stalin's Yerevan had— odd to write the word in any connection with the man—charm. Brezhnev's Yerevan was a shoddy barracks.

In the rose and purple dusk, the city shook off its drowse and gathered in the park by the opera house. But not for pleasure. Patriotic speakers raged, their tirades amplified through broken speakers as they warned the brown-eyed crowd against ancient enemies. You did not need to speak Armenian to understand: They faced the Turks again, this time in their degenerate Azeri guise. Ancestral lands were being stolen, men murdered, women outraged. You could almost hear the mortar shells landing in Shusha's old Armenian quarter and artillery rounds blasting away Stepanakert's Christian heritage.

The Armenian government's official line insisted that the fighting was strictly between the embattled population of Karabagh and Azeri aggressors, that Armenia itself was not a party to the conflict. Our diplomats relayed the official position, then locked themselves in after sunset, safe in their guarded hotel beside the president's fortified mansion. A few kilometers away, the city howled like a wounded animal.

Oh, yes, Armenia was at war. That tattered crowd had not gathered merely to hear nationalist speeches. Families were saying farewell to truckloads of men headed off to the front. (They always left at sunset.) One vehicle carried young men with uniforms but no weapons, another ferried a platoon of mixed age who had weapons but no uniforms, while a third held regulars. More trucks lined the rising boulevard, each the center of a dozen family dramas. Patriotic music blared as mothers and wives clutched their men, unwilling to relinquish them to war. Always, the men broke away at last, each with his own inherited flurry of gestures. There were always more women by the trucks and more men by the opera house where the speakers raved. Those sullen men had not yet volunteered. They smoked their cigarettes angrily.

Back by the trucks, old women in black headscarves comforted young women in tight skirts and scuffed high heels. Tears wrecked make-up. The men on their way to the fighting joked and laughed among themselves to keep from crying. The crowd was feral, bloodthirsty, bereft.

I could not speak Armenian, but understood the lyrics of the folk-singers who performed between the bellowing speakers and the plaints of operatic harpies with piled hair, the call-to-arms of the men with artillery baritones: "On to the front! Our sacred Armenia is threatened! Off to the front, where the Turk waits! Victory, or death!"

Such men and women always cry "On to the front!" then go home to their beds, satisfied at having done their duty.

Trucks pulled off, streaming black exhaust. A young girl collapsed and was caught by two old women.

A tourist amid the agony of others, I walked up to the opera house each night. Sometimes the crowds were smaller and less wretched. It all depended on how many volunteers had been mobilized, how many more men had been gathered in from the villages and towns to the northwest, how many more urban apartments had been drained of young males to feed the struggle to open the Lachin corridor to Karabagh, to rescue embattled brothers and take revenge, at last, upon the Turk.

The Turk is the Satan of the Armenians, having overshot the Lucifer of Scripture. Every political muddle and every exchange of shots in a remote valley is colored by the history of genocide. Proudly claiming to have been the first Christian kingdom, Armenians once ruled an empire twenty times the size of their rump country of today. From the Caucasus to Cilicia and the Mediterranean, the ruins they left shamed the cultures that came after them. Even when their days of greatness and independence had passed, when their grand medieval capital, Ani, lay in goat-fouled ruins and their last king had bowed, the Armenian people supplied the artists and architects, the grand viziers and generals, the engineers and merchants who brightened the glory of the Ottoman Empire and then struggled against its decay—until the sum of lost wars and the Sublime Porte's follies grew too great for any genius to redeem.

With their empire in its death throes, the Turks turned on the imperium's most productive citizens. First in the 1880s and 1890s, and again after the turn of the century, populist frenzies spilled Armenian blood. But those pogroms were mere rehearsals for the genocide executed during the Great War. Armenian colonels and privates—loyal soldiers—were stripped of their uniforms and butchered on the parade grounds before their barracks or shot at the front where they served. Behind the lines, ancient communities disappeared in days. Rape was common, creative torture widespread. The young died first, followed by their elders. Sometimes, only a portion were murdered near their homes, with the survivors driven southward and eastward on death marches into the Syrian desert. At the mercy of Turkish magnates and Kurdish chieftains, pleasing women were culled, along with the more attractive children, male and female. Girls sought to make themselves ugly but found themselves dragged into a ditch or, if they were lucky, carried off on horseback for a single man's pleasure. Eastern Anatolia became a carnival of gallows, shallow graves, and inevitably, crucifixions. To spare bullets, guards simply denied the refugees water. The sun drove sound men mad. The few women who had not yet been raped were raped at last. Those who had been raped and left alive were raped again. And again. Armenian bones formed a highway to the Euphrates.

At least a million died.

Hitler spoke of the lessons to be drawn from the Armenian Genocide—not least that the world stood by and let it happen. Missionaries and a few consuls protested (American and German). Their reports excited skepticism or shrugged shoulders, not action.

For all the horrors of the Balkan Wars that served as an overture to 1914 or the Wagnerian carnage of the Western Front, it was the Armenian Genocide that marked the true beginning of the twentieth century and its cavalcade of misery.

Now the Armenians were fighting again and, although I sought to be objective, I could not help sympathizing with them. I knew too much about their history, but not enough about their contemporary reality. For me, Armenians were Franz Werfel's romanticized heroes of Musa Dagh and I could not fully master my emotions as I watched them go off to war. Standing on the hillside patio before the Matenadaran—their repository of cherished ancient manuscripts—I had seen the teasing ice-cream cone of Mt. Ararat just across the Turkish border, a mountain at the spiritual center of the Armenian world and now held captive by their deadliest enemies. From the slopes of Yerevan, Ararat seemed tauntingly close, a trick of the atmosphere almost convincing you that you could reach out and touch it. Ararat is the world's true magic mountain. (A sense confirmed when I saw it from the Turkish side after I remarried; our honeymoon was a dawdling bus trip from Istanbul to Dogubeyazit on the Iranian border, where the night belonged to smugglers and the day to Ararat.)

That sacred mountain's greater and lesser peaks were now a forbidden zone to the people who had built a civilization in their shadows. Urartu and the Hittite empire left their marks, and the Danishmends and Seljuks left their monuments, but the Armenian kings left a legacy of magnificence, and I was under its spell.

Until an incident reminded me that no nation commands unblemished virtue.

Leaving the park by the opera house as the crowd faded into the dusk, I strolled back down the boulevard toward my hotel. The daily convoy had chugged off, leaving only a few stray clusters of men in improvised uniforms. Greased with a long day's sweat, I veered between fantasies of a hot-water scrub and weary efforts to sort the impressions harvested during an arduous trip up-country. Suddenly, in the mauve light, I came upon a dozen men in black uniforms. I sensed the peculiar discipline of criminals, not true soldiers, and would have been glad to get past them without making eye contact. But a glint on the leader's right breast caught my eye: he had pinned a large metal swastika to his pocket.

I am not in the habit of confronting armed thugs in broken countries, but the sight of that fucking swastika set me off. Any Nazi paraphernalia worn publicly or any hint of admiration for Hitler's Germany infuriates me (some family history there), and the stupidity of an Armenian, of all people, wearing the arch-symbol of genocide kicked my mouth open then left me grasping for words.

Possessed by a greater, meddlesome power, I pushed into the squad of let's-play-SS punks and flipped up the swastika on the ringleader's blouse. He had a wrestler's build and a bully's eyes, but my insolence bewildered him. For an instant. After which his expression grew distinctly unhappy.

"*Shto eto snachit?*" I barked. And it really was a bark. "*Takaya glupost!*" Translated loosely, to capture my tone as well, the words asked: "What's this idiotic bullshit?"

I did catch myself before adding the word *svolotch*, which the dictionary defines as "scum" but which has a richer impact in Russian.

The gang edged in around me.

My fit of valor lasted perhaps twenty seconds before audacity gave way to the conviction that I was in for a thorough beating.

Any courage I had stored up over the years had been expended in my outburst. Still, I had the sense to mask my inward collapse and tighten the muscles in my face so there wouldn't be visible quivering.

Each of the thugs waited for someone else—perhaps their leader—to throw the first punch. I figured that the best for which I could hope would be to end up lying on the sidewalk, which was preferable to disappearing around the corner with Spanky and Our Gang to a quieter spot where they could take their time.

When you're truly afraid, go on the offensive.

"I'm an American officer," I told them, projecting a self-confidence I certainly did not feel. That first statement was true, but what followed was desperate stream-of-consciousness lying. "I've been sent to Armenia to study the situation and decide whether the United States should support your country in Nagorno-Karabagh. A lot of Americans want to support Armenia. But we have to know that you're responsible." I gestured toward the swastika but didn't get my hand anywhere near it this time. "If *one* news photographer took a picture of that *snatchki* on your uniform, Americans would turn their back on your country."

There were nuggets of truth in the last line, at least.

The leader shrugged and tapped the swastika. "It doesn't mean anything," he said. "Are you crazy or something?"

"It means a lot, all of it bad. At least to Americans. And to Europeans," I threw in for good measure. I would not have hesitated to describe NATO armored columns racing across the Ukraine to come to the aid of beleaguered Armenia.

He couldn't let me win the debate in front of his boys—who clearly wanted to introduce me to a different form of Armenian hospitality. They seethed with the anticipation of inflicting pain that bullies feel when the numbers are on their side.

Playing my last card, I said, "If you want American help, get rid of that thing." And I turned as crisply as ever I managed to do on a parade ground, pushing my way out of the pack.

I expected someone to grab me and others to start pummeling me. I waited to hear the ringleader's voice, either commanding me to stop or saying, "*Get that sonofabitch and bring him to me.*"

All I heard was a passing truck whose driver missed a gear.

You never look back. The only hope you have in such a situation is to appear a hundred times more confident than you feel. I marched on down the block, crossed an alley, cleared another block and turned left onto a street not yet deserted. At the next corner, I paused, pretending to look in a shop window (not that the shops had anything much for sale). Two of the black-clad boys were following me, all right. But they weren't trying hard to catch up. Out of sight of their leader, they seemed unsure of themselves— gopher apprentices, not yet hardcore criminals. After one more block, they faded into the shadows.

I had been lucky yet again. The roughnecks in Yerevan didn't play nicely. I knew that. Once darkness captured the city, there were gunshots every night. Twice, I saw the trace of automatic weapons fire down a street or alley when I stayed out too late. Nor was it the celebratory gunfire in which so many in the region indulge. The tracers didn't arc into the air, but traveled parallel to the earth, searching for targets.

The city was nearly lawless (although even Armenian gangsters obeyed certain social codes—women were not to be annoyed, for one thing). The government was bankrupt and the police could be bought for cigarettes. Black-market cabals dueled over turf, inflicting torments the elder among them had learned from the KGB. More than once, I woke in the night to a volume of gunfire sufficient to make me imagine that Azeri troops had arrived.

And had the ramshackle Azeri army arrived—impossible, of course—I would have been embarrassed. The hot weather forced me to turn over my sole pair of trousers every other night for the floor matron to wash (I didn't ask how) and return to me, pressed and slightly damp, in the morning. I recall standing on my balcony in my jockey shorts after midnight, watching tracer fire climb the hillside. That narrow concrete porch was as far as I could go. Armenian dignity has a prudish side and no allowances were made for war.

LAND OF STONES,
LAND OF FIRE

I HAD BOOKED A CAR BEFORE ARRIVING IN YEREVAN. ON MY FIRST morning in the city, I went to pick it up at a tourism office. Two women, one quite old, one young, lazed behind their desks, as if already worn out by the day's demands. A flawless layer of dust covered the welcome counter, which had not seen a visitor's elbow in quite a while, and the brochure racks were empty. The fan's blades drooped—the electricity was off again. The elderly woman, who appeared to expect no more from life than a series of calamities, raised her long face and watched me in dismay.

The younger woman knew her game: Too plain to interest Westerners passing through, she concentrated on her cuticles, shooting off an occasional glance to be certain that her assessment of me was correct. It was.

Windows shut, the room smelled of spoiled lunches.

But all that was secondary: I was captured by the gaunt old woman's unnerving resemblance to my late Aunt Clara, who had terrorized me with her aristocratic pretensions and the penitentiary discipline she applied when I was sent to stay with her in the summertime.

Born in the 1890s, Aunt Clara had managed to spend much of the 1920s and 1930s in Manhattan, where she never warmed to jazz; in Santa Fe, where her artistic ambitions were frustrated by an uncanny lack of talent; and in Europe, where the count she'd met at a YWCA dance in Manhattan, and whom she married with alacrity, turned out to have exaggerated his hereditary claims as capriciously as my aunt had inflated her coal-mining family's financial reserves: Two incompetent fortune-hunters collided.

Count Beda—his rank, at least, was real—remains a sleek, well-tailored gent in the photograph I have of him, but that studio portrait also suggests a man of insufficient intelligence to survive as a gigolo. He blackened both of my aunt's eyes and sent her packing, after which she married a car salesman in Pennsylvania. Her second husband, too, found it expedient to trade her in for a renewed bachelorhood; thereafter, she relied upon my father's generosity. (And he may have been the most generous man of the past century, putting Gandhi and his ilk to shame.) When Dad's fortunes were up, Aunt Clara visited frequently. When my father was scrambling to meet a payroll or to dissuade the sheriff from posting a to-be-sold sign on our front lawn, Clara was less in evidence.

A failed painter and a failed writer—like so many others, she found the idea of being an artist seductive, but lacked the hounding passion to create—my aunt had been more successful in the German-American Bund in the late 1930s and retained a soft spot for Hitler all her life (perhaps a reaction to her brush with the Slav aristocracy). When she gave me an American first-edition of *Mein Kampf* for my eighth birthday, my father told her to beat it (for a while—she was always let back in eventually) and he took me to every documentary film on World War II that came to Pottsville. After sitting through grisly footage of Auschwitz at the Capitol Theater, my father grasped my hand in his prizefighter's paw and summarized the matter succinctly. "Ralphie," the huge man in the gabardine suit said, "your Aunt Clara's full of shit."

I had already come to that conclusion on my own; nonetheless, I was forced to take lessons on the violin she presented to me and suffered exile to her shifting lairs for a few weeks each summer to "put some manners on" me. (She moved from one set of rented rooms to another: Kingston, Wilkes-Barre, Hazleton, introducing herself to promising individuals as the "contessa.") My training involved a whack if I wielded my knife and fork as Americans properly do, as well as the demand that I speak in complete sentences. A frown tightened her face when she saw a class picture— fourth grade?—in which I wore a green suit. "Your mother must be spoken to," she declared. "Only Jews wear green suits."

Aunt Clara—who did live into her nineties—was fond of wheat germ and denied me the cheeseburgers I loved or anything containing sugar (which she said was poison). But we walked and walked, and when she briefly paused in her attempts to mold me into something better than I was born to be, there were tantalizing hints of a greater world beyond our Pennsylvania coal towns. She knew things and spoke to me in a condescending tone but with a grown-up vocabulary. She instructed me about architectural styles, the nuances of the subjunctive, and that a gentleman's lips never actually touch a lady's hand. She tried to teach me to bow from the waist, but to this day I lead with my shoulders. ("Like an Italian," she noted disdainfully.) Her greatest talent was, I think, her ability to hate, yet she meant well by me. I was to be the family success she had not been, an artist—although I could not draw—or a violinist, although I lacked any shred of musical talent. Aunt Clara believed she could will me into greatness. Perhaps I could be a writer, a poet? I learned about Goethe and Schiller, but Walt Whitman was only a bridge on the way to New Jersey.

As the years passed and she aged into greater meanness—one incident between her and my dying, bankrupt father haunts me still—I saw less of her, but I proved a consistent disappointment. When I signed up for a summer program at Oxford, she was mortified. Why not Heidelberg? "The English," she said in her icy diction, "are almost as degenerate as the Irish." Upon hearing that I had joined the Army as an enlisted man, she cast me from her life. I don't know if she ever learned that I became an officer—that would have pleased her—and she died before I published my first bestseller. (She would have found my style too plain and the content rough.)

And yet, I wonder how much I owe that rouged, walking cadaver.

Since a 1960 visit to Germany (paid for by my father) to confirm our distinguished lineage, Aunt Clara had spoken glowingly of our Hessian relations, describing the landed estate that had been in the family for centuries (while noting that our ancestors from Saxony and eastward had been of still-higher culture; she deplored the fire-bombing of Dresden in which our relatives had been lost). I was always skeptical of her claims, but during one of my tours of duty in Europe, I traveled at last to Weissenbach, the dreary village southeast of Fulda from which our namesake line fled. My enquiries at a *Gasthaus* met with peasant wariness. An unearthed cousin, an elderly man, suspected me of concealing a property claim. He quizzed me hard then gave me a tour in manure-crusted boots. *Herr* Peter Schminke was very fond of his cows. Pointing out the lot on which our ancestral home had stood, he explained that it had been torn down twenty years before. "*Es war nicht zu retten*," he told me. It wasn't worth saving. During Clara's visit, which the older man faintly and joylessly recalled, the ramshackle house had still had a dirt floor.

Clara died alone, in a senior citizen's home in Punxsutawney. Her possessions were looted—a few fine books, her unbought paintings, and a daguerreotype of a Civil War ancestor. (He was an enlisted man, but I failed to persuade her that he wasn't an officer.) Selfishly, I regretted the loss of Sergeant Ollendick's image more than I did the passing of my aunt. I would have liked to have one of her paintings, for old time's sake, though, the one of purple tumbleweeds done out West. A year later, my mother—who Clara despised—received a shoebox containing effects no junk shop could sell, old notebooks, and a few photos. An unpublished short story about Lorenzo de Medici was hopelessly stiff and effete. As for the snapshots—taken along the rails of ocean liners or standing beside old-fashioned motor cars with men in Panama hats—Aunt Clara didn't look happy in even one of them.

All that personal history coursed through me as I stared at the old woman in the tourist office. She had the same long, blade-hewn face (although Aunt Clara didn't have a mustache), thinning hair combed just so off the forehead and thin, putty-colored lips turned down at the ends. High cheekbones pressed through aged skin and the years had dug caverns above her sunken eyes. She wore the same plague spots of rouge.

I must have looked worrisome, since the old woman made a slight motion to rise from her chair, although she quickly decided against the effort.

"*Molodoi chelovek?*" she asked in economical Russian. "Young man?"

As she spoke, the spell dissolved. She was nothing like my Aunt Clara, once you got past the leanness, eye sockets, and paint. My aunt's eyes were pale, piercing, and merciless, but the decrepit functionary's eyes were brown and weary. Clara was always ready to snub the world, but this woman looked utterly done in.

I explained my business. Reluctantly, she rose. After several minutes of befuddlement—during which the younger woman filed her nails as if working on a prison bar—and following a search through files that spit dust, the old woman spoke to her protégé in Armenian.

The younger woman laid down her emery board and rose, immediately producing my paperwork from an untouched drawer. Then she sat back down to continue perfecting her nails.

"Your car is on the way," the old woman told me. Not quite Armenian, her nose had a distinctly Persian hook, the legacy of some ancient invasion. Judging age was tricky in the Soviet ruins—you had to subtract ten years from the age you assumed for a woman past her youth. Doing the math, I still pegged the office's matron at sixty or more. With her antique, exhausted look, she might have been at the end of one of those genocide-era death marches that ended in the desert beyond Aleppo. Her movements spread weariness like a disease.

"Will I be able to buy gasoline?" After my ordeal at the airport, this had become a serious concern.

"You do not have to worry," she told me. Even her voice sounded drained, suited only to sorrow and lamentation. "Your driver will take care of that."

Driver?

"Excuse me . . . I didn't ask for a driver. In fact, I—"

"Do not worry. There is nothing extra to pay."

"I can drive myself. Really, I prefer it."

She looked at me as if she feared I was incapable of understanding in any language. "The car has a driver. It must be so. That is the Armenian way."

Suddenly, I got it. It wasn't the Armenian way. It was the Armenian security-services way. On my visa application, I had been honest about my identity as a U.S. Army officer—I'd had quite enough of illicit visits to Armenia. The result was that I had been assigned a minder.

I realized that there was nothing to be done. With a shrug, I moved on to the next subject.

"You handle all tourist business?"

"Everything," the old woman, who later insisted that I call her "Miriam," told me. Admitting a formal duty to help me, she did not imply an active desire to do so.

I produced additional paperwork of my own. "My bag went missing—it wasn't at the airport last night."

"We will find it for you," Miriam said unconvincingly. "Our service is very good. Perhaps it will come on the airplane today."

"Can you have it brought here? Or to the hotel?"

"I think it is better if you come here for your luggage. Do not worry. Our service is very good."

As she bent to write a note, I sensed that she had not bathed recently but had dusted herself with lavender. My Aunt Clara had sometimes smelled of lavender—although she was rigorous about hygiene.

"I also need to ask about—"

A starved-looking young man came in, making a ruckus as if he had not yet learned to control his spidery limbs. It was my driver, who apologized profusely for being late.

"I am Lev," he said. He met my eyes, then bashfully looked away. His defensive smile was that of a high-school student ignored by the other kids in the cafeteria.

He certainly didn't look like a hardened security agent. But one of the many things you eventually figured out was that eastern intelligence services were also welfare organizations that employed countless clerks, gophers, janitors, and cousins in need of a job, as well as the hard boys (some of whom I would shortly encounter in Moscow). I understood at once that Lev was somebody's second cousin or an unimportant nephew. His mission wasn't to pump me for information but just to keep me out of trouble—and to make sure I didn't see things his government might find inconvenient.

I was miffed, but tried not to show it. And, in the end, the situation worked to my advantage. A broken-hearted boy is an easy mark.

His ten-month-old child had died the winter before. It had been a terrible time, with no heat in Yerevan. It felt colder inside the city's concrete apartments than outside. The boy had developed a simple cough, a routine child's ailment. But there was no medicine at the hospital—even the simplest antibiotics had run out. Cutting off the supply of medicines was as much a part of the new Russia's efforts to bring Armenia to heel as blocking the delivery of natural gas and coal. The child died as Lev and his wife watched. He was twenty-four and did not know, he told me later, how he would ever make his wife smile again.

Lev was one of those gangly men who seem boyish long after their maturity. His slight biceps erupted in surprisingly muscular forearms, giving him the look of an emaciated Popeye. Instead of a proud Armenian nose, he had flattened, faintly negroid features—and frizzy hair. Most Armenians are unmistakable in their identity, but Lev could have submerged himself anywhere in the Caucasus or the northern reaches of the Middle East. Each day, he wore the same bright-silver slacks: too short and sewn from a heavy synthetic fabric, they appeared to be made of aluminum. He must've been miserable in the summer heat but never complained. When he put on his sunglasses, he looked like a choirboy pretending to be a hoodlum in the bathroom mirror.

I first heard him laugh when we stopped at a ruined monastery in the hills to have a poor-man's picnic. Conditioned to do so, I had clicked on my seatbelt as we started off. (Lev was an enthusiastic, but not particularly reassuring, driver.) Even running with the windows down, we soon were sweating heavily in the rattling heap my hard currency had rented. As I unhooked myself to get out after several hours on the road, I found that the seatbelt had bled a black diagonal down the front of my shirt—no one had ever used it before and the dye and dust had bled to mark me indelibly.

Once he got his laughter under control, Lev told me, politely, that "Men do not wear seatbelts here. It is not the custom. They are thought to be only for women."

And Armenian social culture was sufficiently oriental for women to be relegated to the back seat.

Reduced to a single presentable shirt, I skipped the seatbelt thereafter.

We sat on collapsed stones in the churchyard, munching on apricots and bread we had just bought—stinging hot—from a roadside oven. Writing on a rain-teased January day fifteen years later, I vividly recall the puff of heat from the loaf as we broke it open and the erotic texture and wetness of those apricots. Attended by slow bees, wildflowers decorated the hillside. Crumbling homes peeked through the trees. A laundry line sagged with garments in chemical colors and mountaintops jutted above the next line of hills. A tethered goat complained.

I do not remember the details of that ruined basilica or its name. There are many such sites in Armenia, strong-walled and dense under dunce-cap steeples, built of white stone gone gray and brown and black, and crowned with thick orange tiles. They look as much like fortresses as churches, and they were. The Caucasian isthmus has been crossed by so many invaders that history literally lost count. Campaigns stretch back into legend, but even myth cannot encompass them all. This was a world of God and war (and of gods and wars before that), and I have never known another landscape so dense with ancient monasteries and churches, some still in use—not least for pilgrimages to beg favors of saints not listed in Western calendars. Others sleep, decayed to Romantic-era tastes.

Those churches and cloisters, shrines and ruins were crucial to my plan of operations. I had studied up on Armenian ecclesiastical architecture and excused my desire to pry into the war zone by explaining that I wanted to visit this abandoned basilica or that remote chapel. Generations of Soviet and Western archaeologists had labored to provide me with a map to the war—or to get as close to it as I could.

On another day, when we pressed toward the Lachin Corridor, where the fighting was fierce and atrocity-prone, the pitted highland roads were mile-posted with broken-down brown trucks (I noted a World War II–era Studebaker, a lend-lease ghost) that had given their all, surrounded by unshaven soldiers sucking the last smoke out of cigarette butts, their chests heaving like old Deadheads working a roach.

I could argue my way so far, but there would always come a point—once within the sound of a battle across a ridge—when Lev would "explain" that the road was under repair up ahead and currently impassable. He managed to say this with a straight face as military vehicles sputtered past us.

I wanted to see the fighting. Our embassy, whose handful of diplomats clung to Yerevan like leeches and would not strike out to see things firsthand, relied on the Armenian government for their information about the war. I knew their assessments were nonsense and wanted to get at the facts.

I broke Lev down as far as he dared to go. Together day after long summer day, I tipped him a U.S. ten-dollar bill each evening. It was an enormous sum in those poverty-scorched years, and it won him over quickly. Daily, generous tipping is a technique I've used on multiple continents—"thank" the driver or guide daily, not just at the end. First, it often makes an immediate difference to him and his family; second, in the bad spots it gives him an extra incentive to keep you alive; and third, it inevitably draws him into a sense of complicity. (If you're going to weave between warring factions, hire a driver from one side and a guide from the other, even if you don't believe you need company, and tip them both daily; inevitably, they get along fine, agreeing that their factions ought to be uniting to kill some third party instead.)

There was no way to get into the Lachin Corridor, but I saw enough to grasp how desperate the fighting had become. (The wounded were usually ferried back to Yerevan after dark, but not all of them could be hidden.) Nor was I foolish enough to tip my hand by chasing the war every day. I covered as much ground as I could, heading away from the fighting one day, sidling toward it the next. And there was plenty to see: for a tiny country, Armenia has a remarkable variety of landscapes, from snow-capped peaks and fertile valleys to high steppes and arid plains. Eden lays an hour's drive from grotesque industrial wastelands. Everywhere, the air pants from the heat and geological instability mirrors the region's political disorder: earthquake fissures scar green prairies, sadistic gouges in the planet's tough skin.

If the war that summer was brutal, it was still an order of magnitude less deadly than the earthquake that struck Spitak and surrounding towns in northwestern Armenia on Pearl Harbor Day, 1988. At 10:40 a.m., the world ended for 25,000 souls. No building in Spitak was left undamaged—most were completely destroyed. In nearby Gyumri, the devastation was only slightly less thorough. And the horror came at the start of a savage winter. As we drove through the streets of Spitak in 1992, miles of wreckage still had not been cleared. International relief agencies had contributed temporary housing that slipped into permanence, creating refugee ghettos a heartbreaking stroll away from ancestral homes. (The Italians did the best job of providing emergency housing and general aid, the dying Soviet government the worst.)

The long days on the road followed by evenings chasing after demonstrations wore me down and I began to stretch out our lunch stops—always at another derelict monument to Armenian devotion. Lev explained the symbology of the *khatchkhar*, those peculiar-to-Armenians slabs, intricately worked in stone, that serve as holy billboards. His interpretation was sternly Christian, but the sunbursts and fertility patterns surrounding the stylized crosses reached deep into faith's dark sea. A devout tribute to Christ, each *khatchkhar* also preserved the iconography of burned-out cults and the legacy of Zoroaster.

To recycle a line I applied to Galilee in a later war, the soil of Armenia bears such a heavy load of history it's amazing it doesn't sink under the weight. Perhaps that pressure, rather than mere geology, provokes Armenia's all-too-frequent earthquakes.

Inevitably, Lev took me home to meet his extended family at a goat roast held in my honor. I learned the Armenian rules for checkers and didn't try to keep up with the rounds of brandy.

By the end of my visit, Lev had proven to be a blessing, since he was able to talk us through roadblocks I could not have passed on my own. And I learned why he had such disproportionately beefy forearms: Not far from the capital's streets, many of the roads were broken up as if they had been bombed. (It was only a combination of Soviet construction methods and a culture uninterested in maintenance.) Steering the car through the baked ruts and stagnant-pool craters demanded a level of strength akin to the muscles truckers required in the years before power steering. Lev enjoyed displaying his skill at passing us through the impassable— he was a mess on smooth asphalt, but give him a ditch and the boy was in his element.

Before leaving, I wanted to see Lake Sevan. Although the waters approached the Azeri border to the east, the sector was quiet as far as anyone knew. Neither side had sufficient forces to fight on multiple fronts and, according to the information available, the struggle centered on Karabagh and its lifeline, the Lachin Corridor. While the Armenians had better officers, thanks to a long tradition of military service under czars and general secretaries alike, the Azeris had Moscow's backing at just that point in the war. The "mercenaries" on Baku's side were Russian special forces (*spetznaz*) and Russian Hind attack helicopters—huge, deadly locusts—drove Karabagh's ethnic Armenians from their defensive positions above Shusha. (Later, the Russians would shift their support to the Armenians again, keeping the hatred stoked and the populations conveniently divided.) Both sides fought with cast-off junk in ad hoc units and atrocities were routine—but the Karabagh Armenians had been pushed back, their cities falling or under siege. A weaker people would have sued for peace.

Our drive over a wretched mountain highway to Lake Sevan took longer than the map had promised, but the weather was glorious, with the heat chased by a breeze raiding down off the hills. I was leaving the next day, so the tension had drained off. We clowned by a lakeside church and took photographs of each other, then pushed on to make a circuit of the lake.

I've already told this part of the tale in print, so I won't give the details here—repeating stories is one of the worst sins of the writer and the dinner guest. Suffice to say that, approaching the international border, we came up against a roadblock that even Lev couldn't talk us through. The guards were scruffy and nervous, and we soon received unmistakable evidence that the war was on in this sector, too, with the opposing forces dueling across the boundary line. The pretense on the part of the Yerevan government was that the fighting confined itself to Karabagh, with some fudging in respect to the Lachin Corridor, but Armenia was not making war. This was yet more proof that the fight was between the two states and not just the localized affair our diplomats reported.

Cutting the day short, we returned to Yerevan and I described what I'd found to a female foreign-service officer. She dismissed me as though I were a child making up stories. To her, the official line of the Armenian government was more trustworthy than the word of a U.S. Army officer.

I left the next day. I had checked in routinely with the tourist office to see if my bag had turned up, only to be assured by the morose old gal who had jarred me with her resemblance to Aunt Clara that all possible diligence had been applied to finding my luggage, but thus far, there was no sign of it. She had contacted airlines, the airport staff—everyone but the patriarch of the Echmiadzin Cathedral. She was terribly sorry, but after all, life is hard and misfortune common. . . .

A new driver picked me up to take me to the airport—I didn't need to be "minded' anymore. We were early, so I had him drive me up the mountainside to the statue of the "Mother of Armenia."

Mom resembles a gigantic, sword-wielding monster—a golem from a German-expressionist film. But the view from the heights where she towers over the city is superb and I wanted a last look. From above, the squalor was less in evidence, the lice-ridden refugees were invisible, and holy Ararat defined the horizon.

Abruptly, I shrugged and walked away from the panorama. We were at the scruffy airport in a half hour. I'd bought a number of canvases from a splendid Armenian artist, Avraham Avrahamian, and had to clear their export through an office meant to prevent the theft of antiquities by those who had failed to pay the appropriate bribes. My last two packs of Marlboros took care of the paperwork, with good will all around, and the inspectors didn't bother unrolling the canvases.

Walking back down the hallway, I glanced into a room—idle curiosity.

My lost bag lay abandoned on a high shelf.

Two young attendants, a man and a woman, staffed the lost-luggage closet. In hardly a minute, I had connected myself to the bag with adequate documentation. It hit the counter with an explosion of dust. To the credit of the Armenians, the combination locks were still intact.

"It has been here for a long time," the young woman told me. "We waited for someone to claim it, but no one came."

"Didn't anybody phone to ask about a lost bag? For Ralph Peters? Nobody called from the tourist office?"

They shook their heads in unison: nope.

I opened the bag and gave them my emergency medicines and syringes—pure gold under the prevailing conditions. I had also packed a back-up carton of Marlboros for which I had no use now. The customs inspectors wandered in from next door to see what the fuss was all about and I distributed the cigarettes among my newfound friends. I could have run for Armenia's parliament with a fair chance of success.

"You must come back!" the young woman—who would have cleaned up nicely—told me.

And I did go back, a year later, as a member of a Congressional delegation. The war had reversed course by then; we had a new, larger embassy; and food had reappeared in the shops. It was a lesson in how swiftly a tide can turn: the Azeris of Karabagh had become refugees now, driven from their homes by resurgent Armenians.

I made my first trip through Azerbaijan two years later. By then the strategic tectonic plates had shifted yet again. With an Armenian lobby strong in California and a sense of Armenian suffering during the genocide, Washington's initial sympathies had gone to Yerevan. But it didn't take long for Azerbaijan's oil and gas deposits to register on corporate America—while Armenia had no natural resources. Baku got a higher-profile ambassador and considerably more attention than Yerevan as we sponsored pipelines to the Mediterranean and negotiated exploration contracts.

I had planned to set a novel in Armenia, but despite my attraction to the people and the place, the idea didn't ignite—I never sat down to write the opening chapter. To my surprise, it was the quirkiness and unkempt romance of Azerbaijan that sparked the creative fires. Following my first visit, I wrote *The Devil's Garden*, which captured the spirit of the time and place well enough to enjoy a stretch of popularity both with State Department dissidents and the Lonely Planet crowd.

There are only three things I would add to the novel's portrait of Baku and the badlands down along the Iranian border: The High Caucasus rising into Daghestan is one of the most enthralling places on earth; it's hard not to admire a Muslim country where you can buy a cold beer from a jerry-rigged roadside refrigerator; and Azerbaijan was the first place where I got an inside look at the nastiness of our Saudi "friends."

A dutiful Marine officer from the embassy drove me around the country (I was visiting on an official ticket) and one of our excursions targeted the refugee camps in the shadow of Karabagh's mountains. The West had little interest in their existence, since the Balkans were consuming our rations of pity, and aid programs—never adequate—faded away. In the summer's heat, cholera teased, unsettling the bankrupt national authorities. (The disease flirted through the capital's back streets, too.)

The camps, such as they were, had been sponsored by various countries and international charities. The camp organized by the Turks was the best run of the lot—the Turks had windy ambitions, since deflated, of achieving hegemony over their Turkic-tongued brethren in the Caucasus and Central Asia. Most other camps managed a minimum of decency, survived the occasional riot, and kept up sanitation as best they could with the displaced mountain folk. Notoriously, the worst run facility was sponsored by Saudi Arabia. It had a reputation for hostility to outsiders, filth, and murky activities.

I wanted to see it. The embassy staff had been forbidden to enter the camps, but as a visitor without diplomatic status I didn't feel compelled to obey the rule. My mission was to assess conditions in the country and I wasn't going to be deterred by bureaucratic timidity.

Following his orders, my Marine escort remained in our vehicle as I walked into the camp. It was a dreadful, derelict place, literally stinking of poverty, but I was welcomed with unexpected warmth.

Not by the refugees, who were sullen and dead-eyed, but by the two young Saudis charged with administering the camp and controlling its thousand or so residents.

They were nervous and languid at once, glad for any company from the world beyond the wire. Abandoned without transportation or money, neither spoke Azeri or Russian, only comedy-act English: They could not communicate with a single one of the camp's inmates. Wearing jeans and cheap shirts, they slumped behind a single desk in their cinderblock office and spoke with the fatalism perfected by Arabs over the centuries. Rarely making eye contact, they stared at a desktop computer. The dead screen was furred with dust and the cables had not been connected. They kept their records by hand in old-fashioned ledger books.

The air was rancid.

Bread. They needed bread.

Bread?

I didn't understand exactly what they were trying to communicate. Once aroused, they were as excitable as they were ungrammatical—they had the Arab "gearbox deficiency," able to shift only between Park and Overdrive. In fifth gear, they did everything but caress me as they begged for help.

It emerged that an official Saudi charity had opened the camp in high hopes of converting Azeri Muslims to Wahhabism. It didn't take long for the senior Saudis sent on the mission to grasp that, Muslim though they felt themselves to be, the Azeris had no intention of giving up alcohol, the local saints they revered, or the various Sufi-syncretic practices handed down from their renegade-Shia ancestors.

As soon as the boss-level Saudis realized that the camp could not be turned into a fundamentalist bridgehead (nobody attended the true-path-to-Islam madrassah and the refugees remained loyal to their mullahs), they looted the funds and went home, leaving the two young men I met with an embassy phone number that didn't work, a hungry camp, and a bread contract that summed up Saudi cynicism toward their fellow Muslims.

Before leaving Azerbaijan, a Saudi hustler had given the contract for supplying the camp with bread to a bakery in Sumgait—on the other side of the country (and, incidentally, the scene of the original ethnic-cleansing riots that poisoned relations between Azeris and Armenians). It was a shameless kickback scheme, since there were plenty of bakeries close enough to supply fresh bread daily. As it was, the camp had never been adequately supplied and, by the time of my visit, there had not been a delivery for over a week. The young Saudis did not know how to contact the bakery and worried that the refugees would turn violent: there were dried beans in plenty, but the people wanted bread.

I lied and said that I'd look into the matter. That calmed them. They didn't really believe that I would help them, but in Arab culture a verbal promise is a temporary sedative—even when the recipient knows it's bogus. My promise was a sign of commiseration, not of a genuine commitment, and they accepted that.

At my request, they took me on a walking tour of the camp. It wasn't as grim as the shit-cloud refugee pens of Africa, but it was sorry enough. People rescue strange things: One ragtag tent had an old television set rigged up to an automobile battery around which a family sat in beggars' rags. Others had brought along shiny rugs, chemically treated to suggest silk, of the sort that decorate countless walls between the Black Sea and the Bay of Bengal. Elsewhere, tent poles had been hung with portraits taken in provincial studios of high-chinned patriarchs with cartoon-villain mustaches and thick matriarchs whose hands, unused to being idle, lay awkwardly in their laps. The inmates glared at us (assuming that I was a Russian up to no good), but never spoke. At the nadir of the visit, I saw how the camp had gained its reputation as a cholera source: the communal latrines stood a softball pitch away from the open-air kitchen, where cauldrons of beans were stewing above wood fires. You smelled human waste, not dinner.

I asked about the infirmary. The Saudis did not want to take me there.

"Two patients." One of them held up two fingers for emphasis. "Very sick."

His comrade gave him an uneasy look.

"Cholera?" I asked.

They shook their heads in ferocious denials that convinced me they feared the worst.

"Where's the infirmary?"

They gestured, warily, toward the declining sun. The clinic was at the edge of the camp, beyond the latrines.

"Is there a doctor in the camp? Or a nurse? Who's in charge?"

"Everything is difficult. Maybe no money is coming. People go away."

"Is there medicine?"

"These things are not good. You are our guest. Why see bad things?"

"These things are nothing," the other added. "A little sickness, nothing. These people are always sick. They are dirty people. But please to help with receiving bread."

The Saudis were relieved when I turned back toward their office. They asked me to stay for tea, but I made excuses. I wonder what became of them.

My Marine companion and I headed back to Baku, stopping along the way to buy a can of Efes beer for me, a cola for the Corps, and a kilo of fresh-picked cherries—which we rinsed in water drawn from a village well, cholera be damned.

I encountered Saudi troublemaking with ever-increasing frequency thereafter, in return trips to the Caucasus and Central Asia, in Pakistan and Turkey, and after I took off my uniform, from Indonesia to West Africa. Everywhere, the Saudis took an interest in human suffering only if it offered them an entry point for missionary activities. And any Muslim who wouldn't sign up for the full, hypocritical program of Wahhabi puritanism was welcome to die. Their "aid" was heartless, ever aimed at dividing societies, either splitting conservative Muslims from more liberal compatriots who also bowed toward Mecca or, as in Kenya and India, attempting to isolate Muslim communities from the mainstream of a mixed society.

Bribing in Allah's name, the Saudis crowded out moderate religious schools, paid parents to remove their children from government-funded classrooms, discouraged the pursuit of university degrees in practical fields, and generally did their best to excite a sense of injustice on the part of local Muslims. In my experience, no power on earth has done more harm to civilization over the past generation than Saudi Arabia. Even as Saudi princes laughed about hiring the best military in the world—ours—to defend them, they spread anti-American and anti-Western hatred far more effectively than the old Soviet Union or Mao's China ever managed to do. Bought, Washington politicians and lobbyists on both sides of the aisle defended Riyadh as SUV drivers poured money into the Kingdom's bank accounts. We not only sold out, but sold out cheaply.

But those other encounters with the Saudi genius for exporting hatred still lay in the future. I wasn't done with Russia.

September 1992–August 1993

AMONG THE MISSING

"*MOZHNO?*" I ASKED, GESTURING TOWARD THE MAP. MAY I?

The Russian colonel nodded. "*Pozhalista.*" Please.

Even with his permission, I hesitated. Then I picked it up. The lines had been drawn with a crayon and a smear divided Poland between Hitler's domain and Stalin's. I was holding the map on which the foreign ministers of Nazi Germany and the USSR had worked out the Molotov-Ribbentrop Pact. Their agreement plunged Europe into the Second World War.

An hour's drive outside of Moscow, the decaying Central Archive of the Ministry of Defense held plenty of other treasures, as well. We three American officials were honored guests and the staff had laid out a display of one-of-a-kind documents that traced the evolution of the Red Army from its Civil War roots through the end of the Great Patriotic War. There were mementos from the days of the Red Cavalry's exploits (transmuted into literature by Isaac Babel), as well as manuscripts from the early 1930s, when Soviet military thought led the world—until Stalin's paranoia led him to purge the officer corps, condemning his finest commanders and staff officers to execution or, at best, the GULag.

A series of operations orders from different stages of the Great Patriotic War told the tale of the Red Army's destruction and resurrection more eloquently than any narrative could do: the orders for the desperate 1941 defense of Moscow were crude and scribbled in pencil; front-level plans from mid-war were competent, if still unpolished; by the time of the Berlin Operation in 1945, the Russian plans could have served as models for any staff college in the world. It was an unforgettable lesson in how an army learns under wartime pressures, and I thought wistfully of my old friend and mentor, Col. Rick Armstrong, who had studied the Soviet military's history for decades but never had the sort of opportunity that fell to me that day.

The uniformed historians at the Podolsk archive wanted to please us in that brief window when naive officials on both sides imagined that an era of cooperation between Washington and Moscow had begun. The problem was that none of the documents helped me with my mission.

It was the most wretched mission of my years in uniform. And it didn't concern the Red Army's soldiers, but our own.

During my Armenian vacation, Jim McDonough was notified that the deal for me to remain a bit longer at Ft. Leavenworth was off: I was to report to the Pentagon immediately.

The Army Staff always struggles to protect its cattle from rustlers, and political developments had sent an invisible lariat sailing in my direction. The Office of the Deputy Chief of Staff for Intelligence meant to get its brand on me fast. So the personnel system herded me into the Pentagon corral as quickly as it could.

I walked into a bitchy network of fiefdoms where desk officers formed petty alliances reminiscent of tales of English boarding schools. Mediocrity resounded, although everyone seemed wonderfully pleased with himself. Delaying their labor throughout the day, "iron majors" complained of the need to work late. The officers were self-serving, their analysis superficial, the results negligible. In short, it was the Pentagon as it long had been described to me.

I was assigned to the office responsible for Russia and the states of the Former Soviet Union. (FSU was the acronym of the day.) I imagined that I might make a difference, since I had reached areas of the late empire no other officer had yet penetrated. I also imagined, naively, that I could cut through the office politics by outworking my peers. In the event, I would not be tested for another year—by which time a staff reorganization had turned the office into a far more productive place.

Except for a pile of dump-it-on-the-new-guy work, my desk was still bare when I was told to report to Col. Stuart Herrington in a Pentagon office a few corridors away. That lifted one of my eyebrows: Herrington was a legendary figure, the Army's most successful spy-catcher and interrogator. He had been the last officer to leave our embassy in Saigon in 1975, although another's name appeared in the histories and Herrington's role was the subject of fourth-beer whispers.

I marched down the dreary Pentagon hallways, wondering what the interview might be about. My hackles were up.

Herrington, whom I had never met, welcomed me with the warmth of a car salesman greeting a lottery winner. "Sit down, Ralph! Sit down, let's talk. I've been reading your stuff for years . . ."

It crossed my mind that my buccaneering on the post-Soviet seas might have raised a warning flag on the counterintelligence deck (where the winds of paranoia filled the sails). Had my trip to Armenia excited some bureaucrat anxious for a promotion? My experience with CI officers had not inspired great confidence in their judgment or their competence.

Herrington was an exception, though. I knew that much. He nailed real spies and put them behind bars. As an interrogator, he was considered peerless. (Incidentally, he believed that handling prisoners harshly was counterproductive—he seduced high-value captives with unexpectedly generous treatment, playing to their egos, not on their fears.)

The office in which we faced off was nearly bare. Herrington's desk held two phones, a computer—turned off—and a few documents stacked face down. Cardboard boxes lined a wall. There were no windows.

The colonel smiled. His face resembled a cheerful Buddha's. But for all of their warmth, his features had the quality of a mask.

Herrington's voice turned gentle, a preacher paying a sickroom call.

"You've heard about Yeltsin's claim? That the Soviets held American service members in the GULag?"

I nodded. The news had flashed by a few months before. It hardly seemed a shocking revelation, given the Soviet record of misbehavior. I considered it, literally, a dead issue.

"If there *were* U.S. prisoners," Herrington continued, "we're going to find out what happened to them."

I didn't like the way this was going. POW issues were a sideshow, a carnival for nuts in need of a cause to lend their lives meaning.

He paused. It was my turn to say something. "Did Yeltsin give us any more details? Beyond what was in the newspapers?"

Herrington let my question pass. "This is a top-priority project. I can tell you that there's interest at the highest levels—in the White House *and* in Congress." Sitting back, he anchored himself to the desktop with one hand. Years of interrogations had taught him to maintain uninterrupted eye contact. That all-too-friendly smile reminded me of a dentist I had hated as a child.

I didn't trust anything about him. If this was building up to a job offer, I intended to turn it down as decisively as I could.

"Officially, State has the lead," he continued. "A special ambassador's been appointed. The military's going to do the heavy lifting, though . . . the nug-work with the Russians and the analysis." Then he said the fatal words: "I've been authorized to pull any Russian-speaking officer I want."

———————

I couldn't find the men's room. The old Soviet Presidium building had been designed to awe those looking at it from the outside, not for comfort, and plumbing facilities seemed to be an afterthought. After getting wave-of-the-hand directions, I ended up in a Kremlin basement, striding down empty hallways. I was in a hurry, since I had to get back to the plenary session of the Joint U.S.-Russian Commission on POW/MIA Affairs in the meeting hall upstairs. The official minutes had suffered from too much sanitization in the past and I had set myself the task of making my own shadow translation of all that was said. Moving at a forced-march pace down yet another corridor, I started to sweat in the overheated labyrinth: I didn't want to miss a word of the increasingly testy exchanges.

I had become a convert to Task Force Russia's cause.

I found the fabled men's room at last. And, just as I entered, I stopped, doing a double-take worthy of a silent-film comic. For once, it wasn't vile Russian sanitation that brought me up short. In my haste to get back to my place at the negotiating table, I'd failed to grasp the significance of my day-hike through the building: a U.S. Army officer was on the loose and on his own in the Kremlin's inner sanctum. Not long before, such a thing would have been impossible (as it soon would become impossible again).

I grinned all the way back to my chair.

I had a favorite antagonist at the plenary sessions—where our formal business was conducted—and in the more intimate meetings in security-service offices behind anonymous facades in Moscow's back streets. Colonel Mazurov was a career KGB officer who had transitioned smoothly to that organization's successor, the Federal Security Service, or to use the acronym of its Russian name, the FSB. No casting agent could have produced a finer stereotype of the nasty-on-principle East-bloc agent trailing slime. The cliché was never more apt: when forced to shake Mazurov's hand, you wanted to wash your own.

On the Russian side, he was Public Obstacle Number One from the start. Whenever we uncovered a lead, whether personal testimony from the camps or an archival document, Mazurov and his associates explained it away, either as the false memories of senility or an "obvious" error in documentation. He bullied the witnesses we called, threatening them behind the scenes. And he lied with the confidence of Josef Stalin himself. Although one of the most junior members of the American team, I never hesitated to jump in and punch when the State Department representatives quit the fight—which happened all too frequently. And I always addressed Mazurov as "*Tovarich Polkovnik.*" The term "comrade" was anathema at the moment, identified with the fallen, discredited regime, and Mazurov grew uneasy each time I challenged him— explaining to all present that no one was a "*tovarich*" anymore, that times had changed and this was a new Russia.

That was the public line in Washington and Moscow. My personal conviction that Russia would, inevitably, revert to being Russia was unfashionable. We were going to be jolly friends forever, and any attempt to discuss the complexity of Russia's history and psyche, its ingrained behavior patterns, and its disastrous combination of incurable paranoia and grandiose ambitions met with scorn inside the Beltway. That patsy optimism about the "new" Russia would culminate in the Clinton administration's appointment of a self-adoring journalist and personal friend of the president to direct the State Department's Russia policy—which involved seeing no evil during those crucial years when increasing amounts of evil were there to be seen. By excusing every Russian misbehavior, including the slaughter and torture of the country's own citizens in Chechnya, we guaranteed that we soon would face the antagonistic-on-principle Russia that emerged under Vladimir Putin.

But in the waning months of 1992, there was still a chance for progress, with reasonable goodwill on both sides. Yeltsin's drunken blubbering that the USSR had held American servicemen in the GULag sent Russia's then-beleaguered security services into a panic; meanwhile, the Russian military, collapsing in the wake of its strategic defeat, hoped for beneficial cooperation. And everyone wanted dollars. Anyone who knew Russia understood that the situation couldn't last; in the interim, there were opportunities to be grasped.

We threw them away. Initially, Task Force Russia faced greater obstacles within our own government than it did from our counterparts in Moscow. Hurled into the mission of investigating any truth behind Yeltsin's statement, Stu Herrington's ad hoc office pulled itself together with remarkable speed: military officers know how to organize. When officers receive a mission, they salute and carry it out, even if they don't much like it. Task Force Russia was a gathering-in of strays, rounded up from the far corners of the Department of Defense: my Garmisch classmate, William "Butch" Burkett, who proved stalwart in the cause and quick with black humor on even the brightest day; the passionate military historian Peter Tsouras (who believes God's a Greek, and damned lucky to be one); Pete Johnson, a lively intelligence officer who psychoanalyzed dictators based on their taste in hats; the indefatigable Moe Wright and Paul Vivian; Bob Freeman, a uniquely effervescent Military Intelligence lieutenant colonel; and a pick-up team of other officers and NCOs—including an old pal of Herrington's from the dark side.

Herrington ran the show, although a major general was called back from retirement to give us flag-officer heft during negotiations. I came to admire Herrington unreservedly. Canny and adroit, he was selfless in his commitment to the mission. But I never believed that our general was the right man to front Task Force Russia. We needed a bare-knuckles prizefighter.

Nonetheless, Task Force Russia coalesced. And the Russians proved surprisingly cooperative in the beginning, since they believed their president was interested in the matter. (All too soon, the Russian security services realized that Yeltsin was a political Casanova, romancing an issue at night only to discard it, forgotten, the next morning.) But our own Department of State decided at the outset that their top priority was *not* going to be uncovering the truth about American POWs, but preserving smooth relations between Moscow and Washington. As soldiers, we identified with our brethren who might have been swallowed by the camps. Our diplomats had other interests.

The State Department may be an international disaster, but it's adept at political infighting at home. Calling on a former ambassador to Moscow—aged beyond alertness by 1992—the Foggy Bottom satrapy convinced him to head the U.S. side of the joint commission. It was a part-time job, leaving his excellency plenty of time for golf at his retirement retreat while letting him strut about on the world stage one last time, with an aircraft at his disposal and congressmen with whom to share asides. State had the lead in the negotiations and we in the military could not get the ambassador to take the POW issue seriously. His job was to keep relations with Moscow on an even keel, with no roiling of the vodka-poisoned waters. He did that job all too well.

After only a few meetings, the Russian security services realized they could stonewall us without inciting a protest. For State, the entire business was just an annoyance and our diplomats showed it. In a matter of months, the initial flow of documents from the Russian side dried to a trickle. Taking a cue from our own diplomats, the Russians went through the motions, but that was all.

That just made the military members of Task Force Russia more determined to break through the Russian defenses. We achieved a few successes, some by design, others through serendipity, in locating documents and tracking down camp survivors or retired Russian officers with guilty consciences. Several of the newly independent states of the FSU did all they could to help us—but the crucial information was in Moscow, in the security-service archives.

For his part, Herrington parleyed brilliantly with Gen. Dmitri Volkogonov, the leading Russian military historian, who had just published a disillusioned biography of Stalin based upon once-secret archives. Aged, ill, and cherubic, Volkogonov seemed a grandfatherly man—it was always a pleasure to speak with him informally—but the general had been a hard boy in his day. Designated as Yeltsin's point man on the POW issue, he appeared conflicted. Bewildered at first by the intensity of the American interest in soldiers still missing from bygone wars (hardly a Russian approach to casualties), he began with the common suspicion that we must be after something deeper and were only using the POW issue to gain access to Russia's secrets.

Herrington made the general a believer—aided by Volkogonov's glimpses of his own mortality and a conscience haunted by complicity in the failed Soviet system. Instead of challenging Volkogonov, Herrington let him talk. And our general, to his credit, arranged for him to receive medical treatment in Washington, extending his life by a few precious years. Volkogonov was grateful.

But the process through which we had gone by then conjured those horror films in which the hero and heroine race against time to escape through a vault door before it slams shut. By the time Volkogonov decided to help us, the security services had regained their composure—and the general found himself vilified at home over his published criticisms of the Soviet system.

The ironies multiplied. We had harvested sufficient evidence by the first half of 1993 to convince the better souls from State that the Russians had, indeed, kept at least a limited number of American service members in the camp system for years. Even the ambassador emeritus showed flashes of impatience with the hard, gray men across the negotiating table as he realized, belatedly, that he'd been set up. But it was too late.

To the end, State demanded fuller verification of every lead we unearthed than we could provide without State's backing to go after it. At one point, we believed we had identified the name of a specific ravine within the precincts of a camp in the Far East where American veterans of the Korean War had been executed and buried—in the wake of Saigon's fall, a quarter century after their capture. Our diplomats nervously dismissed the evidence.

Although the organization lingered on long after the founding members had left it, by the time I returned to the Army Staff in September 1993, our mission was a failure. When the Russians had been willing to help us, the State Department concentrated on diplomatic damage control. By the time our diplomats awoke, the Russians were determined to shut us out. It's unlikely that we'll ever learn the full truth.

My initial prejudice against the entire POW/MIA issue proved both accurate and dead wrong. On the home front, we faced the conspiracy claims of fanatics who showed up at every POW-related event to accuse the government of covering up secret prisons in Vietnam. With their defaced field jackets covered with unit patches they had not earned and badges they were not entitled to wear, the activists responded to any attempt at reasoned discussion with ever-more-lurid charges. Of course, when we looked into the military records of the most vocal champions of their "lost brothers" from Vietnam, we found that they either lied outright about their service or exaggerated it beyond recognition. There were "Vietnam vets" who had never been to Vietnam, but had served their draftee years behind desks in Germany or Korea—or who had never served in uniform at all. The POW/MIA issue was a magnetic field into which lost souls gravitated, but they might as easily have become obsessed by UFO "cover-ups" or UN black helicopters.

Then there were the authors of "authoritative" books that had no factual foundations and the pseudo-scholars exploiting the POW/MIA cause for all it was worth.

Who did the phony vets and the buy-my-book charlatans prey upon?

The families of the soldiers and airmen missing in action.

That was the part of the equation I had gotten wrong when I wrote off the issue before joining Task Force Russia: I missed the private pain behind the public circus. Whether or not there were U.S. prisoners, dead or alive, in the old Soviet Union, in Vietnam, or in North Korea, it was indisputable that their families had been victimized not only by the hucksters selling myths of loved ones still living in bondage, but by our government.

The greatest revelation to me wasn't Soviet misbehavior (which one expected), but the callousness with which our government had treated the family members of our MIAs over the decades. Incident reports that could have been shared with them harmlessly remained classified due to sheer pigheadedness, and bureaucrats with other priorities reacted to pleas for information with unforgivable brusqueness. Even allowing for the legitimate security fears of the Cold War era, the inertia that had gripped the system of accounting for our missing service members was scandalous. The families of MIAs were dismissed as annoying kooks who couldn't accept reality, but reality had never been presented to them. The system was especially cruel to the relatives of aircrew members who had disappeared on intelligence-collection flights near or over the USSR during the Cold War. Decades after the planes went down, family members still were begging for scraps of information.

Stu Herrington behaved nobly. By the time we came to the issue, many of the families had been radicalized to a point where they distrusted every word spoken by a government official. Others had become obsessive to a degree that hurt their own cause, given the ease with which bureaucrats could write them off as cranks. Herrington patiently won their trust—by taking them seriously.

His work on behalf of the families required a level of patience I shall never possess. With someone inside the system willing to listen to them at last, MIA relatives would call him at home at terrible hours, frantic and barely coherent. He soothed them as best he could. Disgusted by our government's past behavior, the core members of Task Force Russia made a compact: We would avoid classifying the documents we produced whenever possible; when in doubt, we would treat information as unclassified, rather than operating on the Defense Department's assumption that toilet paper should be stamped "Top Secret." If we couldn't answer the pained questions of the families, we were not going to add to their misery.

As the drafter of our tri-weekly reports for an entire year, I was able to ensure that a maximum amount of information would be available to the public: although a few documents we received from the Russians could not be declassified without their permission, we nonetheless got the key data out, stretching the rules until they threatened to snap—Herrington's ability to game the system proved invaluable. Repeatedly, we were criticized for not classifying various reports or papers, but we stood our ground and won. Today, any citizen can file a Freedom of Information Act request for Task Force Russia's papers and receive access to virtually every word we wrote—and we made certain to write things down so they would not be lost.

What were my own conclusions at the end of that grim assignment? They will please neither the conspiracy theorists nor the it's-all-nonsense skeptics.

We were charged to investigate the possibility that American service members had been confined in Soviet camps after World War II, after the Korean War, during the Cold War—when the secret dueling in the skies for intelligence was extensive—or in the wake of our engagement in Indochina. Based upon the documentation in former-Soviet archives and in our own files, these are what I concluded to be the facts:

- *World War II.* Not long before Task Force Russia came into existence, a claim had been raised that Stalin held back tens of thousands of American prisoners the Red Army had liberated from German POW camps during its march to Berlin. The allegation was nonsense. At the close of the war, Stalin was terrified of offending the United States. (Thanks to British double agents, such as Kim Philby, he knew the atomic bomb was on the way well before Hiroshima.) The Soviet Union had been devastated, the Red Army was exhausted, and Stalin needed time. In the event, the Soviets actually returned *more* American prisoners from Nazi POW camps than we thought they held. Of course, it was a clumsy business: The repatriation process was slowed by the shattered Soviet infrastructure and a global shipping shortage, and there were a few cases of disputed citizenship for GIs born on Soviet territory. Four POWs waiting in a holding camp in Odessa were killed by a collapsing wall and buried locally (with numerous American eyewitnesses to the deaths). Conditions in the transit camps were abysmal—as they were for Soviet citizens outside the wire. But there is no evidence that Stalin held back American POWs in 1945. Wild claims based on sloppy paperwork at our own European headquarters not only fail to allow for the colossal confusion on every side at the war's end, but founder on the inability of the conspiracy theorists to name names: the POWs who returned from German camps never reported missing comrades.

- *The Korean War.* Korea was a very different story. The Cold War had begun as the USSR regained its confidence. We found convincing evidence that Soviet agents culled select American POWs from North Korean camps and took them to the Soviet Union for interrogation. (Multiple reports channeled them through the city of Khabarovsk, a rail junction in the Soviet far east.) The Kremlin's intelligence services had no interest in dragging masses of American POWs back to the USSR, but they sought out pilots and air crews who might possess technical knowledge about our latest weapons. The problem was that, once the Soviets hid American prisoners in the GULag, it would have been awkward to hand them back again, since transporting them to the USSR from Korea was a grievous violation of international conventions the Kremlin at least pretended to respect. So they chose their men carefully, harvesting only those whose value outweighed the trouble and risk involved. I will go to my grave convinced that the Soviets grabbed dozens, if not a few hundred, of our POWs from Korea, held them in camps (where some died of natural causes, due to the harsh conditions), then executed any survivors shortly after Saigon's fall, when the triumph of socialism seemed assured and the POWs had become nothing but a leftover liability.

- *The Cold War intelligence flights.* We never resolved this issue satisfactorily. While some crews clearly died when their aircraft went down, there is inconclusive, but compelling, evidence that members of at least two crews may have been taken alive and consigned to the camps. The intelligence technicians on board the collection flights would have been highly valued by Soviet interrogators; on the other hand, the Kremlin liked to parade its captives—such as Gary Powers—in front of the world to make the case that the U.S. was an aggressor. In the murky spy-swapping world, aircrew members could have been used for trades. The counterargument is that the Soviets would not have wanted us to know what intelligence-related information they might have squeezed out of any captives. Our best chance of getting at the facts regarding these crew members came in the closing months of 1992—but our own diplomats refused to press the Russians. While I do not believe that any of the crew members were still alive at that point—despite the hopes of their relatives—we might at least have learned what became of those men who volunteered to risk their lives in our secret war that "never was."

- *Vietnam.* There is faint evidence that the Soviets may have taken a single American prisoner with a highly technical background to the USSR. And that's it. In Korea, the Soviets had leverage over their desperate clients, but the Vietnamese were nobody's puppets; on the contrary, Hanoi did a brilliant job of playing Moscow and Beijing against each other. The pattern we found was that Soviet security personnel would travel to Vietnam and submit questions to their North Vietnamese counterparts, who would then do the interrogating. The North Vietnamese kept a close hold on their prisoners, whose political and strategic value they understood, and the best a Soviet operative could hope for was to listen to the interrogation from an adjoining room.

Task Force Russia concentrated on the Soviet Union's activities, while other arms of government worked on the issue of POW/MIAs in Vietnam. There was, however, data spillover and, at the risk of angering those obsessed with "leaving no one behind," it would be dishonorable of me not to state my beliefs regarding "the missing" from Indochina: There was no parallel system of clandestine prison camps in North Vietnam holding hundreds of Americans still unaccounted for. I do not believe there are any living American POWs hidden away in Vietnam or elsewhere in Indochina—unless it involves an odd case or two of prisoners who switched their allegiance, went native, and disappeared into Vietnamese society. I trust our own former POWs who claim that their fellow prisoners all returned. And I believe it's a moral crime for charlatans and enthusiasts to keep false hope alive for family members.

In every war, soldiers go missing in action. In Korea, corpses disappeared into the mud and snow during the retreat from the Yalu. In the hellish conflicts in Indochina, not all bodies could be recovered, and some Americans taken prisoner did not survive battlefield wounds, were killed by captors unable to drag them along, or died en route to captivity from abuse or sickness. We will never know what happened to each last soldier from every war. We must make every reasonable effort and even some unreasonable ones to determine the fate of those who wore our country's uniform, but we also must deal with reality, painful though it can be.

Anyway, it's the families left behind, not the missing, who remain as the final casualties of war.

For me, Task Force Russia was ceaselessly depressing. Once assigned, I committed myself fully to the cause, only to watch with anger, then despair, as our diplomats worried more about annoying our old enemies than over the fate of our unaccounted-for service members. Another layer of frustration came from watching firsthand as Russia's political arteries hardened again—while no end of American diplomats and academics, pundits and politicians declared that Americans and Russians would now be best pals forever. The Russians needed tough love, and we gave them unconditional love. Our moral fecklessness and our intelligentsia's genius for self-delusion contributed significantly to the deformation of the "new" Russia.

I spent a great deal of time in Russia and its former colonies that year, traveling to POW/MIA summits and helping Congressional delegations shop (the primary purpose of any CODEL). I visited shabby Russian military compounds and former KGB torture chambers in the Baltics. Celebrating Christmas in Moscow so one of our men stationed at the embassy could go home for a month, I walked from one end of the sprawling city to the other one Saturday, beginning in the frigid dark and ending, cold to the marrow, late in the evening. Despite all, I still loved Moscow helplessly, as a man might adore a ruinous woman whose appeal can't be explained.

I sat before shabby churches in the snow, meditating on history and fate with juvenile fervor. I bought a complete set of Dostoevsky's works in a used book store, but retreated again to the easier language and simpler world of Tolstoy. Characters from Chekhov and Turgenev still could seem more real to me than the bundled scraps plodding through the slush to steam on subway-platform shrines to kitsch. Moscow in winter smelled of armpits and crotches and automobile exhaust. A Russian acquaintance led me backstage at the Bolshoi, where the decay was as startling as the vulgarity of the pimply ballerinas. The rising class of *nouveaux riches* was already in evidence, with BMWs, private clubs, and ravishing whores. Soon, Russia's social structure would replicate that of 1913, with an extravagant aristocracy littering European casinos, resorts, and grand hotels; a miniature middle class struggling for breath; and scattered throughout a deformed continent's slums and muddy villages, the *chornyi narod*, the common people who never had a chance and never will. The salient difference between 1993 and the days before the October Revolution was that Russia's new aristocrats lacked table manners.

The hard-currency price of caviar was still absurdly low, though, and I always took abundant supplies back to Washington, where I met my future wife at the end of March. A journalist, she had just returned from covering our effort in Somalia on a diet of

Army Meals-Ready-To-Eat. Despite her initial doubts about my soundness, she fell in love with beluga and sevruga.

I was glad when the Army Staff pulled me back in. Although the organization would grind on, Task Force Russia was dead. Even now, I cannot think back on that year without sorrow. I saw our government fail us, and I saw the Russians fail themselves. Their endless suspicion and brutal stupidity had worn me down. I was sick of Russians, and sick with a sense of failure.

Through felicity, not design, I soon found myself on missions far from the Russian bog, but I cannot close this chapter without quoting from a document titled "What Went Wrong?" It summarizes the fate of Task Force Russia and the Joint Commission. I don't think I wrote it, but frankly cannot remember which of us did. (We never signed our names to our work—we were good members of the collective.)

"From the spring of 1992 to the late summer of 1993, the optimism disappeared, the good will broke down . . . and, on the Russian side, the initial reservations of some Commission members turned into ill-masked antagonism and repeated instances of stonewalling. When they lied, we did not call them on it; as they stonewalled us, we failed to exert meaningful pressure; and when they have counterattacked, we have backed down. The overriding U.S. concern has been with diplomatic cordiality; when the Russians realized that we were not willing to press the issue seriously, they stopped taking us seriously. At present, the probability is that the Commission will fade into history with an empty joint communiqué and painfully inadequate results."

We failed.

THUG WARS
TO DRUG WARS

As light as a flirt's fingertips, evening soothed the bare skin of our forearms. With the day's sweat dried, Jim McDonough stood beside the runway in full combat dress, waiting for the aircraft that would ferry him and his paratroopers from Italy to Rwanda.

"I wonder what McCaffrey wants," Jim said.

I shrugged. I was the only soldier amid the bustle who wasn't wearing full battle-rattle. And I didn't much like it.

The safety lights of the first C-130 shone several miles out. Then we heard its engines.

"Good luck," I told Jim.

"Wish you were coming along," Jim said. His smile was tight and wry, a relic of bare-knuckled days on the block. "But there'll be a next time."

There would be a next time. In the following decade I would get to know Africa well enough. But I could not know that then and I was annoyed at missing an adventure.

After averting his eyes as a million Tutsis were hacked to death, President Clinton had decided that the United States should make a show of caring. Jim and his paratroopers were ordered to Kigali. As the Hutu butchers fled, blood-doped, across the Zairean border, Paul Kagame's Tutsi troops marched through a landscape of corpses. Reduced from African dimensions to a merely Balkan scale, the killing sputtered on as refugee camps filled. But the terrible work was done. Under hopelessly restrictive orders, Jim was supposed to show that Africa held a place in American hearts.

Handed the mission, Jim called back to the Pentagon to borrow me. I had become a one-man band in the Army, out of tune and out of step, replaying the theme that our future threats would come from ethnic thugs, religious fanatics, terrorists, guerrillas, and state-hopping gangsters. The chief of staff, Gen. Gordon Sullivan, cocked an ear, but Jim *listened*.

I got on a plane as quickly as I could, under orders to support Jim's intelligence preparations while he remained in Italy, but not, under any circumstances, to get on any aircraft bound for Rwanda.

Jim's rapid-reaction brigade was based in Vicenza, a city known for Palladio's architecture and paratroopers. As soon as I arrived, I drew my combat gear. Jim and I both knew that the Army wasn't going to court-martial me for going into a combat zone to support a presidential mission. In the few days left for staging operations, I worked with his intelligence staff, adding what shreds of insight I could to the first-rate work his team had already done. The days were filled with work, while my nights were wretched with Lariam dreams and the shock that comes from updating too many shots too quickly. Nothing was going to stop me from doing everything I could for Jim and his men.

Or so I thought. Hours before we were to board the aircraft, a call came through: I was to return to Washington on the next commercial flight with an open seat. Gen. Barry McCaffrey wanted me for a mission in Latin America. No further information. Just get back to D.C. within forty-eight hours.

There are orders, and then there are orders. Jim and I understood that, while I could have blown off my Pentagon chain of command, no one crossed McCaffrey. As the Commander-in-Chief of the U.S. Southern Command (headquartered in Panama back then) and the most decorated general on active duty, McCaffrey's desires killed my jaunt to Rwanda.

I turned my combat gear back in and watched sheepishly as Jim and his men lifted off. A world gone mad awaited them: a burning city, demented mobs, and dysentery. While Jim, in the best soldierly tradition, promptly exceeded his orders and did all he could to help the new authorities gain a measure of control, I found myself in Venice with a day to kill. As Jim and his paratroopers struggled through Africa's amplification of Bosch and Breughel, I sat over a glass of white wine in the world's liveliest ghost town, wondering what awaited me in Panama.

Staff officers waiting to enter McCaffrey's office quivered like minor aristocrats about to answer to Robespierre. Gen. Barry R. McCaffrey didn't have a mere face, he had a *countenance*. Cut from gun-metal. Hollywood never cast a general who looked more like a general. His graying hair never strayed from parade formation. Black eyebrows bayoneted the air as he turned his head. Skeptical eyes caught details others missed and his lips, tightened to grimness, seemed ever to verge on a question that would demolish a briefing and keep the staff scrambling long after darkness fell. McCaffrey was born to walk point, whether on an infantry patrol or for a nation. Even soldiers who believed they hated him sensed that their chances of battlefield survival improved the moment McCaffrey took command. He punished failure with the coolness ascribed to Rome's proconsuls.

He was, indeed, Washington's proconsul, more powerful than any ambassador, since his brief ran from Mexico's southern border down to Tierra del Fuego. Latin American presidents nodded along with our diplomats, but they listened to McCaffrey. His headquarters at Quarry Heights—an immaculate compound above the squalid bustle of Panama City—might have been a legion's seat at the end of Hadrian's reign.

McCaffrey had a reputation for cutting short careers, but this veteran of multiple wars and multiple wounds simply had no time for second-raters. In Vietnam, he had charged machine guns alone, firing his M-16 while hurling grenades. In Desert Storm, he had been the only division commander with true fighting spirit. Whatever battles McCaffrey faced, he meant to win, so *his* Army had to be strong. He respected subordinates with spirit, those who knew their business and stood their ground, and only whipped those whose weakness begged for the lash. Once you proved yourself, he remained loyal—a principle many leaders preach, but only the finest follow.

I had done an odd job for McCaffrey while he was a three-star on the Joint Staff, but I didn't really know him. And I didn't have any idea what he wanted. What little I could decipher about my mission I inferred from a volley of interagency briefings that hit me as soon as I stepped off the plane from Italy to Washington.

The focus was the cocaine problem in the Andean Ridge, but what McCaffrey expected a Russia hand to do about it remained vague, to say the least.

Arriving in Panama, I found the staff knives out for me. No one likes to have an outside hitter brought in by the boss, with the implication that their own work has been inadequate. A major's rank wasn't much in the SOUTHCOM command structure and the ill-will toward me was thicker than the humidity: when the colonels greet you effusively, it means they want you dead.

An entourage of strap-hangers accompanied me to the general's office. Looking around at the pack and obviously displeased, McCaffrey ordered his executive officer and enforcer, then-colonel Mitch Zais, to clear the room (one more strike against me in his staff's eyes). I should have been nervous, but while I respected McCaffrey's rank and reputation, I didn't fear him or any man who wasn't intent on killing me. Whether in the Caucasus or the Pentagon, cowardice never seemed a useful strategy.

The general told me to sit down. Close to him. When I met his stare and didn't look away, he nodded once, sipped his Diet Coke, and began to explain what he wanted me to do. At one point, his mouth curled and he snorted. It sounded like a gunshot. A moment later, I realized it was a laugh.

McCaffrey rarely let it show, but he had a dark sense of humor, the hard-nosed wryness you imagine among the leaders of the Easter Rising.

He wasn't getting an adequate, tie-it-all-together picture of the cocaine problem. Not from his staff, and not from the alphabet-soup agencies back in Washington. The multi-billion-dollar cocaine industry topped Washington's list of issues with

Latin America. Drug money corrupted governments, financed guerilla movements, distorted economies—and the product ended up as crack in America's slums. McCaffrey's intelligence staff provided him with plenty of data, but no real understanding of the deeper issues involved. He wanted me to scour the Andean ridge, to visit Peru, Bolivia, Venezuela, and Colombia as his representative. I was to inspect frontline operations, sit down with government officials in each country, and assess the effectiveness of the counter-drug operations run out of our embassies. I was to do all this in less than a month, then provide him with a detailed analysis of the situation and a forecast of long-term outcomes.

McCaffrey would loan me a plane and make sure the crucial doors opened. All I had to do was to get a grip on a problem that had eluded a dozen governments, countless staffs, and a legion of profiteering academics.

Luck plays at least as large a role in military careers as it does in gambling, and dumb luck helped me out again. McCaffrey was unaware of my picaresque background, but I'd been drawn by Latin America and its history since the sixth grade, when I wrote a play about the fabled meeting between Jose San Martin and Simon Bolivar. (My classmates gamely played their roles, with my pal Warren as San Martin and me, of course, as Bolivar.) Earned during weekends at Fort Hood, my master's degree had a heavy concentration in Latin American studies, with courses taught by missionaries and businessmen who'd worked down south, and I had taken an eccentric interest in the structural deformities of South American economies. (Unless your tastes ran to strip joints featuring pocked Korean floozies, the cultural life beyond the gates of Fort Hood was conducive to study.)

My personal mission wasn't the toughest job involved, either. Maj. Matt Duffy, jovial and indelibly Irish, drew the task of traveling with me and handling the admin while I pranced around. When my abysmal Spanish fell short, he translated. When I verged on doing something especially stupid, he nudged me to reconsider. And when I felt the need to rant, he took the blast, a better man than I was. I was nastily intense throughout our journey, determined to accomplish the mission but secretly worried the whole endeavor would end up a costly bust. Matt endured the where's-my-helicopter? bullshit and listened as I thought aloud, testing raw ideas. Of course, Matt never received the credit he deserved.

He did have a small revenge by luring me to drink nine pisco sours on my first night in La Paz, at 9,000 feet above sea level, a tactic guaranteed to slow even the most mission-obsessed martinet.

That drinking bout came just before we flew down to check on the Mennonites growing dope.

We flew low over the scrubland. Rotor wash tousled the treetops and wild beasts ran. We banked to follow a river trace, tilting our shadow on the mud and sand. No ground fire was expected here and the gunner relaxed. Beyond the frame of the chopper's open doors, the day was as clear as Heaven on a Sunday.

Our speed cooled the torrid air and dried our sweat.

We were hitchhiking with the *Diablos Rojos*, the Red Devils, a Bolivian commando unit the United States had equipped and trained for counter-drug operations. The Bolivians got cast-off

Vietnam-era Hueys, and we got first-rate gunslingers in return. It was all part of a billion-dollar battle in a bitterly poor land.

We had lifted off from Santa Cruz, the lowland city that serves as Bolivia's secret capital and money center. The new mansions lining the boulevards had not been built with profits from selling bananas and the quality of life was a world away from the struggle of the cane farmers out in the bush. I spoke as much German as Spanish or English and remembered the comment of an elderly Jewess in La Paz. When I asked about the relationship between the German Jews who arrived prior to the Second World War and the "more conservative" wave of immigration that followed the war's conclusion, she stared at me as if I were an idiot.

"*Hier sind wir doch alle Deutschen! Wir muessen alle zusammenstehen. Gegen die Anderen.*"

"But we're all Germans over here! We must *all* stand together against *them.*"

She meant those of Latin blood. The Indians didn't even register.

Yet, La Paz was a city whose veins throbbed with Indian blood. The bowler-hatted women stared right through white faces. Braids as thick and shiny as anacondas swung over rumps padded in the style of the court of the Spanish Habsburgs. It was the first time in my life that I felt invisible. Then, farther down the city's endless slope, I became all too visible, an obvious gringo amid the brown faces attending the university, a starved institution where activism substituted for scholarship and angry students learned nothing to lift them from poverty, merely how to daub paint on stucco walls to demand that the Yankees get out of the

Chapare. (The families of Spanish and German lineage sent their offspring abroad for their educations.) La Paz was the archetypal South American capital of operetta governments and coups, where social formality and the use of official titles rivaled the practice in *fin-de-siecle* Vienna. Now and then, the mob lynched a president from a lamppost to remind the rich that the poor would always be with them. The air was polluted and painfully thin. The chances for the common man were zero.

Flying down to the oddly misnamed Santa Cruz de la Sierra was like flying from Denver to Miami in February. Hot air slapped you as you exited the plane and the sun shone on a boom town. I slipped into a counter-drug conference that coincided with my time in-country, but found it worthless; the conference was held at a resort hotel built with cocaine profits—a fact to which the attendees were oblivious. I didn't think I'd learn much from the lectures.

Better to climb aboard a Huey with the do-it guys with guns, to get away from the cities to where the drug labs were hidden, to the isolated towns where the government's power was barely a facade. There were smuggling centers, ramshackle and lurid, on the broad tributaries of Amazon tributaries, where *alcaldes* of Levantine descent enlivened old clichés with their evasiveness. The contrasts between the Chaco and the Altiplano, between semi-desert, jungle, and the Andes, and, above all, between the people—white and brown, rich and poor, acute and torpid, hospitable and murderous—made Bolivia irresistible. I later used it as the setting for a novel, *Twilight of Heroes*, which may have been the best fiction I wrote under my own name. The book sank like a jilted lover leaping off a bridge.

We had one great advantage in Bolivia in 1994: the military team assigned to our embassy was the finest I've ever encountered in such a setting. The officers knew the country, believed in their mission, and simply were good men. They did their best under awkward circumstances, when the Bolivians often proved more helpful than our vanity-addled diplomats. A cancerous problem we faced in our counter-narcotics efforts in the Andean Ridge was the feudal nature of our embassy system. Each ambassador reigned as supreme lord of his petty domain and the jealousy between embassies was maddening. At a crucial point, our ambassadors to Peru and Bolivia, which were then the two most-significant coca-growing countries, so disliked each other that they avoided speaking. Of course, their attitudes infected their staffs. It was exasperating for McCaffrey to have to cajole our own diplomats to cooperate.

We flew on through a clear sky on a skillet afternoon. The huge throb and churn of the blades seemed to fade as I leaned out over the skids to admire the view. We dropped so close to the water that we chased waves upstream and I spotted the scalloped pattern on a sand bar where a big snake had entered the brush.

Some aspects of the mission still need to be glossed over; suffice it to say that we began the day by lifting off from Santa Cruz and flying a quick dog-leg so I could see one of the Mennonite settlements from the air. After tens of miles of eroded gullies and underbrush-choked heartbreak farms, gem-green fields assembled in perfect order. Oiled machinery glinted in the sun and a rainbow shone through the irrigation spray. A hamlet appeared behind a grove, its old-fashioned houses precisely plotted. With every detail as neat as a cadet's bunk, it could've been the backdrop for a film set in the American Midwest of a century ago.

Nudged from Central America for growing marijuana as a cash crop, the Mennonites had been welcomed in Bolivia—largely because of their reputation for hard work, but perhaps in part because of the sentimental echo of *verlorenes Deutschland* they provided. Frankly, we didn't care that they inserted the odd field of marijuana into their crop rotations. In the great scheme of things, Mennonite pot dealers on the edge of the Chaco were no more than a curiosity, while the crack cocaine gutting our ghettos and barrios posed a strategic threat. And the Mennonites didn't kill people.

For their part, the Mennonites didn't regard themselves as renegades, but as religious believers true to their faith. They didn't touch alcohol, since their reading of Scripture denied it to them, but enterprising young members of the community had pointed out that there was no Biblical injunction against growing and marketing pot.

After an off-the-books stop or two, our flight ended at a river town, where two inexhaustible officers from our embassy sat under a tree with Matt, me, and a mayor whose shabby slacks sported a broken zipper through which swollen, sweat-glossed, hairy flesh played peek-a-boo. His frayed shirt contrasted curiously with his Rolex.

Of course, no coca paste left his community! That was all over in the Yungas, or maybe in the Beni. But not here. And if he ever heard of any drug smuggling, by Mary the Mother of God, he would instantly tell us. Instantly! If necessary, he would report to our embassy in La Paz himself. It was his duty as *alcalde* . . .

General McCaffrey asked me to protect the contents of the report I submitted to him. I have done so and, in consequence, this narrative foregoes certain details. But a few insights bear the telling. One was so simple that only the privileged and well-educated could miss it: as I sat beside that Rolex-sporting mayor at the edge of a town at the rat's-ass end of the world, our made-in-Washington initiatives revealed themselves as nonsense. In the specific case of Bolivia, we were bent on coca eradication and crop-substitution programs. I warned then, and it since has come to pass, that bullying the La Paz government to forcibly destroy a crucial cash-crop of the poorest Bolivians would only undercut the government's authority and polarize the population, leading to an eventual populist backlash.

Diplomats in Brooks Brothers suits condescended to tell me that they were certain the *campesinos* didn't want to grow coca and would leap at the chance to raise legal crops instead, even if their income dropped as much as 40 percent. Academic studies had proven it.

Then you saw for yourself how the people lived. And you tried to imagine their hand-to-mouth existence reduced by two-fifths, their meager rations slashed, and their children, already half-naked and worm-sucked, stripped and sickened beyond their current state.

A Bolivian with manicured fingernails shared our disdain for the peasantry. "You think they're getting rich from growing coca?" he asked, in easy English. He pursed his lips in an imitation of spitting. "Maybe they get a radio out of it. And that's it."

He was a man who had never had to envy a neighbor's radio. You can bury me under an avalanche of think-tank studies and government-sponsored reports, but I will continue to believe that, to a man who has never owned one, a radio may be a welcome thing. And the harder-working *cocaleros* had televisions, too.

As for the imaginary preference of the poor in remote Bolivian or Peruvian valleys for growing oranges or bananas rather than coca leaves, moving such crops to market relied on roads that only existed in long-term planning fantasies. Meanwhile, no one was going to fly into those isolated settlements to pick up avocados or plantains the way the *narcotraficantes* came for the coca.

For all of our professed belief in free markets, our officials thought like socialists.

Having grown up in the rock-music world of the late 1960s, I had seen, very personally, the damage hard drugs do. But I found it vile and just plain stupid for us to put our primary effort into uprooting or poisoning the crops of the poor because we lacked the integrity to face our drug problem at home (of which more in a chapter to come).

Drug-crop eradication can work, if a strong central government *wants* to take on the narcotics trade and if the local economy is sufficiently robust to offer realistic alternatives to farmers. In Colombia, where cocaine production enriched guerrillas who enslaved peasant farmers, aerial eradication had sufficient popular backing to be effective. But in Bolivia, with its inherent political instability and medieval poverty, eradication turned us into the heartless Yankees of leftist caricature.

You cannot take away the livelihood of the poor unless you have the wherewithal to replace it immediately and enduringly. Our military men in-country understood that, since they spent a great deal of time in the countryside. (And they *liked* Bolivians, and respected them.) Our diplomats, who preferred life within the city limits, lived in a world of theories that created victims and called it progress.

As I write, Bolivia has an elected leftist government that is making a poor country poorer still. The sad demagogue in the presidential chair was elected by the coca farmers.

When I think of that mission, I recall flights over a succession of landscapes whose beauty taunts the poor. We traveled back to La Paz in a Bolivian Air Force C-130 transport barely younger than the DC-3 we left behind on a red-dirt strip. We didn't fly over the Andes, but through them: the overloaded old bird lacked the lift to get over the peaks, so we wove between rock walls. I rode in the cockpit and twice tightened my grip as we skimmed glaciers. The pilots were confident—or perhaps just fatalistic—and displayed a bantering friendliness toward the killer ridges and glittering summits. The cockpit's heater fought the daunting cold.

I've never taken a more ravishing flight, not in the Hindu Kush nor even over Iraq (whose beauty is only apparent to those who see ancient ghosts). It didn't matter that my head pulsed from the altitude or that my breath grew labored. As our wingtips teased the mountainsides, I felt yet again the inadequacy of language to describe the beauty God has strewn before us. Even had McCaffrey found my conclusions worthless and hammered me for incompetence, it would have been worth it for that one flight through the Andes.

In Peru, there were flights to the Upper Huallaga Valley and other spots not on the tourist route. At one U.S.-manned radar site monitoring narco aircraft, I found the perfect symbol of American failures abroad: our Air Force had built a remarkable castle of sandbags over concrete, as forbidding as one of Vauban's fortresses. We were hurried inside for our briefing—the personnel at the site lived under lockdown, utterly disconnected from the world around them. For them, Peru meant green specks on a radar scope. We were in the country, but certainly not of it.

We made the same mistake, on a grander scale, from Bosnia to Baghdad. But those are other tales for other times.

From the Peruvian highlands we flew across the Andes again, then spent hours over the Amazon's upper tributaries en route to Iquitos. When we think of Peru, our mental snapshots are of fog-whiskered peaks grinning with Inca ruins, not of endless jungle as green (and serpent infested) as Eden, with nameless brown rivers coiling toward the still-greater rivers that meander into the Amazon. No matter how much you have read about the vastness of the Amazon basin, until you have spent hours flying over jungle and watercourses only to realize you haven't even reached the Brazilian border, you simply cannot grasp the immensity of this least-friendly wilderness. The remotest swamps of Africa appear developed compared to this monstrosity of nature, where you can fly for hundreds of miles without spotting a clearing or a canoe.

Implanted deep in the continent, the Peruvian city of Iquitos is a major port, if one where a cargo of pigs still had to be wrestled up a mud embankment. My little room was vivid with unpaid guests and the water ran brown as sewage, but I lived in luxury compared to the Special Forces officers who came into town to meet me. With intercepts of drug flights on the Andean routes dis-concerting the narcos, we worried about aircraft looping into Brazil, where we couldn't touch them, as well as about the growing two-way river traffic in drugs and precursor chemicals. Our SF team on the ground had a difficult, diplomatically sensitive mission in wretched conditions. But that's what special operators do. My appearance only added to their work, but they were gracious, if a bit wary of the clean-and-pressed guy from headquarters: Men who live with the reality of violence, disease, and routine misery understandably look askance at staffers engaged in military tourism.

After working over a series of maps and discussing mission mechanics, we went down to the river, to an open-air restaurant where you hoped that whatever you ate had been brought to a boil. The SF men loosened up a bit—although they adhered to their orders and wouldn't touch the cold beers they must have yearned for—and we finally got down to an honest discussion of what worked, what didn't, and why. Over river fish and fried plan-tains, they delivered the sharpest analysis I'd gotten in the country. (My unavoidable visit to our embassy in Lima had been worthless.)

Matt knew one of the officers, so he stayed on to chat while I headed back to the hotel to write up my notes. The heat had cracked as the sun fell—which meant that your sweat merely greased you—and I strolled by the "House of Tiles," the city's sin-gle claim to cinema stardom (from the unintentionally hilarious film *Fitzcarraldo*). The city's old heart was clogged with faded McMansions left over from the rubber boom and I played hooky for a half hour, wandering the dirty streets as the dark thickened. Nearing our tiny hotel at last, I strained to make out the details of a wrought-iron balcony across the alley. And I bumped headlong into a gnarl of living things. Or, to be perfectly accurate, they bumped into me.

There was a boa constrictor in my face.

It belonged to a boy so small I was surprised the snake didn't simply suffocate him and swallow him.

The snake's tongue pursued me as I leapt backward. The boy smiled and asked if I'd like to fondle his pet for a small fee.

I declined.

Thereafter, the wildlife in my room seemed less disturbing.

For all of our worries about the drug trade spreading into Brazil, what I took from Iquitos emerged from the neglected architecture of another century—the old townhouses looked far less romantic when I went for a morning run than they had in the twilight. A backwater today, Iquitos had enjoyed a spectacular boom as the world discovered the many uses of rubber. Eventually, synthetics came along, the boom ended, and the city cleared from the jungle went back to sleep. Now it was the beyond-the-end-of-the-line sort of place where stray Europeans washed up, jaundiced males with hair as dull as string and vagabond blonds aging hard in the killing heat. But if a few worn-out backpackers stayed on to bilk Indians out of the pots they lugged in from the jungle, the talented children of Iquitos fled.

Thanks to that twilight stroll and a morning run through Iquitos, to the gilt altars of Andean cathedrals and the nose-thumbing prosperity of Santa Cruz, I took a second obvious lesson back to SOUTHCOM headquarters: South America has been the victim of boom-bust cycles since the earliest colonial years and the cocaine boom was only the latest among many. The continent had gone through the silver boom, the tin boom, the copper boom, the beef boom, the rubber boom, and successive oil booms. Now cocaine was the magic commodity.

Those booms had the same effect on South America as oil wealth has had on the Persian Gulf, destroying work ethics, distorting economies, preventing diversification, intensifying corruption, polarizing societies, and ending with plentiful monuments to vanity—cathedrals, palaces, mansions, haciendas, the Belle Epoque architecture of Buenos Aires and Montevideo—but without the infrastructure, production capabilities, or character to sustain a healthy economy. Found wealth, when immature countries or entire regions hit the natural-resources lottery, is uniformly destructive of the souls of men and nations.

The demand for cocaine might never go away entirely, but new designer drugs and other alternatives were bound to appear and deflate the market. Drug profits are susceptible to fads, and all fads pass. I guessed that the next generation of seductive drugs would come from labs in more developed societies and that, as the demand for cocaine contracted, traffickers would fight savagely for their share of the pie, turning former transit countries into cut-rate markets. The subsequent explosion of drug use would prove far more socially and politically destructive in Latin American societies (especially Mexico) than in the United States, since those societies were not only corrupt to the point of paralysis, but lacked the infrastructure to manage the consequences of widespread drug use. From Brazilian *favelas* to Mexican border towns, lawlessness was bound to soar.

McCaffrey got it instantly when I briefed him, but the meta-cycle was beyond American control. Now, thirteen years on, the scenario I laid out has come to pass, with various designer drugs encroaching on the market and, worst of all, a nationwide contagion in the use of methamphetamines manufactured (at severe cost to the environment) right here at home, in national forests and trailer parks, on remote ranches and in suburban tract homes. The impact on Central American states and Mexico, the classic transit countries, has been savage. The immutable law of illegal drugs is that, when the rich of the First World move on to new tastes, the unsold drugs are remaindered to the poor of the Third World. Globalization works for criminals, too.

The rich of Caracas swooped down from the hills to claim the prettiest girls the slums produced; otherwise, the wealthy and the poor lived under a stern economic *apartheid*. But no such system lasts forever. In 1994, Venezuela still belonged to the privileged. In 2007, it belongs to Hugo Chavez and the lower classes he champions. Unwilling to give an inch to those who chronically did without, the well-to-do opened the door for the election of a man who despises democracy.

You could see it coming, although no one could put a date on the demagogue's arrival. Caracas felt sick in spirit: hedonistic in the park-like suburbs, bitter and suspicious in the slums—of which there were many.

We sat over lunch in a working-class neighborhood, trying to talk about counter-drug operations with mid-level officers. But Venezuela was a sideshow in the narcotics circus and the officers had more important worries. The inequities of the society kept nudging into our conversation, subtly but incessantly. I suspect that those with whom we ate our stew became Chavistas. In contrast, my interviews with senior officers at the ministry of defense conveyed a programmed message that everything would be just fine if we sent more military aid.

Back in the Kennedy years, my sixth-grade textbook described Caracas as a progressive city. It was anything but. Sprawling and unplanned, it lacked the historical gravity that might have centered it. The heart of the city was ugly and fouled, while the green districts where the wealthy had staked their claims had all the integrity of shopping malls designed by a random assortment of cut-rate architects. *We* worried about spillover from the Colombian cocaine war. The Venezuelans were reluctant to worry too much about anything, sensing that their problems had no good solutions. We talked past each other, though amicably. And all the while Chavez was waiting in his barracks to upend the country and annoy a hemisphere.

If our own ill-judged actions made Chavez larger-than-life, Venezuela's upper class made him inevitable. To survive, the rich must be willing to give the poor a little taste of the pie. But the profits from the country's oil patrimony did nothing for those who lacked running water and had to steal electricity.

Our embassy saw no dangers on the horizon.

The trip grew anticlimactic. I worked late in my hotel room, drafting my report for McCaffrey on a laptop and blessing St. Mary's University in San Antonio, Texas, for giving me a more practical graduate education than any Ivy League faculty could have delivered.

On the long drive down to the airport, the word that struck me to describe both Caracas and Venezuela's political environment was "flimsy."

On the last leg of the trip in Colombia, seriousness of purpose collided with absurdity. Matt had gone back to Panama to take care of a staff wildfire and I was at the mercy of the most frightened Marine colonel I've ever met.

I've long been a great fan of the Marines. I admire their relentless fighting spirit and their crispness. While my fellow Army officers debated the best approach to a problem, the Marine technique was to plunge ahead and solve it. I did all I could to build bridges between my service and the Corps.

But the colonel assigned to our Bogota embassy couldn't grasp that the mission was to help me get out and grip the country's problems. His sole concern was making sure that nothing happened to me, since he didn't want to risk McCaffrey's anger. The colonel was a well-meaning man, but you can't crack any country's code if you hug the capital city.

He put me up in his own apartment and panicked when his wife told him that I'd gone out for a run by myself. Perhaps he'd just been in-country too long and had been thoroughly infected by our embassy's bunker mentality. The interviews I had to endure were of little value, and the CIA station chief seemed the least competent man I had ever encountered in such a position. He smacked of tennis courts, not guts and vision.

No one at the embassy could accept the obvious fact that, for a substantial minority of Colombians, the gusher of drug money was a welcome thing, indeed. Our logic ran thus: drugs are bad, so everything that results from the drug trade is bad; therefore, everyone else must understand as well as we do that everything to do with the problem is bad. It was another version of our condescension in Bolivia. In Colombia, we didn't want to see that, thanks to second- and third-order effects, bankers, builders, merchants, workers, and families with no direct connection to the narcotics trade were doing quite nicely, thanks to the trickle-down of drug profits. The money wasn't building a durable economy, but it was paying a lot of bills in the present. And if, unlike Bolivia's *campesinos*, the Colombians already had radios and even televisions, they had nothing against acquiring a refrigerator or a Mercedes.

We were puritans in a whorehouse.

In conversations with Colombian officials in various ministries, I sensed they were merely playing along with us, saying what we wanted them to say—not because they didn't care about their country, but because they knew we didn't care about it. Their desperation would later lead to death squads and support for right-wing militias, before a succession of bold presidents turned the country around. Typically American, we were looking for short-term results in the face of confounding problems of near-infinite complexity. The Colombians just wanted more helicopters.

I wanted to head down-country, but was told "No Americans are going there." I had sufficient experience to infer a great deal, but there is no substitute for visiting the trouble spots for a first-hand sniff. Stuck in Bogota—and restricted even there—I had to put together stray pieces to form a coherent picture.

Yes, there were car bombings and kidnappings. But I was a soldier, and soldiers go where things are going "Bang!"

Somehow, it all worked out. Back in Panama, with Matt in support again, I was able to finish the fifty-nine-page report in twenty-four hours (in an act of military heresy, I wrote clearly and bluntly), as well as producing the charts and slides without which no briefing achieves institutional authenticity. Then it was time to sit down with McCaffrey.

I didn't know if he'd get it, or if he'd decide my ideas were too far out of the mainstream. In any case, the work was done, I'd given it my best shot, and my wife, whom I'd married three months before, had justified a reporting trip to Panama City to her editor. If McCaffrey decided to shoot me at dawn, I at least had one night of sympathy ahead of me.

Five minutes into the briefing, McCaffrey laughed out loud. It was the beginning of our friendship.

––––––––

The great regret I felt on that trip had nothing to do with the drug wars. Before flying back to Washington, I went to visit the canal, one of the signal triumphs of the American can-do spirit. In a well-intentioned fit of strategic folly, President Carter had committed our country to hand it "back" to the Panamanians. So our vital forward bases in Panama were headed for closure and an era would end.

Looking down at the great locks, or simply standing in McCaffrey's quarters at Quarry Heights, I saw ghosts: the spirits of my countrymen who died of yellow fever and malaria, the shades of crusading doctors and brilliant engineers, and the long shadows of generations of my fellow soldiers. The Canal Zone was *American*. To me, we were giving away a piece of our country.

In the end, the Panamanians did a good job of keeping the canal in working order and plans are underway to expand the locks to accept the massive ships that bear the world's cargo today. The country is firmly democratic and its economy is progressing. While a Chinese company holds the contract for port operations, my friend Randy Gangle, a sturdy Marine colonel and the former commander of the 5th Marines, doesn't believe the Chinese pose a threat. And I trust Randy: he not only grew up in the Canal Zone, but recently retired to Panama with his wife, Ellen, her horse, and two dogs the size of dinosaurs.

As for the report I delivered to General McCaffrey, it led him to make a number of changes, and those changes made a difference. But the cocaine boom was too powerful and our government too divided for the difference to be decisive. McCaffrey did more than any other man in his position could have done, but in the end, the mediocrity of the system won—a phenomenon we both would face again.

A dozen years later, the U.S. Southern Command contacted me to come down and give a lecture at their new headquarters in Florida. I assumed that someone had unearthed the report—which was sadly prescient—and wanted me to speak about it.

I was wrong. They were interested in another topic entirely. The report had been forgotten after McCaffrey left and, when the staff looked through their files, no one could find a copy.

1995

PAKISTAN

As I prepared to write this chapter, I dug through boxes decomposing in the basement in search of the trip report I submitted to my Pentagon chain-of-command after my return from Pakistan in December 1995. Rereading the paper after a dozen years, I realized that I could not better it now. So, this chapter presents first impressions of a mission, rather than reminiscences filtered by time.

The unclassified report underscores the fact that the Army Staff was not blindsided by history: Officers sensed the danger posed by radical Islam, grasped the dilemmas of Middle Asia and the Subcontinent, and registered the shock of globalization. It was impossible, however, to persuade the Clinton White House, the intelligence establishment, or even our sister services (except for the Marines) that our enemies, rather than our desires, would shape the future security environment. We saw trouble coming and nobody cared.

The only alterations to the original report are the elimination of the executive summary, which was redundant to the rest of the text; the insertion of a brief portrait of Terry Cook, a remarkable soldier of whose *exploits I was not fully aware at our first meeting; some edits to shorten the paper's inexcusable length; and the correction of a few typographical errors. Otherwise, the words are those I typed up during a hectic Christmas leave.*

Islamabad:
Donald Trump Meets Albert Speer

You arrive at Islamabad's international airport, a smoky, gloomy Third World people box, in that last surreal hour before dawn, your skin as grubby as the terminal's floor, after a flight dominated by cheerfully mutinous passengers whose individual energies were not counterbalanced by any sense of social responsibility. With the long flight enlivened by children auditioning as terrorist under-studies (to the approval of proud parents), the aircraft's tourist hold put you in mind of steerage conditions in eighteenth-century immigrant ships during a dysentery outbreak—albeit without that earlier era's optimism.

Welcome to Pakistan.

The airport lies between Rawalpindi ("Pindi"), an old city sited to take advantage of the trade crossing the Marghala Pass, and Islamabad, younger than Pakistan and created to be a capital. The dark drive from the airport to the hermetic comfort of the hotel passed random Bedford trucks (assembled in Pakistan), their fantastic superstructures top-heavy in the suddenness of headlights. In this proudly Islamic country, the intricate design of the truck bodies, furiously ornate, looks like an unconscious legacy of the

Hindu impulse to layer and adorn. We maneuvered to avoid horse and donkey carts, while putt-putting cars materialized from nowhere and bearded men waited patiently in the cold, roadside sculptures, with their woolen capes gathered over the long blouse and billowy trousers of the national costume, the *salwar kameez*. Even with the windows rolled up, the acrid smoke of charcoal fires burned your eyes and troubled your throat.

Suddenly, with the turn of a corner, the darkly rural gave way to a well-lit avenue, Islamabad's street of government, its construction grandiose to a degree that would have made Ceaucescu jealous. Huge and self-satisfied, the architecture is from the school of Albert Speer working on a commission from Donald Trump. Only a single structure has any appeal, a not-yet-finished secretariat that plays off Pakistan's Moghul roots, off the region's magnificent heritage.

This architectural self-doubt reflects the country's general insecurity about its place in the world. In the markets you can buy splendid old tribal rugs and antiques that would make an interior decorator's heart flutter, but few Pakistanis value their own heritage beyond the occasional public remark. The large home of a retired air force brigadier, for example, came complete with alcohol (legally banned as un-Islamic, of course) and West-aping furnishing and knickknacks that can best be described as trailer-court neo-classical. Like so many of the better-off men encountered in Pakistan, the brigadier appeared lost between one world that did not satisfy and another world he did not understand.

There is rarely a sense of the beauty and greatness of the local, while even those resentful of the West succumb to the most trivial of things Western. The history of the lands that became Pakistan is an enormous layer cake of successive empires and intermingling cultures, with architectural remnants from the Gandharan Buddhist, Hindu (desecrated), grand Moghul, and neo-Mughal British imperial eras (the British period endured long enough to become an organic part of the local tradition), but when it came time to build a capital city from the dust up, the Paks chose the worst of the West. Even the huge Faisal Mosque, claimed as the largest in the world, owes more of its design to shiny trinkets won at an amusement park than to Islam's building heritage. As with the entire city of Islamabad, the mosque's ramshackle extravagance is an act of cruelty in a poor country where the per capita income of $400 exaggerates the income level of the average citizen, since wealth is concentrated overwhelmingly in a feudal clique.

Yes, the rich. Islamabad's servants live down in Pindi or in a few outlying, technically illegal settlements. Islamabad is a geometrically plotted concentration of ostentatious mansions as unbalanced in design as they are in morality. The air is not as pestilential as in Pakistan's other cities and the cool, lovely Murree Hills rise just to the north, with the lower Marghala Hills an immediate backdrop nestling the city as the mountains do Fort Huachuca. Pakistanis joke that "Islamabad is a great city—it's a shame it isn't really in Pakistan," but it is, in fact, not a great city, nor even a good one. It is, however, a place where life can be more easily endured and where the irresponsible rich can leech off the nourishing government while hiding their vices behind guarded compound walls. In Islamabad, you can live cleanly and eat well, hardly ever seeing a beggar.

The Monstrous Government

Prime Minister Benazir Bhutto, icon of merrily naive Westerners, is a feudal landholder who keeps indentured servants in antique bondage. Her husband loots the country with an avarice that would embarrass a Russian mobster. Ms. Bhutto presides over a swollen population (130,000,000) in which illiteracy is rising, women are treated as morally suspect beasts, and only the irrigated fertility of the Indus River plain keeps the under-employed population fed. Ms. Bhutto has been described by insider Paks as "the epitome of thirteenth-century feudalism." Unfortunately, the only serious opposition leader is characterized by the same voices as "the epitome of nineteenth-century robber-baron capitalism." There is no enlightened leader on the horizon.

Much has been made of the execution of Ms. Bhutto's father, Zulfikar Ali Bhutto, by General Zia's military government, and he has somehow been transformed into an imagined martyr of democracy. Yet, he was a cynical, corrupt, and divisive man—a thorough politician—whose most-enduring legacy to Pakistan may be his destruction of its potential competitiveness in the international marketplace.

Along with the excellent buildings, roads, and railways, all of which remain indispensable, the British left the people of Pakistan (and India) one casual-but-great gift: the English language. Today, English is the global language of business, education, automation and electronics, military operations, diplomacy, and whether the world likes it or not, culture. The ability to speak English is a passport to opportunity. Yet, to please Islamists and blustering nationalists, Bhutto the elder closed or gutted the country's best schools (especially those run by Christian organizations), reduced the status of English where he could not eliminate it, and made Urdu, a congealed barracks language, the official tongue of government and instruction. In doing so, he robbed his people terribly.

The effects of the demotion of English are only now becoming evident. While the elites still speak it, and often very well, it is withering at the sub-elite levels from which fresh blood must be drawn for the bureaucracy and military, as well as for the professional and entrepreneurial classes. Pakistan is tumbling backward. It is analogous to the situation in our own inner cities, where competitive English is no longer spoken and the inchoate victims of an indulgent educational system find themselves unable to share in the wealth of a society that demands English-based literacy to steer the vast electronic fleets of its business empire. The ability to wield the English language effectively, no less than the willingness to work hard, is becoming indispensable to material success. Pakistan was born with a marked advantage over other underdeveloped states but chose to cast that rare advantage aside.

This suits the great landholding families. Just as there was a struggle in nineteenth-century England between obsolescent landed wealth and the new money of the manufacturers and mine owners, so there is a worldwide struggle now between old and emerging elites. (In Latin America, this sometimes takes the form of a contest between landed money and drug money, but those families will intermarry over time.) The land barons of Pakistan and the tribal chiefs who continue to control the uplands and deserts do not want an educated population, rightly judging education to be inimical to their interests, which thrive upon ignorance of the world no less than upon conjured hatreds.

Pakistan's elites also recognize the power of religion as a tool to prolong the status quo while codifying injustice. The West applauds "democracy," but non-Western elites, in Pakistan and elsewhere, pillage the illiterate and uninformed under its banner. The government and the wealthy also collude to keep multinational corporations at arm's length through punitive laws, corruption, and the absence of reasonable systems of contract law and taxation. Foreign investment would be good for Pakistan in general, raising standards of living and education, but it would devastate the inept and dazzlingly corrupt businesses of those who need not now compete with world offerings of machines or medicines. Paid journalists never tire of warning of the evils of the foreign, and it is astonishing how much a liberal on the take can sound like a mullah on the make.

The Military: Island of Competence

It is always suspect when an Army officer praises a foreign military while castigating the overarching elected government, but only the Pakistani military has a truly national orientation that surmounts family and ethnicity. The military is the most effective and efficient organization in Pakistan. It also appears to be the only significant institution that gives a damn about the welfare of the people.

The Paks preserved much of the British military legacy, from their manner of marching, through the numbers and names of fine regiments, to the upright notion of what an officer should be. A cardinal difference, however, is that the Pakistani officer corps traditionally has been an educational elite, as well, which is an accusation impossible to level at British officers. The officer corps also has a strong, if inconsistent, Western orientation. This may be changing.

I went to Pakistan to lecture on "The New Warrior Class" and on Russian monkey business in the Newly Independent States of Central Asia to a variety of military schools and garrisons. The trigger for the invitation was a series of briefings I gave to senior Pakistani officers during a visit they made to the Pentagon. Because my opera-length presentations were delivered at an intimate roundtable session with the U.S. Army's chief of staff, Gen. Gordon Sullivan, the Pakistani generals wildly over-estimated my status, viewing me as a potential conduit directly to the chief of staff's ear. They decided to win me over to their view of our relationship (and they did, to an extent).

But there were also deeper reasons for lavishing attention on an American staff major. A crisis is looming in the Pak officer corps—the recent, inept pre-coup was a warning. The generals in power now speak better English than do most U.S. flag officers and understand the world beyond their borders with broad sophistication. They are professional and dedicated to a progressive view of their country. Such men are able to operate above the common rhetoric and the crisis of the moment. Despite the mutual misunderstandings surrounding the Pressler Amendment [which withheld U.S.-manufactured military equipment for which Pakistan had already paid and severely restricted ties with the Pakistani military], such men realize that Pakistan is ultimately reliant upon the West for future development as well as for its ultimate defense against the Indian leviathan.

The officers who are now of company or field grade are a different story. Except for the elite of the elite, such as those attending the staff college in Quetta, they are the products of the Bhutto legacy and the Islamist General Zia's further gutting of the education system. Their English is weak and degenerate, and they are less capable of gathering objective and technical information from abroad. They have no firsthand experience of the inner ethos of the old British officer corps and content themselves with mimicking the externals. They matured on a diet of anti-Western rhetoric from political leaders, journalists, and the religious community, and the self-righteousness (and unfairness) of the Pressler Amendment played into the hands of the West-haters and West-baiters. The officer corps is becoming ever less cosmopolitan, less sophisticated, less knowing. By cutting off Pak access to our military education system, we lost potential advocates and voices of reason. In the garrison towns, I was bewildered by the naivety about the world revealed in the questions from officers up to the rank of brigadier.

We might have been from different planets and, once again, I was confronted with the chaotic effects of popularized information, media-delivered, on Third World males who do not possess adequate frames of reference or mature sorting mechanisms. Some of these officers were perfectly willing to believe that the earth is flat, as long as the West insists that it's round, and they shared the Greek or Iranian readiness to blame the CIA every time the plumbing breaks. Their vision of America is a *melange* of Hollywood excesses and politico-religious castigation—of casual and calculated disinformation—filtered through terrible self-doubt and a sense of powerlessness over things beyond their line of sight. One of the most consistently astonishing aspects of dealing with individuals from the developing world is the level of omnipresence and competence they attribute to Western institutions even as they attack Western culture as inferior and doomed. They cannot reconcile these extremes into one great West, so they deal schizophrenically with two revolving Wests. There are hundreds of millions of David Koreshes, Randy Weavers, and Oliver Stones out there who insist that a malevolent American mega-state is eager to take over their neighborhoods.

We are losing the Pak officer corps; more vitally, their own generals fear they are losing their subordinates. There are more and more Islamist beards on the captains and majors, and their close-mindedness may soon make us nostalgic for the clarity and restraint of the generals we have nearly abandoned.

Another reason why I was invited to Pakistan was to show those up-and-coming officers that America and the Pentagon still care about the Pak military. Even more vitally, I was to demonstrate that U.S. officers do not all have horns, AIDS, and Zionist tattoos. I was not much of a substitute for F-16s, but the Pak generals are doing their best to cling to ties they recognize as vital. We should push to bring increased contingents of Pak officers to our military schools for the next several years—we need to make up for lost time—and we should look for opportunities to send more U.S. officers to Pakistan on exchanges. Relatively low investments could bring disproportionate dividends, or may at least ameliorate some of the damage done not only by mutual folly, but by the trend of worldwide cultural confrontation.

A Pakistani officer corps that becomes more insular and actively Islamist could be very dangerous, indeed. It will be less respectful of democracy, regionally troublesome, and hostile to our interests. It will aggressively pursue an "Islamic bomb." (Even now, the Paks cannot understand our double-standard on the nuclear issue—we are falling over ourselves to expand relations with India, which is a confessed nuclear power, no friend of U.S. interests, and a country that has dismembered Pakistan in a series of wars.)

Pakistan matters to us strategically. It may not be the country we want it to be, but we have a coincidence of regional interests, from an independent Central Asia to a stable subcontinent, and from checking Iranian excesses, through developing alternative trade routes from the Asian interior to the littoral, to finding an accommodation between the West and Islam. The Paks cannot see how we could in good conscience bail out of the Afghan problem after making endless promises to the contrary and flooding an already volatile region with weapons—leaving Pakistan to cope with the violent aftermath and millions of refugees.

We are witnessing an ugly and unnecessary revolution in the making.

The Ghosts of Quetta

"Quetta" derives from an ancient word for "fortress," and the site has been garrisoned in some form since the Bronze Age. The British reinvigorated the town in the last century, establishing first a cantonment to shield the Boland Pass from real tribes-men and hypothetical Russians, then a staff college that saw the likes of John Masters and Bernard Law Montgomery (the latter as commandant). A 1935 earthquake spared the sprawling cantonment area while leveling the town, but Quetta is the sort of bleak but strategic site that will always be rebuilt, however grimly. It is a charmless place in the conventional sense, but a magnet for adventurers.

Quetta is in Baluchistan, a vast and barren tribal realm that drifts northward into Afghanistan and westward into the snake-scoured deserts of southeastern Iran. We flew down on the embassy's C-12, with our Army attaché, Lt. Col. Terry Cook, at the controls.

Terry Cook was one of the great behind-the-scenes soldiers of our time. A literal cowboy born on the edge of the North Dakota badlands, he joined the Army as an enlisted man and surfaced as a staff sergeant on a beefed-up Special Forces A-team in Angola, seventeen Green Berets pitted against 17,000 Cuban troops and East German advisers; after that, the excitement picked up. Despite a wound to his left eye, he became a Mohawk surveillance-aircraft pilot, then learned to fly helicopters, and as an officer, hovered on the Honduran/Nicaraguan border, where he navigated over unmapped jungle and arrived at his first destination to find nothing but "fire, smoke, and bodies on the concertina wire." Then there was El Sal. Terry flew night missions into every country where we officially weren't, delivering arms and calling in fire support for battles that never made the official dispatches. For a break, he turned to Pakistan, studying at the Quetta staff college and kicking off his long series of cross-border excursions into Afghanistan, where he soon gained access denied to our diplomats by playing *buzkashi*, the bone-breaking Afghan version of polo, on

horses borrowed from warlords. Assigned to our embassy in Islamabad, his genius for making personal connections on every side
aroused only jealousy from a series of ambassadors; his prescient
reporting infuriated the apparatchiks of the Clinton administration; he penetrated the Pakistani nuclear testing program only to
see his messages spiked; he tapped into the Taliban and, even after
the State Department forced him out of the country for calling
things right too often, he brokered a deal in the wake of 9-11 for
terrified Taliban moderates to hand over Mullah Omar—but the
Bush administration rejected the offer. (As of early 2008, Mullah
Omar remains at large.) His final job on active duty pitted him
against terrorists in the Philippines; they're dead, Terry's a retired
bird colonel.

Rising from the Pindi airport, we soon had the white rampart
of the Karakorams to our right-rear quarter, with the Hindu Kush
at my shooting elbow. Afghanistan, harsh and spiritually remote,
paralleled our journey as we turned south.

Maj. Ivan Welch, a fellow Foreign Area Officer and a classmate
from Officer Candidate School, was visiting from India and he
tagged along with us. Eccentrically educated and boundlessly
entertaining, Ivan is the sort of FAO who can lecture you on
poetry, pedophilia in the Indian officer corps, or the local geology
wherever you happen to be. He assured us that the high mountain
deserts of Baluchistan are a geologist's dream, but I saw only a
hard, lifeless place of the sort settled as a last resort by desperate
men fleeing the blades of vicious conquerors. Nearing Quetta, the
brown valleys had the look of skin around an old man's eyes. And
yet, there is an austere beauty to the terrain. Circling down into

Quetta was a bit like flying into Tucson, approaching an oasis sheltering at the foot of boney peaks. Quetta sits in a high bowl and the valley floor is spiked with the conical adobe chimneys of low-tech brick factories, with the squat-built town and the military camps beyond.

An accompanying officer (AC) and a military police escort got up in red ascots met us at the terminal and rushed us toward the staff college, sirens warning civilian vehicles out of our way. At each roundabout or intersection, more MPs halted traffic—such as it was—and let us hurry through. We shot past a sheep market and a roadside bazaar, past women in full purdah, with only a web of fabric smaller than a diver's mask letting them see and smell and breathe in the world. There were far more men in evidence than women, most of them displaced Afghans, drably dressed and dark-visaged, with Roman noses and little interest in us. They had a marble dignity that simply did not allow us to matter, sirens or not.

Sprawling, increasingly permanent refugee camps haunt Quetta (and Peshawar), and many Afghans, successful in trade, will never return to their gun-swept country. Others miss no chance to fight on for one faction or another. This is Taliban country, the party of Islamist purists that stands for stern rule and ending educational or vocational opportunities for girls and women (for its part, Iran recently banned music lessons for anyone fifteen or under, fearing the Kreuzer-Sonata syndrome), and Terry Cook claims you can spot a coming Taliban offensive because the fighters flock to the money-changing bazaar to buy dollars so they can enhance their armaments. Then you can tell how the offensive is going by marking the flow of the wounded back to the Red Cross hospital for refugees.

To a welcome of much saluting and cracking of heels, we arrived at the School for Infantry and Tactics, where I was to give my first lecture. Video cameras and still photographers recorded our arrival, and a smartly turned-out sergeant major complete with swagger stick opened the door as if he meant to tear it from its hinges. After another round of saluting and heel-whomping—more British than Sandhurst—a jovial colonel passed us to Major General Nazeem, the commandant and a graduate of our own staff college at Fort Leavenworth. Nazeem offered the exemplary Pak military hospitality to which I would become accustomed—an embarrassment of generosity—and we took coffee and snacks in his large, spartan office. Above the nut-brown paneling behind the commandant's desk, a huge picture of Jinnah, the Father of Pakistan, haunted the room, but there was neither computer nor typewriter, only phones and buzzers, a pattern I would see repeated. Administrative technology has so rapidly become second nature to us that its absence is jarring. We spoke of the military equivalent of cabbages and kings, but my eye was drawn again and again to the dusty mountainsides and the pure blue sky beyond the office window: this was hard country for hard men.

The lecture went to over 200 officers. I always approach lectures and briefings as a performance, determined to capture and hold the audience, and I find them draining. But none has ever been so wearing as those I gave in Pakistan, where every word had to be precise and subject to no misinterpretation. I gave frank talks on awkward subjects, and this was an Islamic state with a serious information deficit. The follow-on questions ranged from the sincerely engaged to the lunatic, but as I wrapped up something happened that impressed me. The primary lecture, "The New Warrior

Class," deals with present and future conflict, focusing on the ruthlessness of the violence now encountered by soldiers and civilians alike. When I had answered the last question as best I could, Brigadier Tariq, the deputy commandant and chief of instruction, took the microphone to thank me. Then he pointed out to his student-officers that the purely military challenge posed by "warriors" was all well and good, but it was critical to look beyond the moment to the deprivation of various kinds that led people to violence. I would hear this theme again and again from senior officers, but never from Pakistani politicians.

Afterward, a young captain approached me and declared that he was a Punjabi Christian. He needed to reassure himself that Protestants and Catholics were not in a constant state of violent conflict in the West. I assured him that the Thirty Years' War was over and that even the muddle in Northern Ireland was more about social and economic segregation, secular myth, and sheer criminality than it was about religious dogmas. He was greatly relieved and, after assuring me that he was Church of England, we spoke of the worsening lot of Christians in Pakistan as Muslims grew ever more radicalized.

Returning to the commandant's office for tea, I wound up discussing religion there, as well. The Christian and Islamic worlds are so nervous about each other that it's an inevitable topic. I am fascinated by the efficacy of religion as an ordering mechanism in society and as a system of resource allocation (consider the distributive authority of the Hindu caste system in light of India's chronic shortages), and we agreed that, apart from theological content, the social habituation of religion is indispensable to society. Odd to have arrived at a point where an American officer's knowledge of religions is as important as his knowledge of weaponry, but that's today's reality. We talked for hours with the general reminiscing about his time in the States, and the conversation turned desultory as the afternoon waned. But the general was reluctant to end our meeting. I sensed that he was clinging to this brief contact with a world far from Quetta.

In the evening, Terry, Ivan, and I escaped the thrall of military hospitality and we headed for the old heart of the town. We were joined by Capt. Scott Taylor, the U.S. Army student attending the Pakistani staff college that year, and he struck me as a born Foreign Area Officer, the sort who always has his nose under a new tent. He never misses a chance to get down into tribal country or to cross the far passes, and his Urdu is quick. Like Terry and Ivan, Scott is the sort of rambunctious officer crucial to distant campaigns—and generally unrecognized when the official histories are written.

On our way into town, Terry regaled us with stories of dynamiting his way through avalanches on remote northern roads, of crossing into Afghanistan to discuss flowers and fanatics with Dostam or tactics with Massoud. He had more trouble with bent-on-blood mobs in Karachi than with the war flickering just across the mountains.

Quetta is a wanderer's delight: teeming, labyrinthine, not undangerous, polluted, colorful, noisy, and ferociously alive. Like Peshawar, Quetta looks more to the northwest, to the great deserts of Central Asia, for its culture than it does to hothouse India, and the gaunt men in their Chitrali topee headgear, with their big hands molded to hold a Kalashnikov, are of the blood that fought every would-be conqueror as much for sport as necessity. The central network of bazaars is rich with fruits and vegetables, and burlap bags spill treasures of nuts and dates. But the streets are sick with fumes: all Pak cities except Islamabad are the victims of motor rickshaws and ill-tuned trucks and buses. The exhaust makes a twilight of a bright afternoon—imagine a city of hub-to-hub lawnmowers roaring away.

The central slaughterhouse, a manmade cavern just off the main drag, was a hygienist's howl from Hell. At the end of the day, a cat licked a crimsoned sheep's skull and an eternally baffled donkey's head lay on the sidewalk, the skin of its severed neck collapsed like a blown-out paper bag. Munching pistachios, we walked through pools of coagulating blood, in a smell of entrails and battle.

There was one last trick to the bazaar: if you want a new L. L. Bean sweater or a London Fog jacket, you can have one for about a dollar. Relief agencies send in great lots of last year's fashions, donated or purchased cheaply for the refugees, but Afghans stick rigorously to their traditional garb. The refugees don't refuse the clothing, but take it and sell it to less particular Punjabis or Sindhis or tourists who took a wrong turn a few thousand miles back.

The next day I lectured to a full house in the staff college's sand-table room then sat down for the inevitable tea with Major General Saeed, the college commandant. He threw me with his observation that the "neutron bomb" would be the perfect answer to the dilemmas of urban warfare, since it would kill all the people and leave the buildings intact, but his remarks to the effect that we need to stop focusing on killing the common fighters and go after the enemy leadership responsible for initiating the carnage might have been lifted telepathically from an essay I had just published. He was also very much attuned to the criticality of Human Intelligence in urban operations, as well as to the need for cultural awareness in distant interventions.

The staff college hall is worth a visit just for its displays of old Lee-Enfields, sabres, trophies, and equestrian bronzes, but the officer's mess is richer still. Above the heads of liveried, neo-Raj servants, faded tiger skins deck the high walls, along with antique weaponry and the heads of very large wild animals. Not PETA-friendly, but a grand place with much upholstery, old wood, a chummy British gas fire, and good carpets, all bound to delight anyone who has read his Kipling. We ate a robust curry and a fine chicken jalfreezi (alas, no beer!), and sixteen of us, mostly colonels, ate and talked over the lectures, Malaysian political maneuvering, Afghanistan and Iran, the role of U.S. forces in Japan, Russia, macro-economics, and the drug trade. These officers, assigned to teach the army's rising elite, had good minds above their buff, be-ribboned sweaters and mustard-colored slacks.

As we left, I saw that the long table in the anteroom was covered with caps straight from the British army of 1942. The Brits have left so much behind in so many places that it must have been grand to know them before the great wars of the twentieth century bled them out.

Peshawar and the Khyber Pass

Beyond its genteelly rotting stucco cantonments, Peshawar's polluted core is architecturally uninspired, but riveting on the human level, with its dense street life, its catacomb-like bazaars, the cheap, hot-colored, savory food, and the occasional bombing. (Over Christmas week, a blast in a market killed twenty-four and wounded forty.) Every self-respecting establishment has at least one old man with a Kalashnikov guarding the premises. Peshawar has a Moghul fort, massive and improved under the Raj, ant-hill traffic on its boulevards, alleys leprous with garbage, an over-whelmed U.S. consulate, Afghan refugee camps that stink of per-manence, and enclaves of well-guarded, tasteless homes where the ruling class admires itself.

Peshawar's a frontier city. At its southwestern edge, the tribal lands begin, vast, raw tracts where the government has limited authority (and sometimes none). Begun long ago and improved by Britannia's engineers, the Grand Trunk Road once ran uninter-rupted from Delhi to Kabul. Today, two clamped frontiers and plentiful local disorders annoy the route, but it still pulses with life recognizable from the loving descriptions in *Kim*. With an armed escort and a tribal officer, we left the city's crush and headed toward the Khyber, the most famous pass in the world and perhaps the most troubled.

As you enter the tribal territories, the houses disappear behind dun-colored walls with guard towers. These are the family com-pounds, the *keelahs*, which long have served as protection against invaders, robbers, the government, and especially, tribal feuds. Roadside shops sport faded Pepsi signs to lure the packed, confetti-colored buses to pause. The irrigated vale withers to sand and rock, and the landscape browns as you climb, its monotony interrupted only by minute oases or the green lines where a mountain stream splashes down. A huge, ancient Buddhist stupa on a knoll could pass as a ruined observatory.

The first old British fort appears, followed by others, each built within supporting distance of its neighbors. Many are little more than blockhouses, but a few are major posts. Picturesque from a distance, their romance existed only in movies and memoirs, in stories written up by fleeting visitors, and novels concocted by those who never set foot in the East: service in such posts was harsh and dull and lonesome, a training ground for drunks, and bacteria killed more soldiers of the Queen than fell to bullets. Only the frontier's menace bridged fact and fiction, but the actual wounds were not as clean and the hero was apt to shit himself to death.

All of the forts are still in use by the military or occupied by tribal constabularies.

The dusty mountains close in and grizzled men with automatic weapons stroll by the roadside. If you are lucky enough to drive by as a family-compound gate opens, you glimpse fine buildings, rose gardens, satellite antennae, and expensive jeeps or automobiles. These establishments belong to the powerful men of the tribe, some of whom deal in opium and heroin, although there is plenty of money to be made in the arms trade or conventional smuggling, from the shabby bicyclists who peddle down from Jalalabad with boxes of crockery for a few rupees, to F.O.B. televisions shipped into Afghanistan only to be smuggled back again to avoid the Pakistani import tax. At the height of the Soviet-Afghan War, the compounds often had heavy weapons mounted on the walls, but at government prompting, the machine guns and mortars are now kept out of sight until needed.

Approached from the east, the Khyber itself is not as forbidding as other renowned passes; its notoriety stems from the vigor and ferocity of the Afridis and other tribesmen whose domains straddle it. These Pathans, who speak the Pukhtu rather than the softer Pashtu dialect prevalent to the south, sometimes have been fought to a standstill, but they have never been fully conquered. Even the toughest invader ultimately comes to an accommodation with them. To us, their way of life is primitive, intolerant, and obstinate, yet it is hard not to admire the unbent nobility of those who truly would fight to the death over matters of honor or to defend their way of life. With their code of *Pukhtunwali*, the Pathans are disarmingly hospitable—even an enemy cannot be turned away, should he appear in the doorway asking food, shelter, and protection, and a guest is pampered. A slight, however, is never forgotten and never forgiven, and tribal feuds (tribal law and the *jirga* still prevail) spark along for generations. The mountains are severely impressive and, for all that we fairly may decry in their customs, so are the men of those mountains.

On the far side of the high point of the pass you come to the garrison of the fabled Khyber Rifles and the town of Landi Kotal, the last settlement before the Afghan border divides a world that declines to be divided. Landi Kotal is pure Wild West, its broken-down main street lined with tea houses (instead of saloons), general stores that generally sell weapons, and a sharp-eyed, well-armed population that never smiles. The garrison below is not expected to halt the smuggling from which the people thrive, but merely to keep individual truculence from becoming collective violence.

Just beyond the straggling town and above a rock face painted with regimental crests, the bastion of Michni Post overlooks the valley that enters Afghanistan. The grand and sudden vista suggests the drama of the Khyber at last, canceling any disappointment with the dowdy landscape on the Pakistani side of the pass. The border crossing hides in a stand of trees, but the hubbub of commerce is surprisingly evident.

We received a formal briefing from a captain in the picturesque dress of the Khyber Rifles, orienting us to the watchtowers and flashpoints, to the local tribes and the intrusions of history. Any military romantic feels moved when he stands at the edge of the Khyber peering into Afghanistan, with the purple-gray mountains an ancient barrier in the distance and the towns farther up the road bearing names such as Jalalabad and Gandarmak (Gundamak), the latter the spot where the British retreat from Kabul climaxed in a massacre, with a lone survivor returning to tell the tale of the empire's first effort to discipline Afghanistan. The country is windswept and wild, but not as cold in December as one might expect, although the thin, clean air carries a challenge. Standing beside the twin-barreled gun that guards the air corridor, I was perched on one of mankind's great frontiers and my sense was of my personal triviality.

Upon our return from Michni Post, the commandant of the Khyber rifles hosted a lunch. We pulled up to the accompaniment of a tartaned pipe and drum band playing an Urdu march. The officers' mess was a museum of Jezails, the old tribal arms from which the Khyber Jezailchis received their name before they received their Sniders and became the Rifles. The Khyber has drawn many visitors and the signed photos in the mess record the visits of Jackie Kennedy (not yet Mrs. Onassis) and Richard Nixon, Margaret Thatcher and Princess Diana.

We were prepared to leave promptly after our curry, but the pipe major raised his baton again. Colonel Saddique, the commandant and a Guards-Club combination of soldierly rigor and languor, led the way to rattan chairs at the edge of the broad lawn before the mess. Suddenly, the pipes broke off and drums thumped behind a tall hedge. A platoon of tribal dancers—soldiers in mufti—burst through a gap in the greenery, performing a highland dance in exuberant disorder. The troupe was followed by another, whose members did a sword dance. Designed to impress visitors, it worked. Ghosts wafted down from the mountains to see what the fuss was about.

We drank green tea in the cool air and, after the dancers faded away, we talked. The commandant spoke of a recent counter-drug expedition to one of the high valleys. He had gone in with rounds chambered, expecting uniform hostility, but the locals had thanked him for taking on the drug chieftains. Conditioned by Latin America, I wondered if the grateful parties just hadn't been getting their cut. Effective druglords co-opt the population.

Back in Peshawar, we joined a party of Pakistani air force officers for dinner at Namuk Mandi, the old salt bazaar. After priming ourselves with Indian whisky at a brigadier's home (in the presence of a teetotaling but tolerant air vice marshal), we drove to the old part of the city where you don't meet gringos after dark and women make themselves scarce. Namuk Mandi is now a street of competing restaurants, each grubby little cavern displaying the cleanliness of medieval Palermo during a plague. Lamb and chicken, greased and salted, scorches in great cast-iron pans set atop fiery grills. Before it can begin to cool, the flesh is devoured by stone-faced, quick-eyed men crowded onto *charpois*, the rope beds whose discomfort keeps tempers short between the Euphrates and Ganges. Hot nan stacked and steaming beside abundant salads is meant to balance the patrons' diet, but all of the right hands plunge into the communal pots of meat until they're empty.

We sat in near-darkness behind our chosen "restaurant," with rotting buildings and a wall of ruined tires for a backdrop. Taught by my wife that raw onions ward off distempers in the developing world, I was the only customer who even picked at any vegetable matter. The finger-sliming meat was splendid and the torn bread used to scrape out the brown pot residue was better still. We sat and talked and laughed, and I thought, yet again, that there are some things you just won't get from room service.

Although there certainly are beggars in Pakistan, you are not under constant assault as you are elsewhere. Most Paks remind me of the Turks, too proud to beg. But this is also deep Asia, and when you do encounter beggars, they are often unspeakably pathetic—like one lurching back and forth on a wooden wagon bed in a narrow alley, his fingers stumped and his skin a raw ruin, eye sockets emptied of eyes to make room for white cheese. No one paid him much mind.

The next day took us to the Warsak Dam, where the Kabul River wanders out of the highlands before watering the Vale of Peshawar. The point of the visit to the dam, with its museum-piece generators and silting problems, was to underscore Pakistan's need for "peaceful" nuclear power and the engineer did his patriotic duty by delivering a tirade that left me cold. The drive was worthwhile, though, since it took us through nontribal villages, where the women trek the shaded roadside in full purdah—animated tents. Fruit groves and wheat fields cover the drier ground, while thickets of sugar cane cluster in the bottoms. The villages are poor and crude, their inhabitants often ragged, but there is plenty of food here, a great advantage over neighboring countries.

Returning to Peshawar, we left a sunny day behind and drove into a gray cloud of pollution. Dried donkey manure and human waste peppered the wind, mixing with the endless dust and exhaust. As we wound through the alleys leading to our backstreet inn, our route was blocked by a donkey collapsed in its traces, its owner whipping it remorselessly in an attempt to hurt it back to its feet. But the animal was gone, dying, and its baffled eyes looked inward. Its master's rage could not extract a single bray of pain. The scene was pure Nietzsche-in-Turin.

There is a good museum in Peshawar, another Brit legacy. The ethnological collection is fine, but the core of the holdings is Gandharan Buddhist, from the centuries just before and after Christ. The displays bring home the cosmopolitan nature of antique empires that developed astride trade routes. Although Buddhism long remained dominant among the people of the Vale, with the highland tribes in thrall to local gods (the Pathans only came over to Islam as the Renaissance shook Europe), the art carries the influences of a variety of cultures and strong hints of other faiths. Alexander's personal trace has been exaggerated into myth, but the Greco-Bactrian empire left in his wake sculpted Buddhas and Bodhisattvas in Greek togas and, although the Roman Empire's boundaries never stretched so far, fashion followed trade, as it does today. There are Roman influences on some later sculptures. Indian, Nepalese, and Chinese traces show, too. In their heyday, the Greco-Bactrians centered their realm on the Amu Darya, the Oxus, on the other side of the Hindu Kush, and theirs was a busy, swirling, absorptive, tragically unrecorded world.

We move more swiftly today, but we grossly underestimate the amount of cultural exchange that occurred from the earliest periods of history. Word gets around, and so do goods. Just as trade develops economies, it also spreads culture. (One can imagine the traditionalists of Gandhara deploring "degenerate" Roman influences on temple statuary much as today's Pakistani elders complain about McDonald's or MTV.) This has always been a small planet, and the clash of cultures we face today is nothing new. Alexander's bastardized-Greek detritus flowed down the Indus, and the Moors of Spain were culturally of a piece with the Turco-Persian magnates of Samarkand. I do not mean this as an argument for multiculturalism, which destroys empires, but only as an observation on the limited nature of our historical perspective. Seeing a Greek or Roman hairstyle on a figure ripped from a temple on the Indus seems, at first, a bit like finding a Hershey Bar on the moon—but only because we have been educated to such a narrow view of history.

The Fate of Woman

It's a man's world out there. If there is one single thing that is repulsive and self-defeating about Pakistan that looms over all of the state's other problems, it's the lot of women.

Confronted with the deplorable conditions under which their womenfolk are kept, Paks quickly point to their prime minister, Benazir Bhutto. But it's an error to think of Ms. Bhutto primarily as a woman. Her true role is as the only available representative of a political and land-holding dynasty. She represents not her sex, but her social and economic kind.

For most women in Pakistan, life is circumscribed and miserable. In the West, our spouses or lovers may also be our best friends, and in the healthiest relationships there is not only passion, but conversation about God and the world and the price of corn flakes. In Pakistan, a wife may be an ally, but it is hard to imagine any wife as a best friend. Men and women live in great separation, psychic as much as physical. The woman is simply not a full-fledged human being in the sense that the male is. While a woman's chastity is respected (and occasionally exaggerated), this has nothing to do with her human rights, but with her status as an object—the property first of the family that spawned her, then of her husband. She is rarely educated (almost never to serious effect), seldom employed beyond the home, and possesses, at best, the freedom of the pet dog, but without the master's unstinting affection.

Some aspects of human progress can be reduced to simple mathematical formulae. Any society (and there are many) that refuses to exploit fully half of its human resources cannot function at the level of a rival society that opens a full range of productive and creative endeavors to all of its capable citizens. Further, societies such as Pakistan's (especially the tribal areas) waste a great deal of emotional and physical energies keeping women down. In today's hyper-competitive world, any society that refuses women access to education and the work force simply cannot compete. Nor is it acceptable to argue that, since unemployment is rampant, the women would only be vying for the same jobs as men who need to feed their families. When productive energies are unleashed, jobs are created. Many of the positions held by Western women today did not exist a generation ago. Given a chance, capable and willing hands create their own opportunities. Societies that oppress or enslave their women are doomed to economic failure. All the power of Islam can't change that law.

Of course, the lot of women varies in Pakistan, although it only approaches the openness of Western society among the super-rich. The average Pakistani woman is illiterate and has minimal contact with men, whether she likes it or not. And many probably believe that they like it. Social conditioning is a powerful tool and it would be a mistake to imagine that every Pak female is burning to cast off her purdah rags and roar out her liberation. They, quite literally, don't know what they're missing. Anyway, life is hard, medical care infrequent and inadequate, and all behavior must meet the stringent rules set down by custom and temperamental males.

At the bottom end, the women of the tribal areas (and Afghan refugee camps) live at a level not much higher than that of breeding animals. As mentioned above, female circumcision, the excision of the clitoris to prevent agreeable sexual sensations, remains normative among many highland clans. This is where the innate male terror of female sexuality finds its ugliest expression.

The lot of women in the tribal areas is so harsh that even other Pakistanis can be moved to criticize it. During one discussion, a Punjabi employed in service remarked to me that he cannot imagine treating his wife the way women are treated by tribal friends he has visited—and that's saying something. He pointed out that most brides are still purchased in the uplands and are strictly property. Often, the woman never leaves her *keelah* after her marriage, and that family compound becomes her entire universe until the end of her days—or at least until she is well beyond evident sexuality. The Punjabi once complained to a tribal friend about the friend's imprisonment of his wife, but the tribesman matter-of-factly told him that, if his wife were allowed out, she would run away. Even if she were recovered thereafter—which she would be—she would have compromised his honor. In highland clans, she would have to be killed. The men of the mountains still avenge the dishonor of a sister by killing her and only then, and only perhaps, killing her violator. Certainly, you see some women on the roads or at the vegetable stalls in the high country, but they are few and shrouded from top to toe, eerie creatures who carry their prisons with them.

Somber multiculturalists will instruct you that these women are most comfortable fully covered and untormented by harassing males. I can only suggest that such champions of female slavery try out the lot of a Pathan tribeswoman for a few years. (Sadly, his treatment of women is a terrible blot on the Pathan, who is so anachronistically noble in other regards.) Today, many Pathans no longer live under tribal law but have joined the military or gone into urban businesses, and their wives are accorded greater respect and privilege—still within carefully observed parameters. The situation is less humane among the Afghan refugees, who treat women as beasts.

The Islamic world between Morocco and Pakistan is so fraught with male fear, self-doubt, self-loathing, and reality avoidance that it has condemned itself to endless mediocrity. Make no mistake: one of the primary reasons why the West has *again* taken off in triumph over other civilizations is that Western women have struggled their way into the workforce and our males have generally, if sometimes grudgingly, accepted them. A society such as Pakistan operates at a very low fraction of socio-economic efficiency, while, even allowing for an enduring *Lumpenproletariat*, Western Anglophone countries employ their human capital at an unprecedented high level. Our wealth and power owe far more to the Pankhursts or Susan B. Anthony than to Bill Gates and Warren Buffett.

Finally, a society in which men do not interact socially with women is deadly boring, visually drab, and a spawning ground for pederasts. In the long run, women's emancipation in the West is doing at least as much for the welfare of men as it does for women—and maybe more. Call us all Lucky Jim.

The Grand Trunk Road to Pindi

From Peshawar, the Grand Trunk Road descends to Nowshera, where the ornate roadside buildings left behind by evicted Hindus decay under the neglect of their present inhabitants. Nowshera is yet another garrison town, long vital but less fabled than Peshawar, and cantonments still shape its life. The countryside is lush and the people stay busy with the toil of primitive agriculture. Filtered through ranks of eucalyptus trees—imported by the British—sunlight dapples the great road and teases your eyes. The Kabul River rushes down, acquiring a series of local names as it blends with other torrents, until it reaches its confluence with the Indus. Because the Indus is dammed just above their intersection, the collision of the waters is striking. Robbed of its silt, the Indus flows bright blue, while the Kabul has gathered mud. There is a distinct, subtly shifting line, almost turquoise on one side, milk-chocolate brown on the other, where the waters meet. From that point, the reinforced Indus sweeps down to fertilize the Punjab.

We crossed the great river above Attock Fort, an antique bulwark still in use by the Pakistani army. The run-down maze of battlements guards the riches of the Punjab against the old chaos that bursts, now and then, from the mountains. The view bleeds history.

On the far bank, to my distress, we picked up another military escort. Smartly uniformed, the soldiers moved with an exaggerated alacrity that could only result from haywire nerves, methamphetamine use or a legacy of British drill. We raced the last hour to Pindi and Islamabad with lights flashing atop the jeeps and sirens blaring, an intended compliment, but an embarrassment and annoyance to me—not least because Terry had cold beer in the Toyota Land Cruiser's cooler and I had planned to toast my crossing of the Indus. I could not crack one open now, since it would have been bad form to bolt down the barley under the eyes of abstemious Muslim military policemen.

Poor is relative. The villages and towns we passed would mortify our own poor, but by local standards, they were well off. Bright markets stood beside the ubiquitous, muddy bus terminals, vending a primitive plenty. Shouts and warlike gestures led to ultimate concord on the price of vegetables.

We crossed the Marghala Pass, a low-lying corridor through a range of hills and the traditional dividing line between the hegemony of sober Pathan culture and the simmering spice of the Punjab. A cobbled stretch of the old Moghul road commemorates the marches of forgotten armies, but the modern highway runs just below the tower erected in memory of Nikkal-Seyn, that same Nicholson who died heroic and young after a series of boy's-book exploits on his empire's frontier, inspiring so much loyalty among the locals that he was posthumously, if briefly, worshipped by a cult named in his honor. Casually brave and immeasurably resourceful, the best British military agents and political officers operated brilliantly beyond the day-to-day reach of bureaucracies, their genius diminished only by the walloping ignorance of their distant superiors.

Then the already-fraying pomposity of Islamabad began again.

Taxila and Flashman's

During the sixteen-day trip, I had one open day. Terry arranged a vehicle and driver, and I recrossed the Marghala Pass to visit Taxila, site of at least three great and long-gone cities (as well as a center of Pakistan's modern defense industry). Taxila includes the neat ruins of a city where Buddhist, Jain, Hindu, and cult religions flourished side by side (as far as we know, and we don't know much), the slight remains of a hilltop palace, a well-preserved Buddhist "university," a complex of stupa shrines, and no end of romantic bits tucked into the green hills as if laid out for a scavenger hunt. I was the only visitor.

At the formal museum, a guard who was better informed than many a licensed guide took his time explaining each display, ensuring that I understood the signals telegraphed by Buddha's hands and the rank structure of the Bodhisattvas. For a child of the sixties, it was as good as the evening I spent in Peshawar listening

to the reincarnation of Charlie Parker, a young sitar player fingering evening ragas into the late hours.

At the city ruins, an old man with an official belt buckle and a
bad eye insisted on guiding me. With little English and far less
knowledge than the museum attendant, he managed to entertain
when he wasn't trying to sell me poorly made imitation statuary.
We walked across fallow fields and climbed the hill to the palace
ruins, where he wanted to break off a piece of a frieze for me to
pocket. Horrified, I stopped him in time, wondering how many
treasures had gone missing just that way.

As we made our way back down the main street of the old
city's ruins, an addled man looked up from scalping grasses with a
sickle and grunted—he was mute—then gestured for me to give
him money. When he realized that I would not do so, his grunting
grew wild and his brown eyes strained at their sockets. I walked on
beside my temple-defacing guide, but soon heard footsteps behind
me, their pace quickening to a run. Now, it's a tricky business
when a deranged mute comes at you with a blade.

I turned and stared at him as you might back off a dog. My
guide waved his arms and jabbered, which probably had more
effect. My would-be attacker seethed but his spastic moves with
the sickle began to weaken. Fixed on me, his eyes passed from rage
to fear, as if he had come after a stray goat and met a demon.

Abruptly, he slunk off, honking like a sad goose.

Leaving the town of Taxila, where the locals hawk ceramics of
incomparable ugliness, we headed for Pindi. I wanted to eat at
Flashman's, given the hotel's Raj mystique. The lobby was terribly
run down, unrecognizable as the preferred retreat of yesteryear's

choosier Brits. But the food in the scruffy restaurant was superb, fiery, and cheap. At a table by the window, eight pretty local girls dressed in a mix of traditional and modern dress were having a lunch of more laughter than food. The manager was obsequious toward them and they clearly were the not-unspoiled daughters of prosperous fathers. The girls were the most decorative thing in all Pindi, a living bouquet of vanity.

Rawalpindi is of less interest than it should be. An Anglican church is as threatened by fumes as by the local radicals, and traffic jams are the city's varicose veins. Everything but alcohol is for sale in narrow shop fronts, and donkeys drawing carts trot by advertisements for computers. Military cantonments occupy the best and best-tended property; the rest is frenetic blandness. The visitor notes that one of the advantages of the flowing male dress is that its wearers can squat down anywhere and piss without exposing themselves. And they do. No gutter is too public. (Life is rather more difficult for Pak women.)

The Murree Hills and the Intelligence School

Snow crowned the Murree Hills, an hour's drive north from Islamabad. The pre-alpine slopes seem lovely, until you learn that their bareness is the result of ruthless timbering. Not long ago, these mountains were lush with pines; now only a few green patches remain, struggling tufts of hair on a cancer patient. The town of Murree was born as a summer hill station for the Brits and remains a favored retreat for Pakistanis. The road twists up from a warm valley past the snow line. Spectacular vistas open from hairpin turns and small, disorderly settlements thrive on open-front shops that lure travelers with plastic junk and snacks. (Wrappers are discarded on the spot.)

The military intelligence school perches on a slope just below Murree, housed in yet another old Brit compound. The commandant, Brigadier Tajwar, has a million-dollar view from his office, but all else is poor. A space heater fought the December chill and we sat passing compliments and discussing cooperation. Outside, the air was cold to brittleness, and the overnight snow cleansed the landscape under a sudden blue sky. The old stone buildings held the chill inside and the temperature kept the students wide awake.

Again, I was struck by the junior officers' deficient knowledge of how the world works. These were *intelligence* specialists, yet, following the ritual exchange about the glorious past and humane present of Islam, with a side discussion about the need to differentiate between fundamentalists in the theological sense and violent extremists who pervert the message of the Prophet (Peace be upon Him), the questions acquired an almost sexual intensity and were voiced with the passion of frustrated adolescents. When asked why the United States wants to keep the people of Pakistan in poverty, I pointed out that our national ambition is to sell things, and that you can't sell much to people with no money. We veered from Marx through Schumpeter to Robert Reich (who resembles Marx in his skilled diagnoses and disastrous prescriptions), but the angriest students had no interest is counterarguments. They could not bear the condition of their country, but could not accept responsibility for its failures, either—the classic paradigm between Cairo and Karachi. Growing impatient at last with their determination to absolve every Pakistani of the slightest blame for their homeland's condition, I schoolmarmed them a bit about the shabby behavior of their own elites, then pointed through the windows at the deforested hills below, asking if Coca-Cola had done that.

Such young men throughout the developing world live behind two paralyzing barriers. The first is their lack of access to objectively packaged information, and the second is their rejection of any facts that might seep through to shed light on their own inadequacies. And, frankly, I find myself wondering how we can expect them to greet the truth, when the truth is that their country will, at best, muddle through the decades in irredeemable mediocrity, forever unable to compete with Western civilization, which is experiencing yet another renaissance that will again increase our wealth and power.

We expect such men to face the facts, but the facts facing them are unbearable.

The levels of civilizational performance are so disparate that the self-aggrandizing fantasies of Arabs, Persians, and Paks constitute their only sources of dignity. Like children, they make it all up. We may be witnessing the emergence into daylight of a human tendency previously evident in the more esoteric branches of religion: the rejection of the hard reality of things in favor of a purportedly superior perception which, in the strongest temperaments, bends reality into the desired shape. While a rock is a rock in Newtonian reality, perceived realities fall into a gray area that allows a great degree of reinvention. The bullet may kill the fantasist as surely as it does the pragmatist, but the environmental perception of death differs—and that perception can be either paralyzing (in the liberal consciousness), or empowering (in the fanatic temperament). And thus the teenage Iranian Revolutionary Guards, half of them without weapons, rushed into Iraqi kill zones, chasing the hot gals of Heaven.

If you think culture and religion don't have military implications, try making peace with a true believer.

How will we define victory when our enemy rejects our interpretation of the meaning of events not only propagandistically, but earnestly? When our enemy views the immolation of his kind as a triumph of the will of God? I suspect that we'll face a sort of "war of the worlds" in the coming years—not between planets, but between cultures that exist in different intellectual and emotional dimensions, a duel of souls. It will be interesting to see how the Army we plan performs when confronted with an enemy who interprets every defeat as a victory.

From Pindi to Kashmir

We went down to Pindi to brief the General Staff. The highlight was meeting Maj. Gen. Mahmud Ahmed, the Director of Military Intelligence and a man of both firm religion and fine intellect. A mustache from a portrait of a Moghul sultan lends dash to his burly figure and his back is as straight as an uncomfortable chair. Like his predecessor in the post—now–Lt. Gen. Ali Kuli Khan Khatak, commander of the praetorian-guard 10th Corps—Major General Mahmud illumines the British prejudice in favor of "the martial races of India." The Brits differentiated between classes, castes, and ethnicities in their Indian empire as thoroughly as Hindu Brahmins, and they convinced themselves that there were "martial races" possessed of innate qualities denied the people of Bengal or those from the southern reaches of the subcontinent. Perhaps this distinction arose because the population of southern India had enjoyed relative peace for centuries, while northwestern societies were trained for war by the frequent invasions they suffered. To the Brits there was, of course, also an aesthetic attraction to the taller, stronger, lighter-complected northerners.

Whether there are martial races or not, the Brits recruited the bulk of their best "Indian" units from the north and the northwest. There were Sikhs from the Vale of Kashmir, rigorous Jats and, of course, the Gurkhas from the Himalayas (the latter neither tall nor Aryan in feature), but the majority of the recruits for elite units came from the Punjabis and Pathans and a few other war-prone groups. (On the other hand, the most-decorated unit of the old Indian Army was the Madras Sappers and Miners, whose other-ranks were dark and short and scrawny.)

Anyway, if you picture a strapping, in-his-prime Indian Army man out of Kipling, you have a portrait of General Mahmud.

Lieutenant General Ali, the corps commander, provided a helicopter, an old, bug-snouted Alouette flown by a wiry, confident major, to haul Terry and me to the Line of Control in Kashmir. We flew low over Pindi on a clear morning, heading west over child-infested compounds and dry washes where gypsies had pitched their tents. Turning north and tracing the end of the Marghala Hills, the pilot skirted the vast monstrosity of the Faisal Mosque, giving us an overview of Islamabad's network of mansions and the barren monumentalism of the government quarter.

Topping the first ridge, we already saw the Himalayas in the distance, beyond the lower snow ridges of Kashmir. Above Murree, children waved from the dirt courtyards of their schools and women at work paused to shield their eyes and scan the sky to find us. Low, tin-roofed buildings pocked the hillsides and plateaus, thickening into towns where old caravan routes crossed the saddles in the ridges. It takes a full day to drive into Kashmir on the abysmal roads, but the journey by helicopter takes hardly an hour. We dropped down out of the snow hills and turned east along the Jhelum River Valley, Muzaffarabad on our left at first, then lost behind our tail rotor. The country grew even more spare and poor and beautiful as the river narrowed to force a gorge, exploding with seltzer rapids.

Our pilot took us straight into the helipad at Sawan Kucha, still out of the line of fire of the Indian forces along the LOC, where we were met by the local commander, who clutched his beret to his head as the prop wash tried to snatch it. Brigadier Ghulam Labi looked uncannily like Spinola, the Portuguese general who surprised himself with a coup (although Brigadier Labi lacked the monocle affected by the Latin). The brigadier drove his own jeep to Chakothi, with me in the passenger seat for a private chat, while Terry rode in the trail vehicle with Lieutenant Colonel Khalid, commander of the 641 Mujaheddin Battalion, the "Koh Shiken," the "Breakers of Mountains."

Chakohti lies at the end of the line, a village where life is as harsh as a mirror on Sunday morning. A small garrison compound shelters in a hollow behind the spur that shields the settlement from Indian direct fire and low-trajectory artillery. Brigadier

Ghulam told me to look at the poverty of the people we passed, adding, "We can't afford to keep up this level of military expenditure. We have to find a solution to this problem with the Indians. These people need education and jobs."

Apart from any propagandistic intent, I read the brigadier's comments as heartfelt. He was one of those unusual men who never smile, yet make you like them instantly and enduringly.

After the mandatory tea around Lieutenant Colonel Khalid's sweat-popping office stove, we hiked up a mud track to reach the observation post and briefing point. Although the visit was intended to be all business, I couldn't help thinking what a splendid place it would be to hike if ever the barbed wire and land mines, the artillery revetments and guard bunkers were gone. The OP consisted of a machine-gun pit, a low cement wall and some trenches. Without pausing to catch his breath from the climb, Lieutenant Colonel Khalid began a terrain orientation, pointing out the counterpart Indian OP that would be watching us and commenting that the new battalion facing his own was an Indian Gurkha outfit. Beautifully on cue, the Gurkhas sent us a burst of automatic weapons fire, followed by a few heavier-caliber rounds that scoured the valley walls. The shooters were out of effective range and were only saying hello, but the Paks ducked. Doing America proud, Terry and I merely stood tall with our arms folded, as pukka sahib as could be, and smiled at each other. The firing stopped.

I don't mean to imply that the Paks cowered. They're infernally brave officers. I think, rather, that their reflexes were situational, protective of us. Anyway, they were embarrassed, made a great fuss about the danger, and ordered a corporal to move the briefing charts back a few yards.

The view reminded me of the gorges of the Caucasus, albeit with Indian bunkers back in the hardwood trees. The demarcation line lay down a broken road in a deep, green valley shadowed by snow-capped ridges. In the winter, troops manning the highest outposts had to rotate teams outside of their bunkers to shovel furiously throughout any snowstorm in order to avoid being buried alive.

Terry told me that most of the firing these days is initiated by the Indians, while the Paks tend to hold back (there was no return fire that day). On the other hand, it's the Indian slice of Kashmir that's in tumult and the Indians believe that the Paks support the secessionists and terrorists.

Split shortly after Partition, with one-third allotted to Pakistan and two-thirds to India, the division of Kashmir took little account of ethnic affinities, but bowed, in haste, to the whims of a local ruler and satisfied London's wish to be rid of a vexing concern. All sides feel cheated, as each side always will. We Americans like to imagine that there is always an equitable solution waiting to be found, but that's as much a fantasy as any extant in the Muslim world.

In old Kashmir, Muslim, Sikh, and Hindu vied for power over the centuries and, in the bloody days of Partition, the Sikhs, a worried minority of 5 million in India's ocean of humanity, sided with the Hindus. As the British withdrew and Gandhi and Jinna played games far more cynical than Western romantics can bring themselves to acknowledge, all sides committed atrocities. Yet, as in the bestiality of the Yugoslav crack-up, there was a hierarchy of cruelty. As populations shifted at empire's midnight, the Sikhs were the most savage actors, slaughtering all the Muslims they could corner and taking special delight in tormenting women and children. British eyewitnesses report that, while the Muslims killed Sikhs and Hindus, the order of magnitude was lower and the Muslims generally did not rape. The Sikhs and Hindus raped with a great and documented enthusiasm that sickened the hardened British war veterans forced to witness it.

Today, some Paks hope that, following U.S. diplomatic successes (such as they are) in the Balkans and the Middle East, we will turn our negotiators loose on the Kashmir problem—which is even more intractable than the Balkan mess. All sides have been wronged, and each has wronged the other. India will never allow a secession of Kashmir in favor of Pakistan, nor will Pakistan hand its slice of Kashmir to India. Nor would either side tolerate a reunified, independent Kashmir, since it would unleash centrifugal forces elsewhere. Should Kashmir leave Pakistan, would the Baluch, Sindh's Mohajirs (Muslims who came as refugees at Partition), or the tribes of the Northwest Frontier be far behind? As it is, only the army holds Pakistan together, and its recent difficulties in Karachi, where it failed to impose civil order, left it jumpy. India, too, faces internal divisions—exacerbated now by the growing economic disparities between the better-educated and more industrious states of southern India and the proud, but less competent states struggling in the north.

We marched down from the OP by a different path, with the Paks hurrying us across a finger of land where we were exposed to machine-gun fire. I felt the warning was largely for effect.

Back at the little garrison, the staff had mustered a few dozen locals who had been wounded by Indian fire as they worked in the fields or clung too long to hovels near the border. A girl of perhaps five years had a badly shot-up thigh that had been doctored practically, but not artfully. Old men limped toward me waving crippled arms. It was both a put-up propaganda job and a display of authentic misery—the latter compounded by the ringmaster approach of the sergeant major charged with keeping the victims in order. Despite the stage management, the people were electrified by the opportunity to pour out their tales to an American officer (clearly believing that I would carry their stories to President Clinton). I would have liked to pay them the respect of listening to each sufferer's story, but the Paks, as always, had a timetable for the visit and, anyway, the weakest were shoved out of the way by the less damaged. I wondered if the lot of them had been promised a few rupees for their appearance.

We deserted the poor for a grand spread at the officer's mess, but clouds lowered over the mountains, threatening to strand us. In haste, we set off back to Sawan Kucha, only to find our way blocked by one of those brightly colored buses. Front wheels thrust over a brand-new ledge, the vehicle's chassis clutched what remained of the road: a rock fall had dissolved it into the gorge. It would not soon be repaired and what otherwise might have been a fine hike back to the helipad would have brought the clouds down over us before we reached the rendezvous point. With the Paks a bit nervous after a recent shootdown, we turned again and headed back for a disused helipad within the range of Indian antiaircraft guns. Narrower than a tennis court, the pad gripped a ledge above the rapids and would have given a U.S. aviation safety officer a stroke. On top of all else, a powerful headwind came up, buffeting the canvas on our jeeps.

In one sense, the road's collapse was a stroke of luck, since it gave me more time to speak with Brigadier Ghulam. He was a thoughtful man and had seemed well-informed at first, but when he turned his questioning to Bosnia it was clear that he'd been told that Washington favored the Serbs and, along with the other Christian powers, had abandoned the Muslims to genocide. He had gotten our policy exactly backward, so as we waited for the Alouette to refuel and fight the headwind to reach us, I laid out our policy then took him back to the Bogomils and gave him an orderly synopsis of the disorderly history of the Balkans. He kept repeating, "But I never knew that, no one tells us that."

And so we circle back to the incredible information deficits in a world suffering an information glut—and how easily even intelligent men can be swayed if the propaganda exploits their predispositions.

Just as I was sharing some of the Sarajevo tales of a Canadian friend, Maj. "Dutch" Ruiters, we heard the *chop-chop-chop* of the old Alouette. A tough customer, the pilot was balancing his machine on the winds. He swooped in quickly and we leapt aboard, buckling in while his crew chief did the minimum required to get the little bird airborne again. An old mountain hand, the pilot swung the machine around hard in the lee of the helipad and then, after flirting with the sheer walls of the gorge, rode the gale back toward Sawan Kucha and the more peaceful world beyond.

As we lofted back above the snowy ridges, where the houses on the northern slopes sank into an early twilight, I thought suddenly of Christmas and my family. My reverie was only a few minutes old when, thanks to the miracle of flight—which still amazes me—we broke into the blue skies above Murree. In short order we were on the ground in a naval headquarters compound in Islamabad, with a captain complaining politely and obliquely that the Pressler Amendment had repossessed his ship.

Lahore

Lahore was my last stop. I was met at the airport VIP lounge by an accompanying officer (the ubiquitous AC), a plain-clothes security officer, a coordinating officer, and a police constable, the latter charged with leading our six-vehicle motorcade that included a motorcyclist riding point and an ambulance in case I stubbed my toe.

Thereafter, things got even sillier.

As a major in a very practical army, I was sensitive to the expense in money and manpower of our automotive extravaganza, but the Paks were nervous because of the murder of two U.S. consular officials down in Karachi earlier in the year. On the other hand, if you want to create an irresistible target, just strand your "VIP" in an unarmored sedan in an ostentatious motorcade in Lahore's crawling downtown traffic.

We stopped first at the Shalimar Gardens of Shah Jahan, the Moghul ruler known best as a builder. I was startled by the condition of the place, a neglected treasure rotting under poisonous gray clouds thick enough to slow a walking man. The gardens were untended and thin, the famous terraces grubby, and the enclosing walls yearned for paint. I just wanted to move on. Conciliatory spirits might remark that, after all, Pakistan is a poor country, but there's wealth in sufficient abundance to clean up its national treasures, and poor countries, especially, cannot afford to neglect their tourist attractions (something India realized long ago).

One border crossing remains open between Pakistan and India to accommodate third-country nationals. The gate is at Wagha, in the low, irrigated countryside a half hour from Lahore and just beyond a cluster of fever-prone villages whose character advertises the nearness of India. Each afternoon at 1700 hours there is a flag lowering ceremony, and I had been invited to admire it. So off we went down boulevards along which squatters pitched their shelters in front of Raj facades. Their paint discolored like an old man's skin, yesteryear's mansions sank into time behind spear-topped iron fences and tall trees. Abruptly, the paved avenue narrowed to a lane where we repeatedly braked for cows. At the border, white colonial buildings drowsed in the deepening shade.

Lieutenant Colonel Qamar, a gunner seconded to the paramilitary Rangers, took us to the "zero point," a small stone monument demarcating the border and the fate of many millions. Although they're shooting in Kashmir, relations are cordial at Wagha and Lieutenant Colonel Qamar encouraged me to step over into India so Terry could snap my picture. The unconcerned Indian guard watched us as if we were someone else's flock of geese. Then it was time for the ceremony. And a surprise.

There had been a communications breakdown and no one had told me that I would be the honorary commander of the retreat, which is a beautifully choreographed cast-of-dozens affair in which each Pak and Indian action is perfectly coordinated to mirror the action on the other side of the border gate. There is a great deal of heel-smashing, saluting, barked commands, and quick-step, arm-swinging marching. The Indian troops and the Pak Rangers (in their impressive charcoal-gray parade uniforms with high, rooster-fan headgear) have been selected for their size and bearing—and, evidently, for their dramatic skills. Crowds of onlookers turn out every evening.

With thirty seconds of warning time, I found myself standing at attention in the position of honor, with the parade-kit Indians across the way wondering who in the name of Kali (remember the filmed version of *Gunga Din?*) the visitor in the drab uniform could be. Recovering myself, I seized the opportunity to fulfill a childhood ambition—having grown up on those wonderfully muddled movies about the Northwest Frontier filmed in San Bernadino, and on Kipling and John Masters and tales of the Great Mutiny.

The captain executing the ceremony on the Pakistani side quick-marched up to me, arms sailing in half-windmills, then hammered down his bootheels and saluted, requesting permission to begin the retreat.

I raised one eyebrow, assuming the persona of Stewart Granger in *Bhowani Junction*, and returned his salute. In a pukka officer's voice worthy of David Niven in his prime, I said:

"*Do* carry on."

Then I cocked a knee, joined my hands behind my back (clutching an imaginary swagger stick), and savored the moment.

Beautiful and precise, with a generous dose of macho posturing as nostrils flared theatrically on both sides of the border, the ceremony was a monument to the legacy the British left each of these militaries. Oddly, it was just the sort of thing I'm glad my Army does not do, much preferring the matter-of-factness of our marching, the practicality and reluctance of our drill, and the implicit recognition that our soldiers are human beings and citizens, not imperial decorations. But it was a lovely spectacle to watch.

Back in town, I told the AC to send everybody in the entourage home for the night. Terry and I ate good Punjabi and listened for a while to a sitar player who lacked the inner fire of his colleague in Quetta. We had been moving quickly and needed some time to talk and compare the notes we each had failed to take, so we spent an hour or so working in my room. As Terry left, we found that a guard had been posted at my door. It was well-intentioned, but, as an old Russia hand, I'm allergic to excessive supervision and I began to suspect that the local Paks were as concerned about keeping me under positive control as with protecting me. Anyway, I found it all heavy-handed, and the hi-jinx lunacy of the head-of-state treatment had grown annoying.

Informed by Terry that I took an interest in history, the Paks had arranged a sequence of post-lecture sightseeing—for which I remain grateful—that was so over-the-top in its organization that the extremity was beyond protest. First, our motorcade nudged through the cross-town traffic, with the locals peering to see which notable was passing through their lives. Our first stop was the Badshahi Mosque, a Moghul signature piece, the courtyard of which holds 100,000 worshippers. My vehicle braked to a stop at the bottom of a cascade of marble stairs leading to the main entrance. Bless 'em, the Paks had literally rolled out the red carpet and there was nothing to do but carry it off with flair. At the top of the steps they had set out a line of chairs so Major Peters, Conqueror of the East, and his grand vizier, Lieutenant Colonel Cook, could sit down and comfortably take off their shoes before pulling on special slippers to be worn inside the mosque.

The mosque was a fascinating architectural counterpoint to others I have visited over the years, from Istanbul to Samarkand. The Moghuls built big and in their own style, but they went for first impressions over content. With its mighty domes, the Badshahi appears wondrous as you enter the vast courtyard, but the main structure is shallow, constructed only as a focal point for open-air services and to shelter the *mihrab* and *minbar*. The grand perspectives are well-planned, though, and the mosque achieves the aura of a sacred place apart.

A flight of brown birds chased through the yard like bad children.

We moved across a public quadrangle to the massive Lahore fort, whose possession had been contested between Hindu and Muslim, Muslim and Sikh, Sikh and Brit, with each next conqueror adding and subtracting and adding again until the complex became a hodgepodge of beefcake bastions and delicate pavilions, of real battlements and romantic fantasies in fading paint. While much has decayed, what remains is worthy of far more time than our tyrannical schedule allowed. An ornate pleasure pavilion decorated with frescos weathered to gauze and flowers crafted of inlaid semi-precious stones—many pried off over the years—seized my interest to an irrational degree and also captured the members of my escort, none of whom had thought to visit the fort on his own, although it was open as a tourist attraction. My

AC, especially, was enchanted to discover the richness of his heritage in a city where he had been stationed for over a year.

Our first problem of the day arose. The cult of the timetable had proven a false messiah and the hit-and-run visits had left six hours of dead time until my evening flight. Yet, hospitality could not allow Terry and me to wander off on our own, so the entourage remained "at our disposal," making us privileged prisoners. I was asked what other sites I might like to visit. I responded that I was very much interested in the Moghul tombs along the river (we could see them from where we stood). The Paks huddled and checked with their higher-ups, then told me that such a visit was impossible, since it was not part of the plan and, anyway, security had not been arranged. (I could have won a small civil war with the guns carried by our posse.) Anyway, it was now time to visit the city museum, which had been established by Rudyard Kipling's father and was captured forever in the opening pages of *Kim*.

All right. I had been looking forward to the museum and even, a bit childishly, to passing Zam Zama, Kim's gun, retired now to a traffic island in front of the museum, where it's clouded by the smoke of automotive battles. The museum has a famously rich collection. The Paks had budgeted half an hour.

I mutinied.

I'm easily seduced by Persian, Moghul, and North-Indian miniature painting and have visited collections around the world, but the Lahore Museum has the most extensive, and perhaps the best, stock of this art anywhere. About a hundred of the paintings are displayed at any given time, from a collection of several thousand. I decided to move at my own pace. With the museum director and the curator of the painting department delighted that an official visitor actually took an interest in their treasures, I seized the chance to inspect the works in detail and we chatted about the popularity of scenes lifted from the epics of Nizami and the compositional influence of miniature painting on Safavid picture rugs. (This is the sort of thing Foreign Areas Officers do to aggravate their peers who prefer tortilla chips and the NFL.)

At last, I was bullied into the coin vault, the only part of the museum on the master plan. Coins interest me only as testaments to lost empires and old migrations, so we made short work of the profiled heads of Alexander and various shahs and then got on to the Gandharan sculpture. After that came glorious illuminated manuscripts, my enjoyment of everything enhanced by the near-panic of my minders who, although the plan left a gap ahead, were mortified that we had overstayed our allotted interval for the arts. I looked at the exhibits, they looked at their watches. It was more fun than changing the rules on a German in the middle of a card game.

Prodded from above, my AC asked if we would not like to go shopping. Both Terry and I would have much preferred more history, but the AC informed us that, while he was our servant and we could do anything we wanted, we were going shopping now. At that point, I realized that the Paks had mistaken us for a Congressional delegation.

Off we went, lights flashing and sirens blaring, to visit the department store that promised us a ride on the second escalator in Pakistan (it was out of order). With plainclothesmen aggressive in their efforts to protect us, the stop was a grating ordeal. There wasn't any damned thing I wanted to buy and there would have been far less danger and bother in taking us down to those nearby Moghul tombs.

As the day waned, we made our way into the cauldron of the old city, amid smells of frying meat and shit, surrounded by vivid chemical colors in the shop fronts and scabbed facades above. A human chain of fairy-tale blind beggars chanted to God as they snaked their way through the crowd, each fellow's left hand on the shoulder of the man in front. Their leader tapped along with the cane he held in his right hand, while the others clutched begging bowls. Prowling defiantly, Terry and I found an old Hindu temple desecrated by squatters and led our watchers into tenements where disease had left the children too dull to beg. It was not what our minders wanted us to see.

By the time we returned to the vehicles, the air had tangible weight and the pollution at day's end was so bad that headlights appeared to be filtered through a fog.

The Good Captain

My AC in Lahore was a young Punjabi captain from the Baluch regiment, earnest and sad eyed. His English was functional, but he had to reach to express anything complex. He was proud to have been selected as my AC, God help him, and he was as deferential to my wishes as his rigid orders allowed. Nonetheless, I had developed an early prejudice against him. Nothing in Pakistan wore on me so much as the attitude toward women and their public invisibility. During an early pause in the cavalcade of events, I had asked the AC is he had a wife.

"No. No wife."

"Well . . . what kind of wife would you like?"

"Whoever my parents choose. She will be very good."

"Yes, but . . . aren't there some qualities you'd prefer?"

"No. My parents will choose."

"Will your parents choose you a wife soon?"

"They will tell me when the time comes."

This came after another AC up-country had told me much the same thing, after which he had assured me that, although Westerners get divorced, this does not happen in Pakistan; therefore, the Pak system is superior. For my part, I found the passivity and indifference appalling. I wrote off my Lahore AC as another Third-World male, allowing that East *is* East and West *is* West. Thenceforth, our conversation was confined to business and social small change.

We arrived at the airport lounge with over an hour to kill. After sitting dully for a few minutes, I asked the AC if he had any hobbies. He brightened, a neglected child noticed at last by an adult, and told me he liked to read religious verse and love poetry and to write in both forms. I found it baffling that he enjoyed love poetry while declaring no preference as to the characteristics of his future wife, but now we at least had a fondness for poetry in common. He quoted me an Urdu quatrain that had been translated into English, reciting in a gentle voice he had never used in my presence. I responded with an edited version of Auden's "Lay Your Sleeping Head My Love," softening a few of the old bugger's lines to get a Muslim PG-rating. The captain listened with closed eyes, a brief peace on his features, then said, "But that is *very* beautiful."

With undergraduate seriousness, he asked Terry and me what wisdom we could provide him as to how best to live his life. He volunteered, proudly, that he had never touched alcohol or a woman. What, he begged, were our personal credos? Disarmed by such a heartfelt question, we stammered out a few platitudes, which the captain dutifully wrote down. I suspect that he harbored the popular suspicions about Westerners, yet in the flesh we were marvelous creatures from another world. We breathed the same air, had the same immediate needs, and more or less shared a language, but our realties were immeasurably different—so different that the gulf between them may be unbridgable.

I shall never forget him sitting there in that smoky, scruffy VIP lounge, a proud virgin, eyes glowing with poetry, yearning for some meaningful souvenir of the exotic world that had touched his life for two days.

I could offer him nothing.

ELVIS, BUDDHA, AND THE BURRITO OF THE APOCALYPSE

I HAD NEVER BEEN IN AN INDUSTRIAL-SIZE BROTHEL BEFORE. IN fact, I had never set foot in a bordello of any sort, since the notion of paying for sex offends my vanity as much as it does my morals. The bars of Moscow had been aflame with prostitutes, but once you established that you were not a mark they subsided into the décor. This was different.

Perhaps a hundred young women lazed in a barn dressed up, half-heartedly, as a disco. Thailand's version of the brides of Dracula, they wore identical white shrouds. Moments after we entered, fear quickened them.

If I resembled John Calvin stranded in Sodom, my host was an effervescent Caligula. I had never seen a general so merry. But his joviality wasn't contagious (unlike much else in that human warehouse): the girls lowered their eyes and hunched their shoulders, hoping, against the conventions of their trade, not to be noticed. It was evident that the employees knew the customer.

The general had a Thai name, but looked half Chinese. Responsible for the counter-narcotics effort up-country, he was said to be corrupt and murderous. He wished to use us, and we hoped to use him.

Short even by the measure of his countrymen and thickening, the general wore his hair slicked back in a pompadour that would have suited an unsuccessful pimp. At our afternoon meeting to discuss the heroin trade, he had worn his uniform and promised all that was asked of him and more. My sense was that he planned to let us eliminate his competition.

Two Bangkok-based men from the Drug Enforcement Agency escorted me through northern Thailand. They had warned me that the general would keep our session brief. He didn't. The meeting dragged on, breaking up only when it was time for us to return to our hotel and change for dinner at the general's penthouse.

His subordinates, who acted as servants with shoulder holsters, ushered us up from an underground garage into a garish apartment no general could afford, unless he had private means or a lucrative sideline. The furnishings recalled a third-rate casino, but the view over Chiang Mai was lovely. Always quiet, my DEA minders went totally silent. They were young and fit and capable, but the dinner invitation hadn't matched their template, and cops like patterns.

The general made an unforgettable entrance. Sashaying—the word is carefully chosen—past a larger-than-life, gold-plated Buddha, everything about him would have been camp, had he not been so earnest.

His evening attire consisted of a black satin shirt with bell sleeves and baseball-size white polka dots, flared black double-knit trousers as gripping as a leotard above the knees, and Jersey-hoodlum boots with pointed toes. His pompadour shone, higher than ever, and his grin was impossibly wide.

"I love everything American!" he announced. "You see? I have been in your country to study. In 1975. It was a wonderful time for me." He sighed at nostalgia reflux. "You see? I *still* dress like an American."

Dinner was tasty and copious, and it was a novelty to be served by national-police officers. The DEA agents exchanged unsettled glances, but trouble was the last thing on the general's mind and I'd been around enough thugs to read the atmosphere. Shop talk faded and our host slipped into reminiscences, his diction weakening with each additional beer and recollection. For him, the United States would be stuck forever in the disco era, with lurid spotlights, cocaine blonds, and a DJ switching between Donna Summer and the Bee Gees. Nothing that had happened in North America in the decades since his visit had registered on him. Except for fluctuating tastes in drugs.

He spoke with adolescent lewdness of American girls he pretended to have had, giggling at his own imagined triumphs. It was after midnight and I had rendered my country sufficient service.

"I'd like to thank you for your—"

The general sliced off the end of my sentence. "Now," he declared, rising not quite steadily from the table, "I take you for *special* treat. Very big surprise."

I tried to beg off, but the general was insistent. He truly didn't want the night to end. His grand position was a lonely one, after all, and he really did think well of the American civilization of the disco era, perhaps the lowest point in cultural history.

"You go with me in my car," he told me. "Your friends will follow us." With that, we all rode down in the elevator together with a contingent of the general's bodyguards.

Stillness reigned in the basement garage. The general looked about in astonishment. Then bewilderment became rage. As sudden as gunfire, he turned on one of his men and began shrieking.

His car was supposed to be waiting. And it wasn't there.

My host switched off his anger and turned to me. Smiling again, he said, "I must discipline these poor boys. They do not understand what it means to be professional. They embarrass me. In front of my important guest."

The car appeared. We got in and tore off, followed by an entourage with an arsenal.

"Where to?" I asked him.

He smiled, a mischievous boy. "You will see. I have a happy surprise for you."

A few minutes later, we pulled up in front of the whorehouse. The DEA men would have been valiant in a gunfight, but now they merely followed me like pups, compelled by their orders to keep me in their sight and laughably ill at ease.

A squad of bouncers jumped out of our way. Inside, a madam and a gussied-up thug waited to pay their respects. We were expected.

Unlike most Thais, the general wasted no time on civility, but snapped out his desires. Everyone within earshot scurried about, trying to look busy. Abandoned daughters and poor kids from the country—some indentured to pay small debts—the girls watched us in unmistakable terror. God only knew what tastes the general had.

And the depravities he revealed to me were, indeed, of a singular kind.

We were shown into a room with a billiard table, plenty of chairs, and some junk slapped against one wall. The private chamber had all the charm of an unfinished basement. Pretending they weren't really present, the DEA men took chairs in a corner and folded their arms in unison.

The general pointed to a padded chair. I sat. An instant later, a flock of girls materialized, all with gleaming hair and alarmed eyes.

The general looked them over, inspecting the troops. Speaking in Thai, he ordered one of the girls to sit beside me. She was stunning, if your taste runs to childlike women. Mine doesn't.

Twice too many bottles of beer appeared.

I was on the verge of telling the general okay, great night, but the party's over. Curiosity's one thing, but I don't do tawdry.

With four or five women gathered about him, the general barked again. Yet another woman appeared. She rushed across the room to the clutter of junk. It was only then that I noticed the karaoke machine.

If I had been John Calvin a moment before, I now became Robespierre. The mere word "karaoke" brings out a side of me that suggests an ancestor violently active in the Temperance movement: I wanted to pick up an axe and go to work.

The good news was that the general had not brought me to the bordello for an orgy. The bad news was that he intended to sing.

The woman delivered a microphone into his hands, then sat down on the carpet, assuming the posture of an adoring fan. Wobbling a bit, the general swept a hand over his pompadour, then tugged up his double-knits. Those trousers would never successfully impound his belly again.

"I love America too much," he told me. "But do you guess who is my favorite American?"

"John Travolta?" I asked, fearfully.

He laughed. "Oh, no. No, Mr. Peters! It is Elvis Presley!"

He spoke in Thai, more softly. The woman rose again and primed the machine.

I heard the opening bars of "Love Me Tender."

I recognize the greatness of Elvis Presley. But Elvis was unique. Late-night impersonations by corrupt and drunken Thai generals do his memory a disservice. Nor did it help that the general couldn't sing a note.

Of course, the local critics had reason to go easy on him. Consider the effect that threats of deadly force and crippling violence would have on the reviews in *The New York Times*.

Instead of fading, the general's accent thickened as he sang: serenading me, then the girls, then me again (he ignored the catatonic DEA agents). The girls, who certainly had the measure of the performance, set their faces in cartoon caricatures of "the inscrutable oriental."

". . . nevoh wet me go . . ."

We all applauded. From various motives.

Grinning, basking, soaring, the general extended the microphone to me. "Now you must sing!"

I assured him that I lacked his extraordinary talent and would prefer hearing him sing again. It was the response he craved.

The girl beside me smelled of sweat and blossoms. She was terrified of me as an associate of the general's. The heat pressed in. More beers were delivered. I didn't intend to drink any more, but it was good to hold a cold bottle in my hand, the next best thing to ice on the back of the neck.

The woman in charge of the karaoke machine cued another recording. The general gave me a lascivious smile. "Very nice, these girls. Very beautiful." He snickered and tapped his crotch in warning. "But I tell you, my friend, you must wear a thing for protection, or you will be very sorry. They give you a surprise you don't like."

Background music swelled: "Don't Be Cruel."

The general rocked out. He must have studied every available Elvis video—in his short, plump way, he had the gyrations down. His singing didn't improve a jot, but he would've been voted Elvis Number One in a competition held before an audience of deaf mutes. My anger weakened as I struggled not to laugh.

Then, inevitably, he detoured from Elvis's repertoire to give us "Feelings," that trailer-court romantic's version of the "Horst Wessel Lied."

"Hound Dog" followed, almost a relief.

The night ended with a whimper, not a bang: A defect stopped the karaoke machine just as the general assured me that I'd never caught a rabbit.

He took the breakdown philosophically, as if his talent had demanded too much of a mere appliance. I wondered if the girls had figured out a way to rig the device.

Disappointed that I didn't want to spend any private time with the honey he'd chosen for me, the general gathered us up. We left without formality or payment. The general never paid for anything. This was his feudal kingdom and he ruled it as a lord. Back at my hotel, he insisted on having one more beer in the lobby. The night manager was a young woman whose poise and dignity had impressed me earlier. Faced with the general's unexpected presence, she became a frightened courtier, delivering our drinks herself, and then at the general's command, kneeling to give him a foot massage. I suspect she was praying that he wouldn't drag her off for the night.

After my DEA minders had gone upstairs, the general leaned toward me and said, "Will we go to have some fun now? Any woman you want! No problem."

I told him I needed some sleep.

Later, someone knocked lightly on my door. I ignored that offer, too.

If my morals had needed reinforcement, they got it the next morning when we visited a clinic for AIDS victims. The two-story barrack was crude, but clean, the patients baffled by their physical erosion. Bare chested and tattooed, young men sat on their cots, staring into infinity. The women who were not too frail to respond cowered in shame, as pensive as the Magdalenes of Georges de la Tour. Many were intravenous drug users, but others had, no doubt, heard Elvis impersonations after midnight.

I ran in the high mountain desert. Winter air kept my bare legs pumping. Up ahead, dawn struck the Huachuca Mountains, revealing hidden canyons and colors kept secret from the mature daylight. Despite the altitude, I ran faster and farther than usual, high on the perfect air and the seductive lonesomeness (*not* loneliness) of the landscape.

I expected a phone call when I got back to my room.

A lecture invitation had brought me from the Pentagon back to Fort Huachuca. My relationship with the Army's Intelligence Center and School became predictable as the years passed: I would be invited to speak to liven up the moribund curriculum but inevitably proved too much for the nervous chain of command, after which I would not be invited back until the staff turned over and someone would scratch his head, wondering why I had not been back to speak for several years. And the cycle of anticipation, horror, and hostility would begin again. (As I write, I've been through the turn of the wheel four times—it's *Groundhog Day* with prairie dogs.)

The night before that memorable run I had watched the 1996 State of the Union address in my motel room, just outside the post's main gate. When President Clinton announced that General McCaffrey would retire from active service to become his Director of the Office of National Drug Control Policy—the "drug czar"—I figured I'd get a phone call in the morning. McCaffrey would need people he could trust amid the political hacks bound to be dumped on his office. I was sorry, though, that the president's election-year need for cover on the drug flank had robbed

McCaffrey of his destiny to become Chairman of the Joint Chiefs of Staff.

When I returned to the motel, there were two messages on the voicemail account, both from Lt. Col. Francis X. "Pancho" Kinney, who had not liked me in Panama, but was doomed to become a friend. I called back and Pancho told me that Jim McDonough would serve as McCaffrey's strategy chief. If I signed on, I could remain on active duty in mufti on a one-year loan from the Pentagon. My role would be the same as the one I'd played in Latin America, but on a global scale.

Later, McCaffrey told me that he'd agonized over accepting the appointment, since he didn't want to take off his uniform. He only agreed after his father, a retired three-star, admonished him that, when a president calls, a soldier salutes and steps forward. McCaffrey achieved far more in his thankless new position than will ever be known to the American public. Yet, even his efforts were not enough to overcome the cynicism of the Clinton administration, which had even less interest in fighting the international narcotics trade than it did in fighting terrorism.

The sole reason I went to ONDCP and the Executive Office of the President was the chance to serve under McCaffrey again. I expected to be disgusted by the administration's innards, and I was.

The previous year had taken me not only to Pakistan, but to Croatia, Azerbaijan, and back to Russia. An effort was underway to groom me for further promotions and I spent ninety days on the Joint Staff designing a special project, but the primary purpose of the job was to give me a Joint Staff efficiency report from another senior general. For my part, I took the mission seriously and developed a gorgeously simple "black" plan that would harm no one in peacetime but, in the event of a crisis, would allow us to gut the Russian officer corps. Then–Lt. Gen. Wes Clark, who was better attuned to politics than to our national security, rejected the plan as "too cynical." He feared that, if word of it reached the State Department, the Clinton regime's Kremlin-huggers would be outraged.

Clark was obsessively fit, privately troubled, and consumed by inchoate ambitions—all of which managed, in a perverse way, to make him pitiably likable (if McCaffrey was raw steak, Clark was cotton candy). But Clark, while physically brave, suffers from chronic bad judgment. The public relations debacle of his cap-swap with a Serb war criminal and his subsequent botched response to the Russian airfield grab in Kosovo were merely the incidents that reached the public. I still recall him falling-down drunk in Moscow after a dinner with his Russian counterpart, despite being warned that he needn't keep up with the Russians vodka for vodka. There was a fat female singer present, and a camera in Russian hands.

Wes Clark suffered from "smartest guy in the battalion syndrome." Always the brightest officer in each unit he passed through on his way up the ranks, he arrived in Washington convinced that he would always be the cleverest person present. In D.C., the sharks devoured him, and he never even realized he'd been bitten. Thereafter, he imagined that he might become President of the United States and his embarrassing quest for attention reminded me of Joe Chapin, the antihero of John O'Hara's novel, *Ten North Frederick*.

My brief spell on the Joint Staff, intended to prosper my career, started me thinking that I might want to leave the Army. My year at ONDCP didn't help my morale.

Our leased office space was just around the corner from the White House, but by Washington's measure those two-hundred yards might as well have been twenty miles. Physical proximity to the President is the decisive indicator of one's importance. We were beyond the Arctic Circle. And the political hacks thrust upon us, a sad lot too embarrassing to be allowed inside the White House itself, grabbed all the best igloos.

My first clash with a Clinton appointee came when an unhappy woman of the sort who gives feminism's critics free ammunition lectured me on the importance of always using gender-neutral language. She didn't care a bit about the contents of the strategy paper I'd drafted, but she was livid that I had used the word "mankind" instead of "humankind." Meningitis-serious, she grew furious when I couldn't keep a straight face.

My next brush with Clinton-era behavior involved a civilian on the hardware side. Assuming that all military officers were stupid beyond disdain, he teamed with a contractor to seek my support for a purchase that was so obviously crooked—none of the numbers matched—that even his fellow dead-enders wouldn't initial it. I didn't sign, but eventually someone did.

These were ant-level annoyances compared to the challenges McCaffrey faced. He brought a total commitment to every task assigned to him and, on the positive side, his organizational skills, quick mind, and commanding presence allowed him to bring the first semblance of order to our government's disconnected counter-narcotics programs. But even McCaffrey could not take on powerful lobbies in an election year.

Among the military officers assigned to ONDCP, I was the only one who had personal experience with the effects of hard drugs on friends and family. In the late 1960s and early 1970s I'd been deep enough in the music world to have a roster of dead friends and institutionalized acquaintances, as well as recollections of lovely young women who shriveled on meth or heroin. I tried, without success, to communicate three essential premises to my colleagues:

First, after all of the sociological studies have been conducted and all of the academic explanations for drug use have been elaborated, people take drugs because drugs make them feel good. If drugs made them feel bad, they wouldn't take them. But the notion that drugs give *pleasure* was politically incorrect (certainly a bizarre twist within the Clinton administration). Those of us with privileged lives and plenty at stake had good reasons to avoid the addiction trap, but for those at the bottom of the socioeconomic food chain, with no prospects of bettering their lot, taking drugs was not a completely irrational decision—better to feel good briefly than bad always.

Second, there indisputably are addictive personalities. But we were forbidden to suggest such an idea. I knew from personal experience that some individuals were far weaker and vastly more susceptible to the lure of narcotics than others. From alcoholics to shopaholics, the biological or psychological vulnerabilities are simply there in some people while absent in others. Yet, we had to pretend that all human beings were identically prone to becoming skid-row addicts. That meant research funds could not be targeted to help the likeliest victims and programs were diffused to the point of uselessness. That pleased the soccer momsters, who worried about pot in suburban high schools, while leaving the poor to rot.

My third premise was that there's quite a difference between smoking an occasional joint and mainlining heroin twice a day. The hoary argument that marijuana leads inevitably to a crack-cocaine habit (and, of course, to prostitution for blond suburban teenagers) is equivalent to insisting that sipping a glass of Bordeaux means a lifetime in thrall to grain alcohol. But we weren't allowed to differentiate between soft and hard drugs, a nonsensical position that became personal when, with the presidential election nearing, the president's henchmen—who pioneered new continents of cynicism—ordered ONDCP to give priority to defeating a California ballot initiative to legalize the medical use of marijuana. Jim asked me to work on it. I told him I couldn't and wouldn't. It was a matter of integrity, since if any of those I loved were terminally ill and believed that smoking pot eased their sufferings, I would condone their drug use. And I refused to work on a program that amounted to busting cancer victims at a time when our inner cities and destitute rural areas were being ravaged by genuine killer drugs. Of course, I realized that the legalization lobby was exploiting the sick to open the door a crack. And no, I don't believe that illegal drug use is a good idea (my life has taught me otherwise). But I was prepared to resign my commission before I would help drop the weight of the federal government on the sick to aid a political campaign.

Jim put someone else on the job and never said another word about it.

_____

"Take this," the DEA agent told me, "and put it on."

He held out a flak jacket.

We stood in an alley in the badlands of Los Angeles, counting down to a raid that involved the LAPD, state counter-narcotics officers and the DEA.

I pulled on the vest: dead weight in the heat.

"Jack" stepped closer and lowered his voice. "Put your hand in the pocket. Right side."

I did as instructed.

"There's no safety on it," he told me. "Don't take it out unless you need it. This is going to go down fast, and let's hope it goes down clean."

The law forbids military members from taking part in law-enforcement activities within the United States unless directed to do so by the president. On the other hand, it's nice to stay alive.

I had been in Mexico, quietly, and had followed the border from the waters off San Diego to the land ports of entry in the lower Rio Grande valley. It was a miserable realm, in which poverty stumbled upon sudden, illegal prospects of enrichment. Our radars tracked low-altitude flights that shot across the border to unload their cargoes at dirt strips in the desert, and smuggling gangs better-armed than our Border Patrol splashed across the river in the darkness. There were tunnels, murders, and billions of dollars in prize money, but a street-punk's life wasn't worth a hundred bucks. It was easy to net the little fish and toss them in the tank for twenty years, but borders, extradition hassles, lawyers-for-sale, and remorseless violence kept the big fish safe more often than not.

My first impression of the DEA down in the Andean Ridge had not been favorable. But the agents I encountered on *la frontera* or in our cities were remarkable men, brave and capable. There was constant tension—which McCaffrey worked to overcome—between the DEA and the FBI, with the latter accusing the former of being cowboys and DEA agents deeming their FBI counterparts too prissy to get dirty. The DEA concentrated on making busts now, the FBI on building complex cases. We needed both skill sets and both mentalities, but the structure of our government and human nature often set them at each other's throat. Both agencies wasted a great deal of energy attempting to woo me, as McCaffrey's scout, to their view of the world (FBI agents were better organized, but the DEA boys were more fun).

Jack stepped away to speak with two men from the SWAT team. Returning, he told me, "Might've been tipped. This one may come up dry. But be ready." He glanced at the pocket of the flak vest.

I intended to stay out of the way of those who had work to do. Being a hot dog accomplishes nothing and risks getting good men killed. I was just a tourist in this world.

At the designated time, cop cars and SWAT vehicles converged out of nowhere. Those of us on foot ran for the targeted building. I stayed a car length behind anyone with a weapon up, in order not to block their fields of fire. The SWAT team led the way, very fast, very smooth, all shotguns, carbines, and body armor.

The warrant was for a "restaurant" that pretended to sell take-out seafood. You called in for a tuna sub or fried shrimp if you wanted, say, uptown coke or downtown crack.

The legal system in L.A. had dragged its feet on the warrant. After all the planning and coordination, the place had been emptied just before the raid, with cigarette smoke still wafting behind the counter. It was a disappointment, but those cops worked in a world where tip-offs went both ways. On that particular day, the million-dollar phone call went against them.

They had a sense of humor, though. Fifteen officers and agents from a cluster of agencies spread themselves around the seating area while one Latino cop tarted up his accent and took telephone orders for the next hour or so. The customers were bewildered when they came in to pick up their goods. The cops didn't say a word, but let the would-be patrons figure it out. And they did. I still recall the ghastly look on one well-dressed woman's face. She had double-parked her Jaguar outside.

I gave back the vest and Jack—who looked like a tough, old television cop—dropped me at the Rampart District police headquarters. Rampart's officers had run through their share of scandals and would face more, all of which delighted the press. I sympathized with the cops. The daily stresses they had to face were outrageous. Their critics had no sense of what those streets were like.

Rampart had come a long way, all of it downhill, since the hippy-trippy flash of Richard Harris singing about MacArthur Park melting in the dark. By 1996, the park was crack-central and Rampart's official population of 200,000 had more than doubled, thanks to illegal immigration. The Los Angeles government did not support the police but protected illegal immigrants, and mid-level drug dealers had no trouble enlisting new arrivals to push crack on the sidewalks in the middle of the day. A bust put the illegals in jail overnight, after which they were told to show up in court on a given date and dropped back on the block. The city's sanctuary policy forbid law enforcement officials from questioning the immigration status of those they arrested.

The Korean community and the Latinos vied for control of Rampart block by block, with no love lost on either side. The place was filthy, reminiscent of the developing world at its most feckless. It was plagued with drugs, addicts, and diseased whores. And it was extremely violent.

I spent a Saturday night riding with the district's police captain. He didn't put on a we're-doing-great show. Instead, he took me on a tour, beginning as the damned crept out of the underworld for the evening. His radio got busy as it grew dark and never paused thereafter.

Of the many stops we made, two still stand out. A unit called for back-up on a domestic dispute. (My best friend from childhood, Dale Repp, became a police chief in Pennsylvania and told me that family blow-ups were the most unpredictable calls his officers had to answer.) We pulled up to a four-story apartment building from the Raymond Chandler era, the place where the guy down on his luck always holed up. If it looked shabby from the outside, the inside was far worse. The moment we opened the first of the double doors, the sewage smell hit us. We heard shrieking on all sides, as if we had entered a primitive madhouse, but the shouts and screams had nothing to do with the domestic spat. It was just the standard level of pandemonium, the way the residents communicated. Trash covered the hallways and a junkie-hooker passed us with a zombie gaze.

We climbed the stairs. The stink of shit worsened. I had sniffed the layered odors of East Village crash pads in the 1960s and recalled the stench of Russian public toilets, but I had never before smelled anything so wretched. (I had not yet been to the dockside slums of Mumbai.)

And I heard barking.

Two patrolmen waited for the captain on the top floor. The man involved in the fight had fled and the woman who had called the cops cursed their arrival and walked out herself.

"Get this," one of the cops said as we approached an open apartment door. "That dog hasn't been walked in weeks."

No sight or smell has ever sickened me to vomiting. But the stink of that room came close. Berserk, a German shepherd bashed itself against the bars of a too-small cage. The cage's floor was thick with shit, as was the animal's fur and the floor of the apartment.

"Call Public Health," the captain said.

"They won't come."

"Call them anyway."

As we left the building, the cooking-grease reek of the street seemed like Alpine air.

There was litter everywhere in Rampart, and the worst of it was human: cast-off life. Nothing good was ever going to happen to the bums and terminal addicts and the hustlers and the hookers teetering at the gutter's edge. In their world, dope made sense. And prep-school grads were never going to figure it out.

After a hurried meal of take-out noodles at midnight, the report of a double murder crackled in. We drove uphill. Fast. I expected to find deserted streets, to encounter a sense of fear, to see police lights swirling in a ghost town.

I didn't have a clue. Murders were entertainment down in the 'hood. Entire families had turned out for the fiesta. Instead of wails

of grief and women on their knees, we met yelling children running between parked cars, late-night nerve-happy. Knots of men
stood drinking beer while women gossiped as casually as if they'd
met at the grocery store.

The bodies lay covered on a scrap of lawn. The cops did cop
stuff, measuring and writing, taking photographs, and asking questions. Nobody seemed upset.

The well-to-do La-La-Land citizens who glamorized the poor
and sympathized with criminals never visited Rampart's human
safari park. Not even for a drive-through. They stayed up north in
their boho-billionaire canyons or lazed along the oceanfront in
Malibu. It's easier to idealize a killer when you can't smell him.
And so the street cops got it from both sides.

Even so, our cops had it better than their Mexican counterparts who tried to stay clean. After a nuclear-burrito lunch in El
Paso with an FBI man who had local roots (we ate at the edge of
the forlorn downtown where Pancho Villa used to stroll for ice
cream), the district's DEA chief drove me across the border in an
unmarked car. We followed a convoluted route to a safe-house
deep in Juarez where a vetted platoon of Mexican anti-narcotics
police were on ice. All volunteers, they genuinely cared about
their country. We trained and equipped them. And in less than a
year every one of them was dead, sold out by their comrades.

The oddest event of that very odd year also happened in El
Paso. McCaffrey decided to bring together the federal, state, and
local agencies that dealt with our Southwest border and El Paso
seemed a good location, smack in the middle of the drug war's
front line. At first, a select group was to assemble for a working
meeting. A political appointee sent down as the advance man

failed to do anything but run up a motel bill, so at the last minute I flew to Texas to pull the conference together.

To my chagrin, the session metastasized. McCaffrey had persuaded cabinet members and agency heads to speak, including the Secretary of the Treasury (on money laundering) and the Attorney General. Suddenly, everyone with a badge or a department pass wanted to attend. The first room I'd booked was too small and we had to move the event onto Fort Bliss (for security reasons, as well). Hotel beds were a problem. Protocol was a nightmare. The egos involved were intergalactic in breadth.

But the Army teaches you how to organize just about anything under pressure. And the local FBI and DEA offices pitched in to give me what support they could. (Thanks, Tom; thanks, Rich.) The DEA special-agent-in-charge and I even designed a logo and he had T-shirts made up for the attendees. *Everybody* likes T-shirts.

Except Janet Reno, the attorney general. Reno was dotty. The Clinton administration loved her because she was too slow to keep up with White House shenanigans. But she had her moments. And one of her moments happened on my watch.

A document folder with the conference logo made its way to her office. The logo consisted of an ONDCP crest flanked by two scorpions to suggest the southwest—we kept it bland on purpose. But the attorney general was horrified. She was certain that senior Mexican officials (who were not, in any case, on the guest list) would assume that the tails of the scorpions pointed across the border at them and we'd have an international incident on our hands. The paranoid wackiness pegged out the meter, but our attorney general's office insisted that every item bearing the logo be destroyed.

It wasn't a battle worth fighting for McCaffrey, who had more important concerns (unlike our nation's attorney general and her staff). We were ordered to shred all the folders and burn the T-shirts.

The DEA SAC was crestfallen. (He'd paid for those shirts out of pocket.) He asked me if it would be okay if he held onto just a couple of the shirts for his agents, promising he wouldn't distribute them until the Washington circus had left El Paso.

I was disgusted at the idiocy of it all. And it was dead wrong for that veteran agent to have to ask my permission for anything: the authority of "the guy from Washington" is generally bogus and usually destructive.

"Don't destroy any of them," I told him. "This is bullshit. Give out as many as you want after we clear out. And I'd like a couple myself."

I still have two of those T-shirts. I've worn them for years while jogging. And the government of Mexico has yet to file a diplomatic protest.

We argued. Politely. All of the arguments were polite in Burma, unless you were a dissident, in which case your bones were broken. The CIA station chief, who was our best connection with the military junta, sat beside me at a low table decked with sweets that no one touched. On the other side of the spread, a row of colonels explained that each of my requests was impossible to fulfill.

The generals who had imprisoned the country and renamed it Myanmar (also re-christening Rangoon as Yangon) would not meet with us, fearing contact with the outside world. The colonels, on the other hand, were aware of the march of events beyond their borders, and I sensed that they harbored their own discontents regarding the generals. One officer, in particular, had intelligent eyes and spoke directly—not a trait often found in ethnic Burmans. Although their ranks were officially the same, the other officers deferred to him. The station chief told me afterward that the colonel in question was the make-it-happen man for Than Shwe, the general who lorded it over the other generals as the head of every committee in the country and the boss of the State Law and Order Restoration Council, with its Orwellian acronym, SLORC (since changed to present a kinder, gentler dictatorship to the media).

For all of the junta's repulsiveness, Burma was a more complicated land than foreign well-wishers acknowledged. "The Lady," Daw Aung San Suu Kyi, had been under house arrest for years because of her outspoken advocacy of democracy and her annoying ability to win general elections. She was heroic (and remains so unto this day). Yet, my concern with Burma was heroin. At the time, it was the world's largest exporter of that iconic, captivating, devastating drug. And The Lady declined to offer public criticism of poppy cultivation or the narcotics trade, while the junta, vicious though it was, fought to suppress the heroin flow. (Later, they would answer the West's rebuffs by exploiting the heroin market themselves.)

The problem was that Daw Aung San Suu Kyi drew much of her support from tribal minorities, and the up-country tribes that surrounded the ethnic-Burman heartland lived off the drug trade. The junta was virulently anti-poppy because the profits bought arms for the tribes on the other side of a simmering civil war fouled with atrocities. The junta's troops were thugs but willing to eradicate poppies. The Lady maintained a ladylike silence on the issue. Not all diplomatic trade-offs are clean.

We were willing to provide limited aid in support of counter-drug operations, but not lethal equipment that could be used on the secessionist Karen or other tribes. Isolated, the junta was desperate for any support, and we had intelligence indicators that poppy eradication was, in fact, happening, at no small cost in Burmese-army casualties. But we had to see it firsthand, on the ground, out in the wilds, with no fakery or bullshit.

The CIA station chief, who was the best of his breed, had been making the argument for months. Now I was arguing on behalf of McCaffrey and the U.S. government. We pointed out that, if the government truly was doing what it claimed, the military should be happy to show us. But the government was madly paranoid and anachronistically hermetic, and didn't want to reveal anything, even positive achievements, to foreigners. The colonels could not understand why we wouldn't take their word for everything, why we couldn't just take it on faith that they were tearing up poppy fields. They couldn't guarantee our safety in the tribal areas, they said, and we would do better simply to trust them.

Just about ready to call it quits, I had a bizarre flash of inspiration. Even Burmese colonels took their Buddhism seriously.

Locking eyes with their point man, I said, "Do you remember the story of Prince Gautama, before he became the Buddha? He had to leave the safety of his parents' home and go out into the world, to see things with his own eyes, before he could become enlightened." I smiled, struggling to appear friendlier than I felt. "We're far lesser beings than the Buddha." Touching the frame of my glasses, I told him, "We have to see things with our own eyes, too."

It was a desperate effort and, while it drew a moment of surprised silence, that was it. We said our goodbyes—politely—and left. The station chief and I retreated to a tea garden in a park by a stagnant pool and took turns shaking our heads.

The funny thing about wielding the Buddha's example against the colonel was that, for all the oh-so-serious reading I'd done about the religion (and the two college years when I meditated twice daily), the story as I told it didn't come out of an esoteric text, but from Hermann Hesse's goofball version of the Buddha's life, *Siddhartha*, a novel so silly that undergraduates cherished it in the 1960s. I had read the brief book at one go, in the parking lot of the Deer Lake Inn back home in Pennsylvania, on a languid summer afternoon when I was about to enter the ninth grade, a victim of terminal dandruff. Even then I knew it was a fraud. (Hesse wrote his romanticized tale before visiting India; when he finally went there, he promptly had a nervous breakdown.)

Just before I was to fly on to Laos, the CIA chief took a call from the colonel. He had relayed my citation of the Buddha's life to Than Shwe himself. The dictator had been so impressed that he had granted permission for me to go up-country.

The junta had dawdled so long that I couldn't go myself—I had to report on Laos before McCaffrey arrived in Bangkok the following week. But the door was open for the CIA station chief.

I had come to Burma on business and so had missed the site I longed to see, Bagan (or Pagan, the evocative name I still prefer). Tantalizingly, a plane that carried me to Mandalay touched down in Bagan to discharge a few jumpy tourists and I did get a quick view over that temple-studded landscape, where at least two thousand ancient shrines remained. I hoped for another view on take-off but only glimpsed a few mottled domes and the brown snake of the Irrawady River, its back flecked with gold by the declining sun.

Mandalay was a revelation. For me, it was associated with George Orwell, John Masters, and Somerset Maugham, but the first thing I learned was that it had become a Chinese colony. The decomposing Burma Road our military had built during World War II now carried Chinese goods toward the sea and Burmans complained that they could no longer afford to live in their city's center, since Chinese immigrants had driven up property prices. You couldn't miss the Chinese presence down in Rangoon, and I knew that Chinese intelligence had built an intercept station on the coast, but the intensity of the nonviolent invasion only became clear in Mandalay.

The strategic imperative, as seen from Beijing, was obvious. Burma not only provided a back-door trade route to the greater Indian Ocean, but opened a strategic lifeline in case a Pacific conflict arose with the United States over Taiwan. The Indian Ocean and its contiguous seas were the most distant and most difficult theater for our Navy to reach and the Chinese believed that our overextended lines of communication would even the odds in a future confrontation.

In Washington, bureaucrats shrugged. Burma was a one-issue country, and the issue was The Lady.

Flying back to Rangoon after dark, the pilot of the tired aircraft couldn't find the city. It was entirely blacked out, thanks to a sudden storm and subsequent power failure. The old plane was not equipped for a blind landing.

Hoping to reassure the passengers, the pilot announced, in struggling English, that we would divert to the nearest airfield in Thailand. It was possible that we would have enough fuel to reach it.

Just as we banked out over the sea, Rangoon lit up, as if it had been playing peek-a-boo.

Before I left for Laos, I had an encounter of a heartening sort. In a vile hotel dining room near the harbor, I met three elderly Americans who didn't fit the pattern of foreign visitors. They explained that they were World War II veterans of the Office of Strategic Services, the OSS, the fabled forerunner of the CIA. During the war, they'd been dropped among the up-country tribes, far behind Japanese lines, to organize resistance and sabotage. They had fallen in love with their hosts, who had protected them at great cost, and now, after successful careers, they returned frequently to Burma to help the tribespeople.

Their deeds were inspiring, but their tales were grim. AIDS was ravaging the tribes in an unreported humanitarian crisis. The burgeoning Chinese cities across the border were wells of the disease and migrant workers carried it back to the villages. Thereafter, it spread through a variety of means, most perniciously through "vitamin injections." The tribespeople had come to believe that medicine administered through syringes was magically powerful, so charlatans traveled about selling vitamin shots and using the same never-sanitized needle on sixty or seventy people in succession.

But the world only wanted to know about the undeniably brave and conveniently glamorous Daw Aung San Suu Kyi.

In the closed realm of Burma, time hadn't stood still—it had slipped into reverse. Apart from a scattering of vehicles and a pair of new hotels, Rangoon might have been an Asian city of the 1920s, if an ill-tended one. Great crowds still moved on foot, the men lithe and fey under parasols, the women and children spackling their faces with tan paste made of tree bark, a primitive sun block. The dominant Shwedagon Pagoda had not altered for centuries, and Buddhist monks were far more common than soldiers. Up-country, the jungle licked at temples rotting at the edge of Mandalay. More monks wandered and begged, and only a snake-ball of electric wires on a downtown street reminded you of the century the rest of the world would soon leave.

Yet, even wrecked Burma retained more infrastructure than Laos, thanks to the British. The Brits build roads, railways, schools, and offices. The French taught local hires how to cook. As a result, Vientiane, the capital of Laos, drowsed on the east bank of the Mekong, with only its "presentation" streets paved by 1996. The triumph of Communism had done little for the startlingly poor country, and the capital seemed like Mayberry, R.F.D., with cassoulet and a glass of tired wine.

By the time I reached Laos, the regime was listless rather than brutal and more frightened of change than of failure. We made no headway on the drug-smuggling issue, which seemed a rich-man's problem to Laotian officials. The best I can say of my time in the city was that sitting in an open-air café by the river at sunset seemed one of the world's ideal spots to have a drink.

If I accomplished nothing on the professional side, my personal outlook grew peculiarly. The development projects we sponsored were making a difference in the lives of the hill people, weaning them gently from poppy cultivation. I flew up in a decrepit Russian MI-8 helicopter to visit the Hmong. My escort was a gregarious rep from the U.S. Agency for International Development, an organization that has not always performed ably. In Laos, however, old-school grand projects had been eschewed in favor of a small-is-beautiful approach, and it worked. Remote villages got wells, simple irrigation, and help getting cash crops to market, along with rudimentary medical care. To an American, it would have seemed nothing at all, but the impact at the back of beyond was enormous. Sanitation in the form of a communal cinder-block outhouse meant a leap of centuries.

But it was the flight back to Vientiane that crowned my journey. With the old helicopter rattling like a Renault full of scrap metal, we flew over the Plain of Jars, a wild landscape that should have been beautiful. Nature was, indeed, fighting her way back, but the earth was pocked and pitted with bomb craters for what seemed a hundred miles. The high table-land had been in the flight path of our bombing runs from our airbases in Thailand to Vietnam and back. Unexpended ordnance—bombs that had not been used on Vietnam—were dropped casually on Laos to save the pilots the risk of landing with armaments still on board.

I'm forced to resort to a cliché: The Plain of Jars looked like the surface of the moon, albeit with wild grasses and scrub trees. The craters had ruptured many a farmer's fields, and the primitive tools available did not permit the earth to be leveled again. Still, the farmers did what they could, and died when their hoes struck unexploded bombs.

The Plain of Jars had been a place of intermittent refuge for Communist guerrillas, so we had something of an excuse for what we did. But an excuse was all it was.

That day, I saw my country's dark side, even more profoundly than I had in Rampart. The United States is the greatest force for freedom, opportunity, and human decency in history. But we go mad now and then. And when we do, we leave desolation behind us.

In warfare, calculated barbarity can be excused. But callousness is unforgiveable.

HUCK VS. AHAB

WHILE I WAS IN SOUTHEAST ASIA, TOM RICKS, THE WAR correspondent and Hemingway look-alike, published an early review of my narco-novel, *Twilight of Heroes,* in *The Wall Street Journal.* Tom can be mischievous, and his column focused on the similarities he imagined between some of the book's less appealing characters and senior figures in the Clinton administration, including a few would-be mandarins at the State Department. As a result, a Foggy Bottom posse formed to demand my immediate lynching. (One of them, at least, identified so closely with Russia that he quite liked the idea of censorship.)

Had McCaffrey been a typical Washington creature, he would've tied the noose for the Friends of Bill and handed me over. But he wasn't, and he didn't. I just moved back to the Pentagon a month early.

But I'd had my fill. A career is like a love affair, and you need to know when it's over. Dragging it on just spoils the happy memories.

I was promoted to lieutenant colonel, but the silver oak leaf couldn't revive my passion. Others were more concerned with my promotions than I was. I wanted the wildness of the world. Americans are either Ahabs, obsessed with one Great White Whale or another, or Huck Finns, forever fleeing Aunt Polly to light out and see what waits over the hill. I was a Huck, and as my bewildered wife observes, it remains inexplicable within the parameters of Newtonian physics that I lasted over two decades in the Army.

I can cite any number of reasons why I decided to retire and move on with my life, and all would be true. I wanted to write things I could not publish as a serving officer. I was weary of being at the mercy of fools. (The proposition that I shouldn't argue with an ambassador seemed absurd.) I was tired of making accurate intelligence calls—based on first-hand experience—only to have the stay-at-homes dismiss my views until it was too late. I didn't want to end up as yet another walking-dead colonel wandering the halls of the Pentagon, terrified of life beyond the PX and the commissary. My bones ached. And I was sick of bad haircuts. But when all else was said and done, I just felt an irresistible itch to move on. I had loved the Army unconditionally, and I didn't love it the same way anymore.

The sharpest indicator I got that it was time to go was simply that I began, for the first time, to calculate which assignments I might pursue, to care more about myself than about the mission. That's fatal for a soldier. I always had gone wherever the Army sent me. Now, I began to feel picky as well as restless. And I had become an adventure junkie. When the possibility of an assignment to Pakistan arose, I was told that I was "too valuable," and, anyway, it wasn't my official area of expertise. I shrugged. But I was not going to vegetate on yet another staff "to rust unburnished, not to shine in use." The Army was too *tame*.

When I mentioned my decision to retire, it surprised everyone. The immediate advice from peers was that I should stay on for at least two years from the date of my promotion, since that was the minimum period of service-in-grade required, with a waiver, to qualify for a lieutenant-colonel's retirement pay. It showed how little they knew me: the notion that I would hang on for an additional year, counting down the days, just to collect a few hundred dollars more each month offended me. For the rest of my life, I'll be paid as a retired major, and I have never wished it otherwise.

The Army was good to me even then, and the chain of command asked what it would take to make me change my mind and stay in uniform. I didn't even consider the offer. Once you make up your mind on so weighty an issue, you stick by your decision. And had I said, "Oh, assign me to X and I'll hang around," it would have seemed as if the whole fuss had been a bit of theater to get whatever I wanted. I had always served with dignity and pride, if sometimes obstreperously, and I intended to leave on my own terms.

Three and a half years later, on the morning of September 11, 2001, I did regret retiring from the Army. But my fate lay elsewhere.

And now, after an interval of a decade, I've set down the little stories in this book. As I reviewed the pages, two things struck me: first, I've been describing a lost world, a time of service profoundly different from the post-9-11 military experience, and, second, no end of worthy and fascinating men and women have been left out. Colonel Jim Cox, a splendid soldier and friend, should have been in the book, but even though we both crawled over the Soviet sickbed, we did so separately and only traveled together to London, where our adventure consisted of a rainy stroll to the Ministry of Defence. Colonel Bill Speer should have made an appearance, too, as well as Colonel Jiyul Kim and dozens of other officers and NCOs with whom I served in the muddy-boots Army. But this is a book of travel stories, meant to entertain. A roster of names might gratify those listed, but it would only victimize the reader. I have done my best to tell a few odd tales and must be content with that.

On February 1, 1998, I woke up as a civilian. And life got interesting.